The Shape of Reason

ARGUMENTATIVE WRITING IN COLLEGE

John T. Gage

UNIVERSITY OF OREGON

MACMILLAN PUBLISHING COMPANY

NEW YORK

Copyright © 1987, Macmillan Publishing Company,
a division of Macmillan, Inc.

Printed in the United States of America

Macmillan Publishing Company
866 Third Avenue, New York, New York 10022

Collier Macmillan Canada, Inc.

LIBRARY OF CONGRESS CATALOGING-IN-PUBLICATION DATA

Gage, John T.
    The shape of reason.

    Includes index.
    1. English language—Rhetoric.   2. Reasoning.
I. Title.
PE1431.G34   1987   808'.042   86-16372
ISBN   0-02-340420-5

Printing: 1 2 3 4 5 6 7   Year: 7 8 9 0 1 2 3

ISBN   0-02-340420-5

The Shape of Reason

✺§ *Preface* ∂✺

When the poet Robert Frost taught writing, so the story goes, he had a special way of getting his students' attention. When their first compositions were handed in, Frost

> gathered them all up, and holding them aloft asked if anybody wanted theirs back after he had read them. After a little hesitation on their part, there was a chorus of "no, no." "Very well, then," he said as he dropped the whole batch in the wastebasket, "here goes. I don't intend to be a perfunctory reader of perfunctory writing."*

Most writing teachers have probably felt the same way. Why should we care to read what nobody cared to write? What is "perfunctory writing," anyway, and what is "perfunctory reading"? Perfunctory writing is the kind of writing students do solely for the purpose of handing it in, and perfunctory reading is the kind of reading teachers do solely for the purpose of handing it back. I don't believe that either is necessary.

I intend this textbook to help college students write seriously about ideas that require their serious attention. Argumentative writing—writing that reasons its way to a conclusion—can also be perfunctory, if nobody, including the writer, really cares whether a conclusion is worth defending. Serious argumentative writing results when students confront real intellectual problems needing real solutions. In this textbook, therefore, issues, ideas, and reasons will always come first. These, and not words and sentences, are the "basic units of

*This version of the story was told by Frost's friend Louis Mertins in his *Robert Frost: Life and Talks-Walking* (Norman: University of Oklahoma Press, 1965), p. 93.

v

composition." The need to say something of one's own to someone who needs to hear it will be the starting point from which all other considerations of writing will follow. This perspective enables students to view the many "tasks" of writing, not as separate procedures to be followed because some rule prescribes them, but as *responsibilities* that result from having ideas and feeling the need to communicate them. This is a book about writing that *earns* its conclusions. It is a book about how someone who has an idea worth writing about can face and struggle seriously with those responsibilities.

This perspective has some consequences in the way in which I approach argumentative writing, many of which are discussed in the chapters that follow. First of all, I address students about their attitudes toward writing and education, since the success of this approach to writing depends on how seriously students take intellectual challenges (in and out of college). I have tried to give students credit for being able to think with me about why they should write in college and how they should do it.

Second, the method in this book treats the writing process as moving from whole to parts, rather than building discrete "skills" in isolation from complete intentions. This means that students are not asked to produce any writing merely for the sake of practicing some part of a whole composition (such as sentences or paragraphs), although they are asked to write thesis statements and enthymemes that represent the whole intention of an essay and the line of reasoning that it will follow. This book does not aim at isolated "competencies" but at the powers of judgment that enable writers to face new and ever more difficult writing situations.

Third, this book asks students to *generate* the structures of their compositions based on the requirements of their specific argumentative intentions, as these are defined by a thoughtful thesis and a well-reasoned enthymeme. Thus, I've used the enthymeme (or rhetorical syllogism) to integrate "invention" and "arrangement" so that the structure of the student's reasoning is what determines the structure of the essay rather than any formula that is independent of the essay's specific content. There are no "empty forms" here for the students to fill up with content, even though the structure of the enthymeme is presented as a practical guide for thinking about the relation between logic and form. The enthymeme is a versatile form for reasoning about one's ideas in relation to an intended audience and for controlling structural decisions.

Fourth, I've situated the process of reasoning through an argument, developing its structure, and drafting and revising an essay, within a context of critical reading and research. Both critical reading and research concern the process of inquiry, a process that underlies successful argumentative writing. I've treated argumentation here as a matter of finding and presenting the best available reasons to assent to a conclusion, not as a matter of "winning" one's case. I've tried to underplay persuasion, as the writer's aim, in favor of *inquiry*. Critical reading is presented here as a necessary prerequisite to inquiry, and research as a necessary extension of that process. Thus, the early chapter on critical reading and the last chapter on research writing place argumentative writing in an intellectual context that goes beyond the composition class. They situate argumentative writing within larger responsibilities that face all educated people: the responsibility of deciding what to believe when encountering the ideas of others, and the responsibility of discovering knowledge in the face of the unknown. To develop the interrelatedness of writing and inquiry, I have included sections called "Implications for Research" at the ends of the chapters on critical reading, the thesis, and reasoning (Chapters 2, 3, and 4).

Finally, I attempt to be honest with students about why argumentative writing matters, and what they can reasonably expect to accomplish by taking the process seriously. They cannot, for instance, expect to "master" writing any more than they can expect to "master" thinking. Argumentative writing should be a challenge. By facing it, students learn the rewards of genuine intellectual accomplishment, but they also learn something about the limits of the mind to comprehend truth. By writing serious arguments, students should not learn that knowledge is easy or that possessing it gives them power. They should learn, however, that thinking is an adventure and that it requires risk. Even as we become educated and increase what we know, we must at the same time learn to live with uncertainty. Facing genuine challenges of reason is the best way to do so.

So, by using this book as it is meant to be used, students need not fear that they will bore their teachers with perfunctory writing. Teachers need not worry about becoming perfunctory readers. At least, this is my hope.

The book contains special features that I hope will make this approach "teachable"—and learnable. I've included extended definitions of important terms, such as "structure," "thesis," "enthymeme," and "style." Each chapter ends with "Questions for Thought, Discussion, and Writing" that call for independent evaluation of the ideas in the chapter. I've written some narrative examples of a student thinking about ideas in the process of coming up with an adequate thesis, finding support for it, and structuring an argument. I've also prepared lists of open-ended questions to guide students through critical reading, drafting thesis statements, and revising.

I've approached style in this book as subordinate to reasoning

and structuring, but I have tried to relate style to argument by adapting
principles from George Orwell's "Politics and the English Language"
and Wayne Booth's "The Rhetorical Stance." I wish to encourage
student writers to view stylistic choices in the same way they would
view all other choices: as responsibilities they face by virtue of wanting to share their commitments.

Students will also benefit from thoughtful discussions of other
matters that do not ordinarily get enough attention in composition
textbooks, such as how to respond to criticism and why they should
seek it, how to face obstacles to revision, and how to relate research
in school to making decisions throughout life. This string of "how
to's" reminds me that I have also sought to phrase my "rules" and
suggestions and procedures in the form of *considerations,* rather than
as prescriptions, so that students understand that the principles of
good writing cannot be used as a substitute for speculation. Students
need to be reminded that "muddling through" is natural and necessary and that no recipes for writing and thinking can guarantee them
results. There are, however, better and worse ways to muddle through,
and I have tried to present honest, serious, and reasonable ways.

Acknowledgments

No discussion of writing, wise or unwise, can be the invention of
one person. It will always rely on the collective experience and thoughts
of many. The best that any individual can do is make a sensible
selection, try to present it effectively, and acknowledge the inevitable
debt. In my case, that debt is enormous and impossible to recount
fully. How can I give credit to all of those who taught me about
argumentation by demanding better reasons when I was being foolish
or stubborn? How can I give credit to all of those who taught me
about writing by forcing me to rewrite my ideas when I was being
confusing or dull? Of all of these, my parents, my brothers, my
teachers, my students, and my friends come to mind. More specific
debts are easier to list.

My approach to reasoning and writing is adapted from my reading of William J. Brandt's *The Rhetoric of Argumentation* (Indianapolis:
The Bobbs-Merrill Company, 1970) and his textbook (with others),
The Craft of Writing (Englewood Cliffs, N.J.: Prentice-Hall, 1969).
Lawrence D. Green's essay based on Brandt's approach, "Enthymemic
Invention and Structural Prediction," *College English* 41 (1980), 623–
34, has been indispensable to me. I have also relied heavily and in
many ways on what I have learned from Wayne C. Booth, especially
his *Modern Dogma and the Rhetoric of Assent* (Chicago: University of
Chicago Press, 1974), as well as his wonderful essays "The Rhetorical

Stance" and "The Uncritical American: or, Nobody's from Missouri Any More," found in *Now Don't Try to Reason with Me: Essays and Ironies for a Credulous Age* (Chicago: University of Chicago Press, 1970). I wish Josephine Miles were alive to hear me acknowledge my indebtedness to her *Working Out Ideas: Predication and Other Uses of Language* (Berkeley: Bay Area Writing Project Curriculum Publication No. 5, 1979) and, even more, so that I could have hundreds more of her poems to read. I was also inspired by my chance encounter with Jack W. Meiland's *College Thinking: How to Get the Best Out of College* (New York: New American Library, 1981), which impressed me with its application of argumentation to learned inquiry.

Knowledgeable readers will recognize that I have also relied on philosophical premises derived from Aristotle's *Rhetoric* and that I have paraphrased Plato's *Phaedrus* and *Gorgias* in a couple of places. There are concepts here from modern rhetoricians and critics as well, most notably Kenneth Burke, Chaim Perelman, Stephen Toulmin, R.S. Crane, and E.D. Hirsch, Jr. I'm happy to be able to admit that I've learned as much about the philosophy of rhetoric from a poet, Robert Frost, who starts this book out and ends it, and from whom I borrowed the title of my third chapter.

Bart Queary coached me through writing this book and helped me by teaching an earlier draft in his English 222 class at Central Oregon Community College. I'm grateful to his students for submitting useful and encouraging criticisms. Other individuals taught me about writing, helped me to think about teaching, and enabled me to write this book: Rick Filloy, Leonard Nathan, Larry Kenney, Terry Busch, Pauline Putnam, and Kathleen Dubs all deserve credit for ideas found here. Many bright and dedicated Graduate Teaching Fellows, who have listened to me as I worked through these ideas for myself on the pretense of teaching them how to teach, helped me to know what to say to other students and teachers. I relied on Mike Stamm's dependable clerical skills to get this book written and much else done; and this book may never have been finished at all had not Beverly Holman's counsel come along when it did. I would also like to acknowledge the reviewers of the book for their valuable comments and criticisms: Martin Jacobi, Clemson University; Arthur Quinn, University of California at Berkeley; George D. Gopen, Duke University; Louis B. Queary, Central Oregon Community College; Victor J. Vitanza, University of Texas at Arlington; Ann Dobyns, The Ohio State University; Richard Fulkerson, East Texas State University; and George E. Yoos, St. Cloud State University. Finally, Robin and Molly Gage made it all worthwhile, as always.

Eugene, Oregon   J.T.G.

❧ *Contents* ❧

❧ *Introduction* ❧

Writing as a Liberal Art

If you were to complete a college education and not become a better thinker than you were when you began that education, you would have a right to feel cheated. The central value of a liberal education (as opposed to vocational training) is to make students better able to cope with the intellectual demands of a complex world, a world in which they are frequently called on to make independent decisions among competing ideas. Such decisions have to be made on the basis of thought—not by flipping a coin or blindly following the crowd or a charismatic leader. An education is supposed to prepare students for making such decisions by providing a basis of knowledge—the content, so to speak, of thinking. But it must do more than provide information, since the overwhelming amount of sheer information available is what makes decisions necessary, and difficult. An education must also prepare students to exercise judgment.

"Judgment" is a vague term used to describe a variety of mostly intuitive mental acts. It applies to all those occasions when we must decide what to *do* with information in its raw form: when we must choose to accept or deny it, to determine its significance or value, to put it to use, or to relate it to other bits of knowledge. If people did not exercise judgment, their knowledge would be a useless hodge-podge of unrelated and equally insignificant bits of information. No educated person can do without the quality of judgment that enables him or her to make sense of all these bits—and yet there are no rules and procedures that can be followed to learn to exercise it. Judgment is learned only by practicing it. It is the act of judiciously appraising, discriminating, sorting, adopting, transforming, and applying ideas.

1

Since all of these activities involve acts of choice, judgment is learned best when one is faced with alternative answers, when problematical situations require acts of judgment to solve.

Judgment is not something that students are assumed to lack when they enter college, or to possess fully when they leave. It is a human activity that everyone does all the time. Judgment may be exercised well or poorly; it is possible to be better or worse at practicing judgment and to learn to practice it better. Everyone practices it better or worse at different times, and no one practices it well at all times. So, your growth as a thinker in college is much harder to measure than the growth of your store of knowledge gathered; it may even be impossible to measure. You may not even feel like a better thinker as you become one, because, after all, as you become a better thinker, the kinds of problems that you think about naturally become more complex and thus you will continue to feel uneasy about your ability to solve them. This uneasiness is nothing to worry about. It is something that you, like all people who care how well they think, must learn to live with.

The improvement that you make in college as a thinking person will probably not be the result of any one course that you take. There will be small, undetectable increments of improvement brought on by the level of challenges that you face. You shouldn't feel cheated if you don't always measure up to those challenges, only if you are not given them. It is only by being in situations that call for good thinking that you will be challenged to produce it. Creating such situations, of one kind or another, at whatever degree of difficulty, should be one of the goals of every course you take. If it is not, you can create such situations for yourself, merely by looking for questions within the material that you encounter. It is your responsibility, as much as that of your teachers, to discover opportunities to do your best thinking. How you accept that responsibility has a lot to do with your attitude. Good thinkers are simply people who seek out opportunities to think better.

Learning to become a better writer happens in the same way that learning to become a better thinker happens. No writing class can complete the job of teaching students to write at their best. All writers, even if they might seem to write effortlessly, are always learning to write better each time they take on and complete a new writing challenge—and each new writing task will be a challenge of its own. The rate at which you become a better writer is just as imperceptible as the rate at which you can expect to become a better thinker; it will happen slowly, in small increments of change. You will not learn to write well overnight, all at once. You will progress in stages that you may not even notice.

Just as you may not notice it when you are thinking better than you were able to do before, you may not always feel that your writing is improving when in fact it is. The reason for this is the same reason I mentioned before: As you improve as a writer, you will naturally take on slightly more challenging writing tasks and find yourself in somewhat more difficult writing situations. As you attempt these, you may continue to feel inadequate to each new writing task, simply because it will involve using what you already know how to do in order to go beyond it. This occasional feeling of inadequacy is nothing to worry about. It is the way you should feel if you are learning. It is only when you feel too satisfied with your writing that you should begin to worry, because at that point you will have stopped trying to write better, just as a lazy thinker has stopped trying to become a better thinker. Instead of worrying about that feeling of inadequacy—which you share with all writers—you need to learn to live with it, to see it as the inevitable result of improvement in a widening range of ideas that always calls for better writing. Good writers are simply people who look for opportunities to write better.

The relationship between writing and thinking is more than an analogy, however. Learning to write well and learning to think well are related in direct ways; learning to write is a way of learning to think. All of the mental acts I listed as synonyms for "judgment," for instance, define the kinds of choices that writers must exercise. Writing, like thinking, is impossible without judgment.

One difference between writing and thinking is that writing is tangible—it results in a finite product—whereas thinking is intangible and just goes on and on (or, sometimes, around and around). But this difference between these two activities is also a reason that learning to become a better writer results in better thinking. Writing is thinking-made-tangible, thinking that can be examined because it is "on the page" and not all "in the head," invisibly floating around. Writing is thinking that can be stopped and tinkered with. It is a way of making thought hold still long enough to examine its structures, its possibilities, its flaws. Of course, all of us have many thoughts that we never attempt to write down. Yet the road to a clearer understanding of one's thoughts is often traveled on paper. It is through the attempt to find words, and to find patterns for expressing related ideas, that we often come to discover exactly what we think.

There is yet another important benefit to thinking that comes from learning to write better, even if this benefit, too, is an intangible one. Writing, as this book stresses, is a process of finding and structuring reasons. Writing can be the cause of our search, not only for the right words in the right order but also for the right reasons. It is in this way that the serious attempt to compose your thoughts in writing will often lead you to the very important discovery not only of *what* you think but *why* you think it.

Writing is a way of learning to think better, then, and as such it is at the very center of what you do as you become more educated. Any student, in any class, can listen, read, collect information, pass multiple-choice tests, and even think deliberately about the problems or implications of the information learned about a given subject. But writing about that information has an effect that none of these activities alone can produce: It causes us to clarify that information, those problems, and those implications for ourselves, to put them into relationships and to explore our reasons for saying what we have decided to say about them. Writing, because it is undertaken as a decision to be clear, forces clarity. But if it is also undertaken as a decision to be *believed,* it forces more than clarity. Any act of writing that does not stop with the mere assertion of a random list of bits of information will force the writer to look for good reasons, and, in the process of looking for good reasons, the writer's judgment is being exercised as well as the writer's composing skills.

Attitudes That Help and Hinder

As a writing student, you can get these benefits from writing if you approach it as a serious thinking process. Once again, success is a matter of attitude. Whatever benefit you get out of a writing class is up to you, since no one but you can control how you approach it. One approach that does not work very well might be called a "vocational" view of the benefits of learning to write. At the beginning of this introduction, I contrasted a liberal education with vocational training. A college writing course is intended to help you to become a better writer because better writing will help you to become better at exercising judgment in a world full of conflicting ideas. Even though you may be in college to establish credentials for pursuing a career, you know that the personal benefit of learning is the experience of becoming a more capable person outside the strict boundaries of that career. But many students are so career-minded that they fail to find any value in course work that does not have some "payoff" in terms of performance on the job, and this attitude compels them to see much of their study as a waste of time. The unfortunate result is that they do not take full advantage of the opportunities to study subjects that have no such payoffs but are worthwhile nevertheless for the experience they provide.

Writing can be seen as either kind of benefit. Students who see it as a mere "skill" valuable only in terms of pleasing fussy professors or employers will get very limited returns on their investment of effort. Students who view writing as an adventurous opportunity to explore ideas and to engage in tangible reasoning, however, will discover that the experience is valuable for its own sake, as well as for the sake of better performance later on.

If your writing class is a requirement, the reason is not because your college means it to be a hurdle that you must jump over on your way to something more important. Rather, it is a requirement because it is meant to provide you with essential means for attaining your educational ends, whatever they may be. If you choose to see it as a hurdle, you may find yourself stumbling unnecessarily. If you must see it as a hurdle, at least I hope that you are a good enough sport to view hurdles as good exercise, even though it takes longer to run 100 yards when they are in the way. But your education isn't a 100-yard dash. It's not how fast you finish that counts, but who you become along the way.

There is another reason students sometimes fear, if not dislike, a writing class. Many students have been in writing classes where grammar and mechanics were viewed as ends in themselves, so that when they write they are made overly conscious of all of the mistakes they might make. For many, learning to write has been a constant process of trying to avoid the teacher's—or the handbook's—list of "Don'ts." Don't do this, don't do that—before you have even had a chance to try out an idea! No wonder writing is seen as a chore rather than a chance to explore ideas. The rules are laid down, like land mines, and it becomes the student's task to dance around them. Grammar, when taught in this way, is one cause of students' never writing anything worthwhile, because it is easier to avoid all the traps by keeping everything simple and meaningless. Worrying too much, as you write, whether your grammar is correct may prevent you from worrying enough whether you have anything worthwhile to say.

Good writing needs good grammar, but good grammar by itself is not good writing. You can say a stupid thing correctly, but it will still be a stupid thing to say. The problem is not to strive for perfection of grammar, but to strive for excellence of thought and then to *use* grammar to make sure that that thought is expressed well. If you say a smart thing incorrectly, you will be less believable. Grammar helps to make you credible, but it cannot make you right. Being right is the first obligation of a writer. Being correct is just one of the responsibilities that comes with having a good idea. You should expect and want your teacher to pay attention to your grammar, then, but you should not allow grammar to stand between you and your ideas.

This Book and You

The assumptions that I have made about the importance of writing have led me to approach composition in this book by emphasizing reason and structure as the central elements of good prose. The book is intended to guide you through a process of thinking and composing that will result in thoughtful, well-structured essays about meaningful ideas. But, as I have already suggested, no book can do more than guide. You will really be teaching yourself, as you think about the ideas in this book and try to apply them.

The chapters are organized to focus on aspects of the composing process, but you will find, as you compose essays, that these aspects are not as separate as this organization suggests. Books about writing must inevitably make distinctions among principles and "stages" of composing that are always somewhat arbitrary and artificial. In this book, the stages are: understanding the principles of structure (Chapter 1), reading and responding critically (Chapter 2), finding something to say that represents your own position (Chapter 3), discovering adequate support as a basis for that position (Chapter 4), using the support you have discovered as a basis for structuring your composition (Chapter 5), making decisions about style (Chapter 6), and revising your writing to ensure that you have made consistent decisions in all these matters (Chapter 7). The last chapter (8) enlarges the context of this process by discussing the nature of research. This arrangement is necessarily abstract and linear, as discussions of any "process" must be. But it is not literal. It merely attempts to represent an intuitive process that writers go through with different degrees of emphasis and consciousness at different times. Making the stages conscious, and focusing attention on each one, nevertheless provides a basis of experience on which to draw as you compose, even though your actual acts of composing will never be this self-conscious or this neatly divided into parts.

Since these chapters focus on aspects of the whole composing act, it is not until you have read all of them (or at least the first seven) that you will be expected to compose the kind of whole, purposeful, well-structured, and well-reasoned essays that I hope this book will help you to write. You will, of course, be writing before you have read all these chapters. It is possible to practice any part of the whole process of writing exclusively, until that part is "mastered," but this should not be your goal. The mastery of writing does not come with the ability to perform any given quantity of a potentially infinite number of limited tasks; it comes from the ability to make choices in the context of whole, complete acts of composition. And, of course, *mastery* is the wrong word to use, anyway. You can "master" limited tasks, but you can only learn to live with the inevitable and recurring feeling of inadequacy that comes when you are writing at your best. And then the satisfactions! It helps to remember that no one is a perfect writer, if that means someone who does not struggle through each stage of the process.

It is my purpose to invite you to struggle with and find your way among real ideas, ideas that matter. The positions you forge for yourself will be your own positions, reasoned about and structured in such a way that I hope you will feel a sense of achievement in each essay that you write. If you enter into the process of reasoning and writing discussed in this book in a willing and thoughtful way, you will be writing essays that represent your best thinking on issues that are important to you. Students who are only asked to write on the teacher's topics and who churn out empty-headed compositions on "My Favorite Movie" or "How to Change a Tire" are doomed to write boring stuff for an already bored teacher. And they are cheated of the opportunity to use writing as a way of discovering what they really think and why they think it. It is my intention to enable you to use writing to learn where you stand in the ongoing discussion of ideas that demand thoughtful attention. It is to allow you to write essays that you can discover in a box or notebook ten or fifty years from now and say, "There was my best thinking at the time, and that's why I am who I am."

QUESTIONS FOR THOUGHT, DISCUSSION, AND WRITING

1. Think about your own attitudes toward your education and honestly ask yourself whether you generally seek challenges on your own or whether you mostly look for an easy way out of an assignment. Perhaps you can describe situations of each kind. What made the difference?
2. Think about an experience you have had in which you felt that what you already knew was adequate to solve a significant problem. Think about another experience in which your knowledge was not adequate to solve such a problem. Then compare what you learned from these two experiences.
3. Describe an experience in which you came to a clarification of your own thinking through writing.
4. Before reading any further in this book, describe the approach to writing you expect it to take. What *responsibilities* will you be asked to take as a writer? What do you feel about taking them?

CHAPTER 1

❧ *A Sense of Structure* ❧

Writing Is Ideas in Relation

Sometimes one word is enough. The word *stop* written on a stop sign communicates its meaning without having to be qualified, explained, or supported by other words. It's absurd, however, to think of somebody having *written* that sign, in the way that a writer *writes* words. "Mr. Faulkner, we have chosen you as the writer for this project. Please compose a sign that will notify drivers that they are to stop at an intersection." Sure. The job was given to a graphic designer instead.

Sometimes one sentence is enough. The sentence "Please form one line" communicates its meaning—in certain physical contexts—without having to be qualified, explained, or supported by other sentences. Someone probably *did* write that sentence, but it was not much of a task. Here's another example of a sentence that is usually found alone, unqualified, unexplained, and unsupported: "Warning: The Surgeon General has determined that cigarette smoking is dangerous to your health." This unqualified assertion, one of several warnings that appear by themselves on cigarette packages sold in the United States, was a much harder sentence to write. There is a long history of composition behind it, involving many drafts, a lot of editing, considerable argument over what words it should contain, and hours of labor. All for one sentence. And most of this work took the form of more writing—millions of words—contained in memoranda, reports, testimony, studies, letters, and other documents, all written to support (or to oppose) the idea that this one sentence asserts. Yes, the sentence stands alone in its present context, but it

8

contains an idea that does not exist in isolation from other ideas. Many other ideas, thousands of them, had to be written to explain and support it, and to convince legislators and the public of its significance. Not only did this sentence result *from* the effects of the meanings contained in many other sentences, but it has also resulted *in* the writing of many other sentences. Since its writing, and since its appearance on all cigarette packages and advertisements, it has caused many people to react with sentences of their own—in more studies, more reports, letters to editors, even comedy routines. Sentences, in most cases, arise out of other sentences and beget still more sentences.

Even though some sentences seem to stand alone, it is obvious that most writing does not begin and end with the composition of a sentence. Sentences are not isolated entities, containing all of their meaning within themselves. They are parts of the meaning of something larger, and whole compositions consist of sentences tied together in meaningful ways. What a writer does, then, is something more than, and different from, writing sentences. The act of writing is also the act of creating relationships, not just between the words in a sentence, but between the sentences in a composition. Writing, as an activity, involves creating relationships among parts, as much as it involves creating the parts themselves. The parts of a composition, whether they are individual words, words grouped into individual sentences, or larger patterns of thought made out of grouped sentences, are meaningful only in relation to other parts.

The relationship among the words of a sentence has a technical name; it is called *syntax.* Syntax means significant word order. It is the syntax of a sentence that gives it meaning, as much as it is the individual words themselves. Consider, for instance, this "sentence":

> Students courses course those basic this enroll with completed in should only.

The words are there, but until we put them into significant relationship, the sentence is meaningless. It is not even a sentence as we know it. The same words, however, with the addition of syntax, can produce this sentence:

> Only those students with basic courses completed should enroll for this course.

Now that the words are put into order, they mean something. What they mean depends on the particular syntactical form that the words have. The above sentence means that students who enroll for "this course" must have completed its prerequisites. But a simple shift of the position of one word in this sentence can change its meaning:

> Those students with *only* basic courses completed should enroll in this course.

This sentence means that students who have not taken any other kinds of courses besides basic ones should now take this one. Another shift produces:

> Those students with basic courses completed should *only* enroll in this course.

This means that students with the basic courses behind them should now take this course and none other. We cannot say that syntax makes *all* the difference in meaning, since if we changed the words themselves we would change the meaning too, but what a difference syntax does make! Without a meaningful order, there is no meaning.

Just as the meaning of this whole sentence depends on the order of its words, the meanings of larger pieces of discourse also depend on the order of their sentences. Sentences not only contain ideas, therefore, but they also have a functional relation to the sentences that are placed with them, and it is our understanding of these relations that gives rise to our understanding of what any piece of writing means. You might say, then, that there is syntax larger than the sentence, just as there is syntax within a sentence, but the significant order of the sentences within a whole composition does not go by this technical name. Some people call it "form"; some call it "coherence" or "organization"; some call it "structure." There are yet other terms for this concept. What they all signify, in reference to writing, is **the relations that hold sentences together and give meaning to the whole discourse.** It is the writer's job to create these relations. Where do these relations come from?

The relations among words within a sentence follow certain conventional patterns in a given language. The "rules" of syntax for English are different from the "rules" of syntax for German, for instance, and this is why a translator from one language to another must not only translate each word but also rearrange the words to conform to the conventional patterns of the new language. The rules of syntax are complicated to study but easy to use if you know how to speak a language, in which case you do not even have to know what those rules are. They are abstract principles, such as "adjectives go in front of nouns," or "prepositions connect verbs and objects," to cite only two obvious ones. (Consider how many such rules and exceptions you would have to articulate in order to describe the actual relations among the words in the sentences we speak. For some linguists it is a life's work. Fortunately, for the purpose of making sentences, these rules are mostly "second nature" to us.)

The relations that give meaning to the sentences within larger structures of discourse, however, do not follow from rules as do the syntactic relations among words. We are able to create these with a good deal more flexibility than we can create syntax, even though the relations we create will still affect meaning.

The rules of syntax demand that only certain kinds of words can function in the "slot" left open in the following sentence:

"The _____ is red."

Lots of meanings are possible, but all of them depend on the slot being filled by some form of noun phrase. We could say "The East is red," or "The new hybrid form of lemon being marketed under the trade name of applem is red," but in each case we will have filled the function slot with the same kind of syntactic unit, a noun phrase. But consider the kinds of sentences that could function in the slot between these two sentences:

"The East is red."
"_____."
"Communism applies more to governments than to people."

Many kinds of sentences are possible, with very different kinds of relations to the one that comes before and the one that comes after. Rather than speak of the sentence (or sentences) that could be entered between these two as fulfilling the function of a syntactical slot, we would speak of them as creating *transitions,* and many kinds of transitions are possible. The desired kind of transition would define the relationship that we wish to make between these two ideas. For example, we could fill in the blank with:

"Some people, therefore, think that all Asians must be Communists."

We would then have *drawn an inference* from the first sentence in order that we might *contradict* that inference in the last one. Or we could fill in the blank with:

"This means that Eastern nations are assumed to be communistic."

Then we would have *explained* the first sentence in order to *support* the last one. Or we could fill in the blank with:

"The West, on the other hand, is pinkish-blue."

Then we would have *created a contrast* with the first sentence in order that we might use the last one to *point out* the silliness of both the first and the second *generalization.* As you can tell, a virtually infinite number of possible sentences of many different kinds might "go" in the blank space. And the function of those sentences would be to link the existing sentences in different ways, to create different sorts of meaningful relationships. The meaning of the transitional sentence, moreover, changes our understanding of the other sentences.

Where, then, do the relations between sentences and ideas come from? They come from *purposes.* Notice that each of the above phrases in italics used to describe the kinds of functions created by the added sentences are the names of actions: draw an inference, contradict, explain, support, contrast, point out, generalize. These actions govern the purpose of the sentences, each version suggesting a different point that the writer is trying to make. Sentences have certain kinds of relations because those relations enable writers to achieve their particular purposes. The transitions that constitute the relations between sentences in discourse result from what the sentences are intended to *do.*

Within the context of a whole piece of discourse, sentences are not merely the bearers of content, then; they also have relational functions. They *do,* as well as *mean.* The kinds of things they do are limited only by the range of actions that it is possible to perform using language: to support, to explain, to contradict, to develop, to add to, to take away from, to illustrate, to generalize, to compare, to infer from, to prepare for, to repeat, to separate, to connect, to affirm, to deny—the list seems endless. Each of these actions is relational. We say one thing *in order to* explain another. We say one thing in order to illustrate, or to prepare for, or to affirm, or deny another. What our sentences do, therefore is defined by what they do *to* other sentences. And they do what they do to other sentences in order to achieve an overall intention that calls for these actions and these relations.

A sentence, then, may be words in relation (syntax), but *writing*—the act of composing sentences that go together—is ideas in relation. Ideas are put into relation in order to achieve purposes. It is the purpose that determines what relations sentences will have; the purpose, therefore, determines what structure a composition will take on. One word is not enough. It is a whole *structure* of ideas that achieves our purpose.

From Wholes to Parts

The structure that any piece of writing takes on results from the writer's overall sense of purpose. If we think of structure as the progress from part to part in a composition, it may become easier to see that some sense of a destination, a goal to be reached, is what gives the writer—and the reader—a sense that the parts are held together in meaningful ways. We feel, as we read, that each new part is somehow justified by what went before it and that together they are progressing toward some conclusion. You have probably encountered writing that lacked this quality, and your response was to wonder, at some point as you slogged through it, "How did I get here?" You had this experience because the writer had somehow failed to make a transition from one part to the next, failed, that is, to connect the parts in a way that suggested forward progress. Thus, both the reader's sense of progress in prose and the writer's control of this quality come from the same source: **a clear sense of an intention that accounts for the necessity of each of the parts and their relations.**

That thought reminds me of an episode in *Alice's Adventures in Wonderland,* when Alice encounters the Cheshire Cat sitting good-naturedly in a tree. She asks the Cat:

> ". . . Would you tell me, please, which way I ought to go from here?"
>
> "That depends a good deal on where you want to get to," said the Cat.
>
> "I don't much care where—" said Alice.
>
> "Then it doesn't much matter which way you go," said the Cat.
>
> "—so long as I get *somewhere,*" Alice added as an explanation.
>
> "Oh, you're sure to do that," said the Cat, "if you only walk long enough."

Lewis Carroll is having fun here with an idea that is central to an understanding of human actions of all kinds, including writing. That idea may seem self-evident, but it sometimes escapes us: Intention determines choice. When we face a choice of one or another way of acting, it is our intention that guides us. Sometimes, of course, we are not certain whether one or another way will, in fact, serve our intention, but the kind of deliberation that we enter into in that case still concerns the relationship of means to ends. What Carroll illustrates is that if we have no intended *end,* then the *means* that we choose hardly matters. In reference to the structure of writing, we might say that if we have no destination to guide our selection of parts and their relations, it hardly matters what parts or what relations we choose. If we have no end in mind to use as a reference point for structural decisions along the way, any structure will do as well as another. Structure is not an *end* in itself; it is among the writer's *means*.

The reason that written compositions have different structures, then, is because they differ in their intentions. We might also say that the reason some writers sometimes have difficulty finding their own structures is because they have not first discovered their own intentions. We might add that the reason writers sometimes seem to be leading us in unaccountable directions as we move through their developing structures is because they have not made their intentions clear to us. The self-evident relationship between means and ends in composing, therefore, gives us three principles that can help us to ensure that the parts of the compositions we write will provide the reader with functionally clear relationships:

1. As we write, we must be clear to ourselves about the purpose we intend to achieve.
2. We have to use our intended purpose as the test against which to measure whether any given part is necessary and whether any given transition is effective.
3. We must make our sense of purpose clear to the reader so that the parts and the transitions between them can be followed as the reader progresses through the composition.

The purpose of a composition is its *whole* purpose, the sum of its parts. Its *structure* is the way in which those parts are held together, to make a whole. It is for these reasons that writing teachers like to say obvious things, like "An essay must have a beginning, a middle, and an end." At first, you may feel that this kind of advice is incredibly dumb, simply because there is no such thing as any piece of writing that does *not* have a beginning, a middle, and an end—every piece of writing has to start, to continue, and to stop. Yet, the terms *beginning, middle,* and *end* do not designate any kind of start, any kind of continuation, and any kind of stop; they are *functional* terms designating the relations of parts within whole structures. The beginning of any whole composition must be where its intention starts; its middle must be where its intention is developed; its end must be where its intention is fulfilled. The following passage starts, continues, and stops, for instance, but it cannot be said to have a structure, since it is obviously only one part of some structure:

ice, then, will not cure that kind of fever. No runner wants to have to wait for

It is not a structure, because it provides us with no sense of purpose. It leaves us asking, "Why *then?* What has just been said to create the need for this transition? *What* kind of fever? No runner wants to wait for *what?* And why should one? And what do runners and fevers and ice have to do with each other here anyway?" What we are asking about is the beginning, middle, and end. And this is the same as asking about purpose, because we want to know about the beginning, middle, and end of *something.*

These questions are not just about intentions and structure; they also concern *ideas.* Our sense of whether a piece of writing has structural coherence is closely related to our sense of what it is trying to say.

The purpose of a composition, and the source of its structural wholeness, is an idea. Compositions contain more than one idea, of course, but the ideas of a composition relate to each other because they serve an *overall* idea. At this point, the word *idea* may seem to you to be confused with the words *purpose* and *intention,* which I used to refer to the guiding principle of a structure. But it is not, really. I am saying that a purpose or intention of a piece of *writing,* as opposed to the purposes of other kinds of structures, can be paraphrased as an idea, the central idea that captures the intention. If we were to say, "The purpose of this piece of writing is to show that . . ." we would complete this sentence with an idea, such as "cigarettes are unhealthy." Purpose combines an action, to *do* something, and an idea, to *say* something.

We perceive the relations among the many ideas *in* a composition, therefore, because we perceive the central idea *of* that composition. We see how its parts fit together because we understand them to make up a whole thought.

Earned Conclusions

The overall, or central, idea that we perceive when we understand the relation of the ideas in a composition is sometimes called a *thesis.* Later, I discuss thesis statements and their role in creating structures of ideas in your compositions (see Chapter 3, pages 47 ff..) Now it is enough to say that the relation between the thesis of a composition and the ideas contained in that composition is a relation of end to means. The purpose of any piece of writing (excluding, perhaps, some literary kinds) is somehow to provide sufficient ideas within its structure to enable the reader to understand and to accept the one idea that has controlled the choice and placement of all the others.

We can speak of many different kinds of actions that ideas perform within a composition, such as to show, or to explain, or to illustrate, or to support—all the same terms used earlier to describe transitions. But one kind of action takes in all such particular actions and makes them necessary, and that action is *to earn*. Whatever else the ideas in a composition do, they are there in order that the writer can *earn* the thesis.

I have chosen the word *earn* to characterize the act of relating ideas to a thesis because it suggests a kind of ethical edge that other words do not. We could speak of the parts of a composition as all providing *support* for a thesis or as all providing *development* for a thesis, but no term of that kind carries quite the right connotation for what is involved when a writer composes ideas. What they lack is the sense of responsibility that comes from having a thesis and wanting to construct a composition that does justice to it. This is because a thesis is not just any old idea picked out of a hat for the purpose of writing about it. A thesis is a special kind of idea, one that we have chosen as the purpose of writing because it is our own, and because something about it makes us want to develop and support and explain it. A thesis is an idea that we have chosen to write about because we feel a sense of commitment to it and want others to feel the same way. It represents more than just an opportunity to compose for the sake of composing, but a commitment that makes composing seem worthwhile. If we were to compose without regard to our commitment to some idea, we would be in Alice's predicament of not knowing which way we ought to go because we don't much *care* where it is we get to. It is when we care about an idea that we have a motive to enter into the process of searching for other ideas to relate to it.

At one time or another, all writers have the experience of writing like Alice, lost in a confusing wonderland of words, thinking, "If I only write long enough I'm bound to get *somewhere*." In fact, it sometimes happens that just writing, when we are not yet certain about "what we want to say," can lead us into unexpected and interesting discoveries. You may have experimented with "free writing," for instance, in which you "just wrote" without knowing, or without caring, where you would get to in the end. In the process you probably stumbled on a thought that seemed interesting, or a purpose that you didn't know you had. There are many ways of coming upon ideas and purposes, and "just writing" can be one of them. Free writing is probably never totally "free"—in fact, it is hard to imagine writing without *some* purpose, even if merely to fill up a page "because the teacher told me to." Anyway, if you have had the experience of discovering what you want to say *as* you were engaged in writing, you also realized that once you made the discovery you became responsible for doing something to all that writing to make it lead up to that conclusion, or for getting rid of all that writing so that you could let the newly discovered idea take over. Unless you were writing a "free association" novel, you realized that although the writing may have been what stimulated you to have an idea, that writing itself could not stand as a composition *about* that idea. This awareness came from a feeling of responsibility, a feeling that once you knew what you wanted to say, you somehow assumed the burden of making sure that everything else you wrote was relevant to that thought.

If you have never had this experience, try it. (This is not an assignment.) Try to "just write" without knowing or caring what you say; let your thoughts follow by whatever means they will. Having done this for a while, see if there are any thoughts in the writing that seem to be more interesting than others, and then pick out the most interesting one. Consider that as the main thought, and then consider whether everything else that you have written can be said to be a composition *about* that main idea. No doubt, it won't be. But there's no reason you couldn't make that thought into a thesis for a composition. To do so would be to decide to make the rest of your writing somehow responsible to the main idea.

This exercise (even if you only imagined doing it, which is enough to make the point) illustrates what is meant by the ethical edge that comes from having a thesis. Having an idea that you find interesting enough to write about makes you feel somehow responsible for writing in such a way as to earn that idea. And it will be that feeling of responsibility that will provide the motive for your search for other ideas that can be written in order to earn it. As we shall see, different thesis statements suggest different ways of structuring compositions. But the search for structure involves the desire to earn a central idea and the sense of responsibility to do so well.

Having an idea that is worth writing about creates the need for finding means of earning it. This is what makes composition an act of self-discovery; it involves not just the physical activity of writing one thing after another, but also the mental search for those means. It is in this sense that writing is an act of *inquiry*, a process of looking into the implications of an idea and its possible support. It is in this way that having one idea leads to the discovery and testing of other ideas. If we take responsibility for earning our main idea, we begin to see that there are many, too many, possible things to say *about* it, and we have to begin testing some of those things to see whether they are any good. In the process of looking for other ideas to put into relation, we accept some and reject others, whether we reject them before we write them down or whether we scratch them out after we have done so. What we are really doing is asking whether the other ideas that might go into a composition about a given idea are good enough. We are judging the quality of ideas, on the basis of whether they do justice to the one idea that controls our inquiry. We are doing more than "just writing"; we are thinking about what we think.

We have come a long way in this chapter, from the idea of syntax to the idea of inquiry. I hope you see, after having encountered all of the stages from this beginning to this end in this chapter, how the concept of structural relationships and the concept of inquiry are related. **Writing is ideas in relation, and putting ideas into relation involves a responsible inquiry into the way that one might earn a thesis that one cares about.** That is the thesis of this chapter. Having read this far, you should have some sense of the way in which this book will invite you to approach writing. You will be asked to look at writing as a way of earning ideas that you care enough about to take responsibility for. If you do this, you will not only be engaged in a process that enables you to write about ideas that challenge you to think at your best, you will also be giving yourself a basis for structuring your compositions in a coherent manner. The structures that you find to support your ideas will not be imposed from the outside, as empty forms you fill in with sentences; they will be structures you *generate* as a result of searching for the best means of support. You will be asked, in other words, to enter into a composing process that every serious writer must confront: the act of structuring ideas. This act entails the two most basic lessons that all writers must learn, whether students in any college class or nonstudents writing in the larger world of ideas. These lessons are:

A sense of structure.
A sense of one's presence in a community of inquiring minds.

Having devoted this chapter to principles of structure, I devote the next to your presence in a community of inquiring minds—by talking about your role as a member of the audience for others' writing. We return to the idea of structure in later chapters; in the next one, we consider reading.

QUESTIONS FOR THOUGHT, DISCUSSION, AND WRITING

1. Find a piece of good writing and try to identify the relationships between some of its sentences. What kinds of transitions hold them together? Ask yourself what the function of each transition is: What

does it *do?* Try this same analysis on writing of different kinds and compare the different uses of transitions in those contexts.

2. Use another piece of writing to think about the following structural questions: Given the writer's purpose, are there any parts of the writing that are not strictly necessary? If so, should the writer have cut them? Why or why not? Based on your sense of the writer's intention, are there any gaps in the structure—places where another part should have been added? Why?

3. Have you ever discovered your own intention in a piece of writing after you had begun to write? What did you do with the writing you had already done as a result of this discovery?

4. What does it mean to you to hear that you should be conducting genuine *inquiry* into your ideas as you write? What does *earning* your ideas mean to you?

CHAPTER 2

❧ *Reading for Reasons* ❧

How We Read

You've heard the old saying: "You are what you eat." What does it mean? If I were completely literal-minded, that is, if I took what I read or heard at face value, I would answer that it means something like "you become the foods you consume." But, literally, that meaning is absurd. I am not carrots and roast beef and pesto sauce. I am a flesh and blood human being, and I didn't get that way from practicing cannabalism! None of us would think to take the meaning of this saying quite that literally. We naturally understand it to mean something else, which it expresses indirectly, by inference. It implies that the kind of food we eat will have some kind of effect on the kind of flesh and blood people we are. A steady diet of ice cream will make a difference. Nutritious meals will help make us healthy. The meaning of this saying could be paraphrased for a long time without exhausting the many inferences that constitute its meaning. Proverbial statements such as this sometimes "ring true" precisely because they enable us to project our beliefs onto them. I assent to "You are what you eat" because I can associate its meanings with truths about nutrition that I already believe. Unless I were being pig-headed, I probably wouldn't stop to ask myself whether I *should* believe the statement. ("Oh, yeah? Prove it!") But I also know that my belief in the statement must have some limit. If I believed it completely, literally, then I would be as irrational as if I rejected it as nonsense. I *decide* to believe it to the extent that I understand it to conform to other things I already know about reality.

I have made an example of this saying for two reasons. First, I want to discuss in this chapter the process of believing what we read:

how we understand meanings in relation to other ideas that we can connect them to and how we can adjust our beliefs to fit what we already know. The act of believing is the result of a decision, and we can decide how *much* belief to give to any idea based on how well it measures up. The process of giving and withholding belief can be carried out in a rational or an irrational way. We are rational when we decide to make up our minds or not to make up our minds by exercising reason. This means that we must figure out how to make our way between the extremes of too much unreasonable belief and too much unreasonable doubt—a lot easier said than done. The above example is too easy, but it does illustrate a process we must go through in some fashion—whether we know it or not—whenever we have to say "I understand" or "I agree."

But I have made an example of that saying also because I want to play with it. Let's begin this extended discussion of critical reading with a statement I have invented by twisting that one around a bit:

"You are how you read."

Now, what does that mean? Literally, it's nonsense. But many phrases that are literal nonsense have meaning, as we've just seen. You might, for instance, have read the twisted version of the saying and said to yourself, "Either Gage is off his nut or I'm missing the boat," even though there are no nuts or boats in sight. Nonetheless, by asserting that "You are how you read," I invite you to consider some inferences behind that statement and to see whether they accord with your reading experience.

Notice first of all that the statement doesn't say, "You are *what* you read." That is no doubt as true in the mental sense as the original version of the saying is true in the physical sense. We "consume" words and we can be changed by them. But if I had put the saying that way, I would be embarking on a different kind of discussion, a discussion of *what* to read rather than *how*. It is very important to some people, maybe to some of your teachers, that you learn to appreciate certain good writers, and it is very important to others that you avoid certain bad ones. "Good" and "bad" in either case might mean a variety of things, depending on who is doing the recommending or the censoring. And, yes, we are all affected by our choice of reading. We learn from it; we add it to what we know. But there are several reasons I would not want to be telling anybody what to read or what not to, at least here. First of all, it would be useless. There are as many lists of "essential reading" as there are people who make them up. And the people who do make up such lists are only telling us about the books that they have read (or, sometimes, that they want us to *think* that they have read), and they cannot include any of the presumably good readings that have no doubt escaped their notice. There is more reading to be done in the world than any person, or any committee, or any school board is able to know about.

More importantly, those who believe that there is such a thing as "essential reading" or "forbidden reading," might think that *just* reading will make you believe or accept something as true; they want to be sure that you read things they want you to believe and not read things they don't want you to believe. They don't want to give you credit, in other words, for being able to accept or reject what you read on your own. They think that you will be the victims of the words you consume. I don't. At least, I think that you don't have to be. (By the way, do you believe me?)

We are not made better or worse simply because we read anything. Rather, we are made better or worse by *how* we read, no matter whether the content of our reading is what we would consider good or bad. One can learn how to be a better person, for instance, from a book that might otherwise be corrupting, if one reads it in a certain way. It is what we choose to *do* with what we read that affects us. Therefore, we are how we read, in the sense that the way in which we go about accepting or rejecting what we read is what determines the way we are changed by it.

Much of what we know and believe does not come from reading, of course. But much does, probably more than we could ever tally. Whether we are habitual readers or casual readers or infrequent readers, we are all readers, and a lot of what we know and think has been the result of how we have read whatever we happen to have read. *Somebody* must be reading all those ads for toothpaste with guileless innocence, even if *we* all know not be believe them. And somebody, similarly, must be reading our favorite self-help book (the one we keep nodding yes to without questioning) as if it were nothing but propaganda. We change our reading habits to fit the nature of the reading matter and our reasons for reading it. It would be silly to adopt the same guarded stance when reading the comic page that we might adopt when reading the advertisements. But might the comics ever be trying to sell us anything? Are they not sometimes asking for our belief in certain ideas? You bet they are. We might change our reading habits to fit the occasion, and we should, but we might not want to give up our ability to think critically about what we read.

Reading is one of our principal sources of information. In college, it might be our main source of information. Information comes to us in many other ways—by word of mouth, on film, over the airways. Yet, we know that there is something inherently more credible about information we find in an assigned textbook than information we overhear in the cafeteria. Hearsay, as helpful as it is in some ways, is not admissible evidence in court precisely because no one is taking *direct* responsibility for its truth. When someone has written information down, we presume that that person is taking some kind of responsibility for its accuracy.

Whether rightly or wrongly, we often rely on reading when we want a "source" for some piece of information. We may not believe everything that we read, but we nevertheless know that if we are to have reliable information, we probably ought to seek it in a reliable written source. Part of becoming educated is learning about the usefulness of such sources. We don't usually study a subject with the idea that we will commit everything we learn about it to memory. We know there are some things about it that we can look up if we have to. We study that subject with the idea that we can go on reading about it with a better sense of understanding.

I've said that we "know" these things. Perhaps I should say we "assume" them. To what extent should we rely on reading as a source of information? What does it mean to have found a "reliable" source? By what means do we decide that a given piece of information is true?

A Case in Point

Let's consider an example, although you should be warned at the beginning that the example is loaded. Let's keep things simple for the moment and not try to deal with controversial matters of belief; let's stick to "facts." Suppose, for whatever reason, you decide to read up on the history of the bathtub, a subject on which you ought to be able to find reliable information. You look up "Bathtub" in an encyclopedia and discover an article that contains this information:

> The Victorian tub was frequently a hooded affair, usually made of wood, copper, or iron. Bathroom fixtures were often disguised out of a desire for modesty. The tub, for example, might have a cover resembling a sofa or chaise longue. Home bathroom facilities gradually became common in western Europe, Canada, and the United States. The White House in Washington, D.C., did not have a bathtub until 1851, and a generation later a bathroom in the house was still a mark of the wealthy class.*

You notice right away, of course, that some of this information is vague. The words *frequently* and *usually* in the first sentence tell us that the author cannot be categorical about *all* bathtubs during the Victorian age. He does the same with *often* in the next sentence and *might* in the next. He's hedging. You might be beginning to ask,

The Encyclopedia Americana (1982), 3, 351.

"What *does* this writer know for sure?" But then he says something straightforward and precise: "The White House . . . did not have a bathtub until 1851." Now, there's what you're looking for, an unqualified fact. You've found this information in an authoritative source, one that would have no reason to lie to you. The source isn't lying, but it is nevertheless wrong. In fact, what you have learned in the article is hooey. The first bathtub in the White House was not installed in 1851. You'll see shortly why I think so.

It is no surprise to anyone, of course, that encyclopedias and reference books are sometimes wrong. Sometimes, they are wrong because the "truth" as it was known at the time of the writing has been superceded by more, better, or different information. The author can't be blamed for not knowing that what was the case at the time of writing might turn out to be wrong in the future. But in the case of the bathtub article, the author of this "fact" has it wrong simply because he accepted it uncritically from some other source.

At some point in reading about the history of the bathtub, if you had pursued it further, you might have encountered a reference to "the infamous bathtub hoax." That might have led in a new direction of inquiry, and sooner or later, you might have come across the following essay, written for readers of a journal called *Menckeniana* for fans of an American journalist of the 1920s, H. L. Mencken. Read it through and you'll see why the encyclopedia "facts" aren't to be trusted.

THE PHILOSOPHY OF H. L. MENCKEN
by P. J. Wingate

He called his piece "A Neglected Anniversary" because he said no attention had been given to the seventy-fifth anniversary of the installation of the first true bathtub—one with pipes carrying in hot and cold water and others to carry away the spent water—ever set up in the United States.

This bathtub, Mencken reported, had been completed on December 20, 1842, in the home of Adam Thompson, a Cincinnati grain merchant who shipped much of his grain to England. During trips to visit customers in England Thompson became familiar with bathtubs and decided to install one in his own home.

Thompson's tub was a large thing made of mahogany wood and lined with lead so that it weighed 1750 pounds. It was supplied with water from a third floor tank and some of the water was heated by running it through a long copper coil in the chimney of the fireplace. Thompson liked his new tub and invited several other wealthy Cincinnatians to try a bath in it. They liked it too and soon there were several bathtubs in Cincinnati and the newspapers there ran stories about these tubs.

Whereupon a surprising reaction to use of the bathtub occurred.

"On the one hand" Mencken wrote "it was denounced as an epicurean and obnoxious toy from England, designed to corrupt the democratic simplicity of the republic, and on the other hand it was attacked by the medical faculty as dangerous to health."

Mencken went on to quote from the *Western Medical Repository* of April 23, 1843, which called the bathtub a certain inviter of "phthisic rheumatic fevers, inflammation of the lungs and the whole category of zymotic diseases."

Nevertheless, news about the bathtub spread and soon tubs were being installed in other cities which developed controversies of their own. Hartford, Providence, Charleston (South Carolina), and Wilmington (Delaware) all put special water taxes on homes with bathtubs, Mencken reported, and Boston in 1845 made bathing unlawful except upon medical advice. But this ordinance was never enforced and was repealed in 1862. The repeal was a slow reaction to the fact that the American Medical Association had met in Boston in 1852. A poll of the membership showed that nearly all the doctors present then thought bathing was harmless, and twenty per cent advocated it as beneficial.

However, the thing which really caused the bathtub to flourish in America, Mencken reported, was the example set by President Millard Fillmore. Fillmore had visited Cincinnati on a political tour in 1850 and had taken a bath in the original Thompson tub. To quote Mencken: "Experiencing no ill effects, he became an ardent advocate of the new invention" and when he succeeded to the Presidency, after Taylor died on July 9, 1850, he had his Secretary of War, General Conrad, install one in the White House.

"This action," Mencken reported, "revived the old controversy and its opponents made much of the fact that there was no bathtub at Mt. Vernon or Monticello, and all the Presidents and magnificos of the past had got along without such monarchial luxuries."

Nevertheless, the bathtub prospered greatly after Fillmore's term as President and by 1860, according to newspaper advertisements, every hotel in New York had a bathtub and some had two or even three.

Mencken closed his story for the *Evening Mail* this way: "So much for the history of the bathtub in America. One is astonished, on looking into it, to find that so little of it has been recorded. The literature, in fact, is almost nil. But perhaps this brief sketch will encourage other inquiries and so lay the foundation for an adequate celebration of the Centennial in 1942."

However, for the next nine years, no one wrote anything else about the bathtub, although Mencken's account was reprinted in over a hundred magazines and newspapers, and excerpts from it appeared in history books and encyclopedias. One item in particular—Fillmore's installation of the first White House bathtub—fascinated historians and it was recorded in a multitude of places. Fillmore, in fact, became known during the 1920's as "the first clean president."

Then almost a decade after he wrote his story for the New York *Evening Mail,* Mencken wrote a follow-up piece which appeared in the Chicago *Tribune* of May 23, 1926. In this new story Mencken admitted that the first piece was totally a product of his own imagination.

"This article" he wrote in the *Tribune* story "was a tissue of absurdities, all of them deliberate and most of them obvious. If there were any facts in it they got there accidentally and against my design."

Mencken went on to say that he had liked his fabrication and was at first pleased when so many newspapers across the country reprinted it. Then he became alarmed because "I began to encounter my preposterous 'facts' in the writings of other men.They began to be used by chiropractors and other such quacks as evidence of the stupidity of medical men. They began to be cited by medical men as proof of the progress of public hygiene. They got into the learned journals. They were alluded to on the floor of Congress. They crossed the ocean and were discussed solemnly in England and on the continent. Today, I believe they are accepted as gospel everywhere on earth. To question them becomes as hazardous as to question the Norman Invasion."

This exposé, itself, was reprinted in twenty or thirty major newspapers and then a very curious situation developed. No one paid any attention to this exposé. Two weeks later the Boston *Herald* reprinted the original hoax as an interesting piece of American history. Of course, no one corrected the history books which had faithfully reproduced parts of it, particularly the item about Millard Fillmore putting in the first White House bathtub.

Mencken made one more attempt to debunk his bathtub hoax and on July 25, 1926, wrote another piece on the subject for the Chicago *Tribune,* once again calling his original story a fake.

Again, very few people apparently paid any attention to the exposé and the original story kept right on gaining credibility and acceptance. And it kept on doing so long after Mencken died.

Dr. Daniel Boorstin, Librarian of the Library of Congress, for example, included the most intriguing of Mencken's "facts" in his scholarly book *The Americans—The Democratic Experience* published by Random House in 1973. On page 353 Dr. Boorstin wrote: "In 1851 when President Millard Fillmore reputedly installed the first permanent bathtub and water closet in the White House he was criticized for doing something that was 'both unsanitary and undemocratic.' "

Dozens of other authors have done the same thing, the two most recent being Barbara Seuling in 1978 and Paul Boller in 1981. Boller's book, called *Presidential Anecdotes* was published by the Oxford University Press.

Also, all three of the national television networks reported in 1976, on January 7 the occasion of Fillmore's birthday, that he had installed the first White House bathtub.

All this has occurred despite the fact that many newspapers have exposed Mencken's fake over the years. For example, on January 4, 1977, the Washington *Post* exposed it once more but the *Post* closed its story on a note of optimism.

"Will this current account" the *Post* asked "destroy one of the nation's most charming myths? Certainly not. It will not even slow it up any more than a single grape placed on the railroad tracks would slow up a freight train.

"So on January 7, let all true patriots retire to their bathrooms, fill up the tub with champagne, invite the neighbors in, and drink a toast to Millard Fillmore, statesman, scholar, patriot, and the finest plumber who ever lived in the White House."

The Philadelphia *Inquirer* of January 7, 1977, carried a similar story which was headlined: "A Dirty Story. Fillmore's Still in That Tub."

And so it goes. The original hoax has become indestructible while all attempts to correct it go nowhere.

Mencken explained all this in his essay which he called "Hymn To The Truth" written for the Chicago *Tribune* in 1926.

"No normal human being" he wrote "wants to hear the truth. It is the passion of a small and aberrant minority of men, most of them pathological. They are hated for telling it while they live, and when they die are swiftly forgotten. What remains to the world, in the field of wisdom, is a series of long-tested and solidly agreeable lies."

In another essay called "The Art Eternal" Mencken stated his views in a somewhat similar manner and said that Americans were particularly resentful of the truth.

"A Galileo," he wrote "could no more be elected President of the United States than he could be elected Pope of Rome. Both high posts are reserved for men favored by God with an extraordinary genius for swathing the bitter facts of life in bandages of soft illusion."

Mencken closed his 1927 essay on philosophers this way:

"There is no record in human history of a happy philosopher: they exist only in romantic legend. Practically all of them have turned their children out of doors and beaten their wives. And no wonder! If you want to find out how a philosopher feels when he is engaged in the practice of his profession, go to the nearest zoo and watch a chimpanzee at the weary and hopeless job of chasing fleas. Both suffer damnably and neither can win."

So it is clear why Mencken did not wish to be called a philosopher.

Nevertheless, he had a philosophy of his own. Mencken believed that the list of eternal truths is a very short one and if a man happens to come across what he believes to be one of these eternal truths he still should not take it too seriously.

As P. J. Wingate's essay makes clear, Mencken enjoyed the idea that people would believe his fictional account of the history of the bathtub. He enjoyed it because it proved that people are gullible, and Mencken, like other great cynics, thought it terribly amusing that this should be so. He poked fun at people's credulity, and by this means, perhaps, tried to make people more skeptical, like himself. Mencken lied, on purpose, in order to argue an implied thesis: that people will believe anything on the basis of authority. His lies were believed because his thesis was overlooked by uncritical readers. Their unquestioning faith in authority proved him right! (It's possible, of course, that Mencken lied when he said he lied. Why do you suppose I am rejecting that possibility, here?)

The many writers of books and encyclopedia articles who repeated Mencken's fictions might have been more skeptical of the "facts" they passed along, but mere skepticism would not have been enough. If they had chosen to *disbelieve* this information, on the general principle that they would doubt everything, then they could not have written anything at all, for they would have nothing to say. The question is not whether they should or shouldn't have believed x, y, or z about bathtubs when they read it somewhere. The question is, *what kind of process did they go through as readers to measure their belief in the "facts" they read?* What kind of critical thought went on in their heads when they faced the decision to believe or disbelieve what they read? Had the original readers of Mencken's essay about the bathtub been more critical—as opposed to skeptical—they might have entertained some doubts about his information. And these doubts might have accompanied the information, so that others, who encountered it in other contexts such as encyclopedias, might share them.

What sort of process am I talking about? Not one, I assure you, that will prevent you from ever being duped or that will tell you when a thing is true. Critical reading can do no more than keep you asking about potentially good or bad reasons, so that when you face the question of whether to agree or disagree, you will be able to make a qualified decision based on your understanding of the quality of the reasons given. **Critical reading is the conscious act of adjusting the degree of one's agreement with any idea to the quality of the reasons that support that idea.** People who believe without caring about the quality of the reasons, as well as people who disbelieve without caring about the quality of the reasons, no matter *what* they believe, are, by this definition, uncritical. All of us are uncritical sometimes. We are more or less critical at different times. When we are reading, however, we should try to read as critically as we can. If we don't, we risk becoming the victims of a writer's reasoning.

When writer's write, they do not simply string together sentences that all directly assert some information. As we have seen in Chapter 1, writing takes its shape from the writer's intention, and that intention is always persuasive in some way. That is, writers want people to believe something. They write with an idea in mind, therefore, but their choice of things to say in addition to that idea depends on what they think people need to hear in order to believe it. Writing is purposeful and *strategic.* Writing that contains information, then, will also contain something put there in order to help you or encourage you to believe that that information is true.

A critical reader must, therefore, pay attention to more than *what* a piece of writing says. A critical reader must also consider *how* information is presented. This is because a writer who thinks strategically is mindful of the *means* that are necessary to reach the *end* that he or she has in mind. This does not mean that writers cheat or want to deceive us. It simply means that writer's intuitively understand that they must convince readers to believe them, and they make use of available means of persuasion accordingly. Information by itself is rarely the *end* of a piece of writing. Information is more likely among the *means* a writer has chosen to make an idea persuasive. Or, to put this another way, writers want more than our acceptance of information as true; they want us to adopt an attitude toward it, or to take a stance with them about the significance of the "facts." Let me illustrate this with a passage of writing that might appear at first simply to report objective information. In keeping with the theme of the bathtub hoax, here is an essay that appeared in newspapers. It repeats certain information that we have already read in Wingate's essay, but you will quickly see that this writer's purpose differs from Wingate's, and so the information is used differently.

MENCKEN AND THE GREAT "BATHTUB HOAX"
by Tom Welshko

In December 1917, H.L. Mencken (we celebrated his 104th birthday Sept. 12) published an article in the New York Evening Mail titled "A Neglected Anniversary." This article purported to note the 75th anniversary of the invention of the bathtub (defined as one with pipes to carry in hot and cold water and others to carry away the spent water), and to recount the history behind its invention and how it subsequently came into common use by Americans.

According to Mencken, the bathtub was invented on Dec. 20, 1842, by one Adam Thompson of Cincinnati. It soon became popular in Ohio and the U.S. in general, we learn. Mencken also states that 19th-century physicians denounced bathing as a health hazard and several jurisdictions, on this basis, banned the tub. Millard Fillmore, Mencken notes, was the first president to install a bathtub in the White House.

The only problem with these facts is that they are totally bogus. Mencken's article has since become known as "The Bathtub Hoax." Yet, 67 years after its first publication and 28 years after Mencken's death, the article and its spurious facts are still being quoted as true.

P.J. Wingate, in the fall 1983 issue of Menckeniana (the Enoch Pratt Library's magazine dedicated to the Baltimore author), lists several references, some as late as 1981, where Millard Fillmore is credited with installing the first White House bathtub. These references are from several major U.S. newspapers and all three television networks. (It must be stressed that many of Mencken's "facts" concerning the bathtub found their way into encyclopedias during his lifetime and will remain there to be quoted for ages to come.)

Mencken himself wrote at least two articles in 1926 in which he admitted concocting the history of the bathtub, but these disclaimers seem to have done little good. He explained why he thought "The Bathtub Hoax" gained so much credibility: "No normal human being wants to hear the truth. It is the passion of a small and aberrant minority of men, most of them pathological. They are hated for telling it while they live, and when they die are swiftly forgotten. What remains to the world, in the field of wisdom, is a series of long-tested and solidly agreeable lies."

I believe this is not why Mencken's bathtub facts gained currency. People do want the truth. However, nature abhors a vacuum. Sanitation is not a polite subject; hence, there are few books or articles concerning the objects of sanitary convenience, such as the bathtub, while thousands abound regarding more polite subjects such as electric lighting, the tele-

Source: The Baltimore Evening Sun (Sept. 12, 1984). Reprinted by permission.

phone or the computer. Mencken simply took advantage of a vacuum that existed in 1917.

Today, the vacuum still exists. The best way to combat Mencken's bogus facts about the bathtub is to recount its true history. These facts, though, are only to be found in the most dusty and obscure books. Obtaining those facts was a difficult task, and they are not as colorful, or as definitive, as Mencken's concocted history.

Of course, receptacles for bathing, where people carried water to a tub, existed from ancient times. What concerns us here is the "mechanized" bathtub. According to several sources, this process did not begin until the 19th century.

Paris was the first city to have a regular water supply, but only for well-to-do districts. This occurred in 1812. Among the earliest bathrooms in the United States were two built in the Van Ness Mansion in Washington, D.C., in 1815. The Tremont House, a Boston hotel, was said to "have an elaborate battery of water closets and bathrooms with running water in the basement" as early as 1827–29.

According to the Sept. 17, 1853, edition of The Illustrated London News, the Mount Vernon Hotel in Cape May, N.J., allowed "every guest to have his bath in his bedroom and there are hot and cold taps for his use when he pleases." As far as there being one person who can be credited with the bathtub's invention—such as Mencken's fictitious Adam Thompson—there is none.

Even as late as the 1880s, though, "5 out of every 6 dwellers in American cities had no facilities for bathing other than those provided by pail and sponge." Bathtubs were luxury items, affordable only by the rich. In fact, the Crane Co. did not begin to mass-produce copper-lined wood bathtubs until 1883 and enameled tubs until 10 years later.

Mencken, though, perpetrated one of the greatest literary hoaxes of all time. No matter what the reason, his bathtub facts will endure.

Now, what has Welshko done in this writing with the information that he seems to have derived from Wingate? In the first place, Welshko is using the information about Mencken's hoax to set up his own explanation for why people are gullible. Wingate simply presents Mencken's view of this problem by quoting or paraphrasing Mencken himself, and he seems to agree with Mencken's explanation since he does not challenge it. Welshko, on the other hand, is reporting the incident of the bathtub hoax for the purpose of *disagreeing* with Mencken's explanation, and you might observe how much of Mencken's explanation he has, therefore, left out of the account. Welshko also skips over certain details of the bogus history of the bathtub because they do not much matter to his intention. He needs only to tell his readers enough to persuade them that there was a hoax and that "its spurious facts are still being quoted as true." Notice that Wingate goes into detail on this point; Welshko just asserts it. Welshko's purpose is to make an argument of his own, and he offers just enough information to give us a context for understanding it.

The argument that Welshko wants to make begins in the sixth paragraph. He is trying to make a case that Mencken's explanation for the success of his hoax was too harsh. Welshko does not want to blame unskeptical readers for their gullibility as much as he wants to credit some kind of universal principle, that "nature abhors a vacuum." This in turn permits him to carry his argument one more step, and to say that the history of the bathtub might be set straight, not by making people more skeptical necessarily, but by recording "its true history." He seems to mean that there will be no problem once he fills the vacuum with the real facts, in place of Mencken's bogus ones. Now look at what Welshko says: "These facts . . . are only to be found in the most dusty and obscure books." He then goes on to tell us some of these facts. Does he expect us to believe him? What reasons does he give us to accept his facts? Is Welshko any more *believable* than Mencken was?

Only an uncritical reader at this point could accept Welshko's facts as true *solely on the basis of the reasons he gives.* At the same time, however, we have no solid reasons to disbelieve him. With our knowledge of Mencken's hoax in the background, we must at least acknowledge the possibility that Welshko might be perpetrating one of his own, having us on for reasons similar to Mencken's. It is possible that Welshko's reference to "dusty and obscure books," without naming them, is a hint to his ironic purpose in this context. It is possible that his reference to *The Illustrated London News* is as bogus as Mencken's reference to the *Western Medical Repository.* (Unless we did a little hunting, we couldn't say whether *either* reference were real or bogus.) But these are only possibilities, not certainties. In order to test Welshko's facts, to know with a greater degree of certainty that we should accept them, we would have to do some independent inquiry, to confirm or to dispute them based on more reading, just as we would have to do to know whether Mencken's or the encyclopedia's facts were to be fully trusted, *or distrusted.* Another possibility is that Welshko did not name some of his sources because he didn't think it necessary, since we would take his word for it that they say what he says they do. Yet another possibility is that Welshko did find his information in "several sources," but that these sources are themselves wrong.

These possibilities in themselves do not dispute Welshko's facts. They simply enable us to adjust the degree of acceptance we choose to give to them. We do not have to believe them. No one is compelling us by force to do so. But we must decide nevertheless how believable they are. To do this, we go through a process of weighing. We weigh our agreement, balancing it against all the other things we know and don't know, against what we know and don't know of Welshko's purpose, against what we know and don't know of Welshko's strategies, against what we know and don't know independently about the history of plumbing, and so on. The more knowledge we have, the better we are able to do this weighing, but since our judgment also involves our consciousness of what we don't know, this process can never arrive at a conclusion that does not balance belief against the possibility of being wrong.

Reading and Belief

Some people are accustomed to think that facts must either be believed or they must be disbelieved—as if belief were like a light switch with only two positions, on or off. My use of the bathtub hoax is intended to illustrate that belief does not have to operate as a simple yes or no choice, all or nothing. Belief can be more conditional; it can be something that we decide to have "up to a point" or "to a degree." And so, the question we might ask ourselves while reading does not have to be "Should I believe it or not?" but instead can be "How much should I believe it?" This latter question implies that the belief we have in any given fact, or in any given idea, is not determined by whether it sounds right or whether the source is an authority. It means that our beliefs are determined by the reasons that justify them. Belief is not a mechanical action, brought about by invariable rules of nature. It is a human activity, the exercise of judgment. With this in mind, we might say that we perform this action better when we know what the reasons are that have led to our belief, and why they are good reasons.

If it seems difficult for you to think of belief in this way, try thinking instead about the words *agreement* and *assent*. These may seem more clearly to be human actions, and they also may seem more clearly to be susceptible to degrees of commitment. And yet, for most purposes, they mean the same as *belief*. If I believe you, I have decided to agree, for the moment, with what you say. I have assented to your ideas. For good reasons, let's hope.

These observations do not deprive us of our ability to believe in what we read. They are not intended to transform you from credulous believers into stubborn doubters. The process of weighing beliefs against the quality of reasons is one that you already go through all the time, whether you are aware of it or not. We all do. The practice of critical reading is the exercise of this kind of judgment on purpose. By doing it, we protect ourselves from being led into belief for inadequate reasons, but at the same time we open up our minds to the possibility of arriving at belief for adequate ones. If we decide to grant or withhold assent based on the quality of the reasons that we are given, we admit at the same time that two things are possible: We admit that we might assent less in the future if we discover that the reasons are not so good after all; and we admit that we might assent more if we are ever presented with better reasons than we had formerly known. This attitude is not pure skepticism any more than it is pure credulity. It is somewhere in between. It is the attitude of an open-minded thinker, of someone who wishes to be responsible for deciding for herself or himself what to believe.

The practice of critical reading, then, can do more than protect us from jumping too quickly to conclusions. Because it is a process of examining reasons and measuring conclusions against them, it can provide us with a way to learn to live with uncertainty. "Living with uncertainty" is one of those skills we must master to get along in this world, but it is also a skill that people do not much talk about. We have just seen that certainty is not easy to come by. It requires that we assume some responsibility for questioning what we read, which might entail a search for more information and better reasons than we are given in a single source. It requires independent inquiry and thought, in other words, which are carried out not only because we want to know what to believe but also because each of us alone must make up his or her own mind.

But the same reasons that motivate this process of questioning also teach us that the process might not ever come to completion. Even when we do feel that we have adequate reasons for our convictions, if we arrived at them through inquiry, we must also know that our inquiry has not been complete. More inquiry is always possible. New ideas, new reasons might turn up. So, although we learn from this process that it is possible to believe an idea up to the point that we have good reasons to do so, we also learn that permanent, absolute belief is probably not available to us about many things. In the realm of theology, we may decide that faith is a better reason than reason itself, and so we may choose to give up questioning for the benefit of something better. But most of the issues that face us, in college and in the conduct of our lives, are not theological issues, and we would not want to give up questioning if that meant we might be deceived about them. If absolute, permanent belief is not available about many matters that concern us, we must adjust to this situation and accept it. It can be a situation to be enjoyed, not lamented, because it is what makes thinking and learning an adventure. It keeps our minds alert and active. It makes us want to continue to learn because we are more able to accept new ideas. It makes us less susceptible to the tactics of people who would like to do our thinking for us. Instead of the easy convictions that come from narrow-mindedness, this process offers us the possibility of continuing to think about things that matter to us.

Critical reading, then, is something we practice in order to acknowledge that we belong to a human community, a "community of inquiring minds," as I called it earlier—a community of language users, in which inquiry and argument are valued for their ability to keep us thinking and talking to each other.

Some Considerations for Critical Reading

The preceding section has offered you some of the philosophical premises about reading and writing, about education, on which this book is based. You are free, in fact encouraged, to question them. But now we must get practical in our thinking about critical reading. If you have some sense at this point what critical reading is and what principles justify your practice of it, let's consider in more specific ways *how to do it*.

What follows is a discussion of some of the questions that a critical reader might consider in order to arrive at an adequate basis for deciding how much to give or withhold assent. Asking the questions will not, of course, guarantee answers. They can only serve as guidance for further thinking. Perhaps you ask yourself many of these questions anyway when you read, even if you never become self-consciously deliberate about doing so. One reason to become more deliberate in considering these questions is to make them habitual; if you can force yourself to think along these lines by consciously asking these questions, sooner or later you will ask them without having to force yourself. They are numbered for convenience, but they are not intended as a checklist, to proceed through in mechanical fashion. They are not, as you will see, quite as separate as a numbered list might suggest. Nor are they equally applicable to every kind of reading; some will be more important than others, depending on the nature of the reading to which you apply them. Use them as a basis for more thought, that's all.

1. *What is the writer's purpose?* What is this writer trying to do to the reader? What is the single most important idea in the writing, the one that makes everything else in it necessary? This central idea

(or "thesis") may or may not be stated explicitly by the writer. It may or may not be obvious.

2. *What question does the writing answer?* The writer's intended audience is assumed to share a concern for some question, which the essay serves to answer in some way. The question may or may not be explicit or obvious. Do I share this concern? Should I?

3. *Why does the writer think this question is important?* There must be some reason the writer has chosen this question to answer. What difference does it make to the writer that the question be resolved? What about the writing tells me this?

4. *How persuadable am I?* Do I already have my mind made up on this question? How willing am I to listen to another point of view? If I agree with the author, can I maintain some critical distance and not agree with the reasons just because I already agree with the conclusion? What untested reactions do I have to the writer's thesis?

5. *What are the writer's reasons?* What ideas does the writer advance in defense of the thesis? What ideas are advanced in defense of *those* ideas?

6. *Where does the reasoning stop?* What reasons are asserted as if they are self-evident? Although some reasons are supported by a further "line of reasoning," it is impossible for all of them to be. If the reasoning depends on these ideas being believed without further support, do I believe them?

7. *Are the reasons logical?* Not all reasons actually support the conclusions they seem to support. What actually connects the reasons to the conclusions? *

8. *What responsibility does the writer take for the verifiability of information?* If the writer cites facts, or studies, or experiences, or sources, is there an adequate basis for checking up on these, or does the writer expect us to simply take his or her word for them?

9. *What has the writer done to put the reader in a receptive frame of mind?* Not all parts of a writing have the strictly logical function of supporting a thesis. Some aspects of the composition, especially its style, will function to create confidence in the writer, or a special bond between the writer and the reader. How do I react to these features?

10. *What am I going to do about it?* If a critical reader is engaged in measuring assent, then I should know how I might be changed by having read and thought about these ideas. To what extent must I adjust my thinking? Do these ideas have relevance to my thinking

---

*We look at logic in Chapter 4. For now, try to determine whether the conclusions follow from the reasons without trying to reduce them to logical formulas.

about other questions? Are there connections between these ideas and other things I believe?

These questions are not exhaustive, of course. And they do not need to be answered definitively, in perfect sequence. Here is an example of another essay, one that depends less on our granting the writer facts and more on our following a line of logical connections. My critical analysis, based on the questions above, follows the essay.

IN WHAT SPIRIT THE AMERICANS CULTIVATE THE ARTS
by Alexis de Toqueville

It would be to waste the time of my readers and my own if I strove to demonstrate how the general mediocrity of fortunes, the absence of superfluous wealth, the universal desire for comfort, and the constant efforts by which everyone attempts to procure it make the taste for the useful predominate over the love of the beautiful in the heart of man. Democratic nations, among whom all these things exist, will therefore cultivate the arts that serve to render life easy in preference to those whose object is to adorn it. They will habitually prefer the useful to the beautiful and they will require that the beautiful should be useful.

But I propose to go further, and, after having pointed out this first feature, to sketch several others.

It commonly happens that in the ages of privilege the practice of almost all the arts becomes a privilege, and that every profession is a separate sphere of action, into which it is not allowable for everyone to enter. Even when productive industry is free, the fixed character that belongs to aristocratic nations gradually segregates all the persons who practice the same art till they form a distinct class, always composed of the same families, whose members are all known to each other and among whom a public opinion of their own and a species of corporate pride soon spring up. In a class or guild of this kind each artisan has not only his fortune to make, but his reputation to preserve. He is not exclusively swayed by his own interest or even by that of his customer, but by that of the body to which he belongs; and the interest of that body is that each artisan should produce the best possible workmanship. In aristocratic ages the object of the arts is therefore to manufacture as well as possible, not with the greatest speed or at the lowest cost.

When, on the contrary, every profession is open to all, when a multitude of persons are constantly embracing and abandoning it, and when its several members are strangers, indifferent to and because of their numbers hardly seen by each other, the social tie is destroyed, and each workman, standing alone, endeavors simply to gain the most money at the least cost. The will of the customer is then his only limit. But at the same time a corresponding chance takes place in the customer also. In countries in which

Source: From *Democracy in America*, Volume II, Alexis de Toqueville, translated by Henry Reeve, revised by Francis Bowen, edited by Phillips Bradley. Copyright 1945 and renewed 1973 by Alfred A. Knopf, Inc. Reprinted by permission of the publisher.

riches as well as power are concentrated and retained in the hands of a few, the use of the greater part of this world's goods belongs to a small number of individuals, who are always the same. Necessily, public opinion, or moderate desires exclude all others from the enjoyment of them. As this aristocratic class remains fixed at the pinnacle of greatness on which it stands, without diminution or increase, it is always acted upon by the same wants and affected by them in the same manner. The men of whom it is composed naturally derive from their superior and hereditary position a taste for what is extremely well made and lasting. This affects the general way of thinking of the nation in relation to the arts. It often occurs among such a people that even the peasant will rather go without the objects he covets than procure them in a state of imperfection. In aristocracies, then, the handicraftsmen work for only a limited number of fastidious customers; the profit they hope to make depends principally on the perfection of their workmanship.

Such is no longer the case when, all privileges being abolished, ranks are intermingled and men are forever rising or sinking in the social scale. Among a democratic people a number of citizens always exists whose patrimony is divided and decreasing. They have contracted, under more prosperous circumstances, certain wants, which remain after the means of satisfying such wants are gone; and they are anxiously looking out for some surreptitious method of providing for them. On the other hand, there is always in democracies a large number of men whose fortune is on the increase, but whose desires grow much faster than their fortunes, and who gloat upon the gifts of wealth in anticipation, long before they have means to obtain them. Such men are eager to find some short cut to these gratifications, already almost within their reach. From the combination of these two causes the result is that in democracies there is always a multitude of persons whose wants are above their means and who are very willing to take up with imperfect satisfaction rather than abandon the object of their desires altogether.

The artisan readily understands these passions, for he himself partakes in them. In an aristocracy he would seek to sell his workmanship at a high price to the few; he now conceives that the more expeditious way of getting rich is to sell them at a low price to all. But there are only two ways of lowering the price of commodities. The first is to discover some better, shorter, and more ingenious method of producing them; the second is to manufacture a larger quantity of goods, nearly similar, but of less value. Among a democratic population all the intellectual faculties of the workman are directed to these two objects: he strives to invent methods that may enable him not only to work better, but more quickly and more cheaply; or if he cannot succeed in that, to diminish the intrinsic quality of the thing he makes, without rendering it wholly unfit for the use for which it is intended. When none but the wealthy had watches, they were almost all very good ones; few are now made that are worth much, but everybody has one in his pocket. Thus the democratic principle not only tends to direct the human mind to the useful arts, but it induces the artisan to produce with great rapidity many imperfect commodities, and the consumer to content himself with these commodities.

Not that in democracies the arts are incapable, in case of need, of producing wonders. This may occasionally be so if customers appear who are ready to pay for time and trouble. In this rivalry of every kind of industry, in the midst of this immense competition and these countless experiments, some excellent workmen are formed who reach the utmost limits of their craft. But they rarely have an opportunity of showing what they can do; they are scrupulously sparing of their powers; they remain in a state of accomplished mediocrity, which judges itself, and, though well able to shoot beyond the mark before it, aims only at what it hits. In aristocracies, on the contrary, workmen always do all they can; and when they stop, it is because they have reached the limit of their art.

When I arrive in a country where I find some of the finest productions of the arts, I learn from this fact nothing of the social condition or of the political constitution of the country. But if I perceive that the productions of the arts are generally of an inferior quality, very abundant, and very cheap, I am convinced that among the people where this occurs privilege is on the decline and that ranks are beginning to intermingle and will soon become one.

The handicraftsmen of democratic ages not only endeavor to bring their useful productions within the reach of the whole community, but strive to give to all their commodities attractive qualities that they do not in reality possess. In the confusion of all ranks everyone hopes to appear what he is not, and makes great exertions to succeed in this object. This sentiment, indeed, which is only too natural to the heart of man, does not originate in the democratic principle; but that principle applies it to material objects. The hypocrisy of virtue is of every age, but the hypocrisy of luxury belongs more particularly to the ages of democracy.

To satisfy these new cravings of human vanity the arts have recourse to every species of imposture; and these devices sometimes go so far as to defeat their own purpose. Imitation diamonds are now made which may be easily mistaken for real ones; as soon as the art of fabricating false diamonds becomes so perfect that they cannot be distinguished from real ones, it is probable that both will be abandoned and become mere pebbles again.

This leads me to speak of those arts which are called, by way of distinction, the fine arts. I do not believe that it is a necessary effect of a democratic social condition and of democratic institutions to diminish the number of those who cultivate the fine arts, but these causes exert a powerful influence on the manner in which these arts are cultivated. Many of those who had already contracted a taste for the fine arts are impoverished; on the other hand, many of those who are not yet rich begin to conceive that taste, at least by imitation; the number of consumers increases, but opulent and fastidious consumers become more scarce. Something analogous to what I have already pointed out in the useful arts then takes place in the fine arts; the productions of artists are more numerous, but the merit of each production is diminished. No longer able to soar to what is great, they cultivate what is pretty and elegant, and appearance is more attended to than reality.

In aristocracies a few great pictures are produced; in democratic countries a vast number of insignificant ones. In the former statues are raised of bronze; in the latter, they are modeled in plaster.

When I arrived for the first time at New York, by that part of the Atlantic Ocean which is called the East River, I was surprised to perceive along the shore, at some distance from the city, a number of little palaces of white marble, several of which were of classic architecture. When I went the next day to inspect more closely one which had particularly attracted my notice, I found that its walls were of whitewashed brick, and its columns of painted wood. All the edifices that I had admired the night before were of the same kind.

The social condition and the institutions of democracy impart, more-over, certain peculiar tendencies to all the imitative arts, which it is easy to point out. They frequently withdraw them from the delineation of the soul to fix them exclusively on that of the body, and they substitute the representation of motion and sensation for that of sentiment and thought; in a word, they put the real in the place of the ideal.

I doubt whether Raphael studied the minute intricacies of the mechanism of the human body as thoroughly as the draftsmen of our own time. He did not attach the same importance as they do to rigorous accuracy on this point because he aspired to surpass nature. He sought to make of man something which should be superior to man and to embellish beauty itself. David and his pupils, on the contrary, were as good anatomists as they were painters. They wonderfully depicted the models that they had before their eyes, but they rarely imagined anything beyond them; they followed nature with fidelity, while Raphael sought for something better than nature. They have left us an exact portraiture of man, but he discloses in his works a glimpse of the Divinity.

This remark as to the manner of treating a subject is no less applicable to its choice. The painters of the Renaissance generally sought far above themselves, and away from their own time, for mighty subjects, which left to their imagination an unbounded range. Our painters often employ their talents in the exact imitation of the details of private life, which they have always before their eyes; and they are forever copying trivial objects, the originals of which are only too abundant in nature.

Having read de Toqueville's essay, what am I to make of it? Below is an example of the kind of thinking that can follow from asking the ten questions suggested as guidelines for critical reading. These are my own reactions, dramatized a bit. Yours are no doubt different. These questions have no right or wrong responses, only "better" or "worse" ones. They are designed to stimulate further thinking. Each response ends with an ellipsis (. . .) to indicate that I could carry each thought beyond what I give here for illustration. The responses are written as if I were "thinking out loud." They might provide some raw material for an analytical essay if I explored them further.

*   *   *   *

1. *What is de Toqueville's purpose?* He seems to want people to believe that great art cannot flourish in a democracy. In the first paragraph, he says that in democratic nations people "habitually prefer the useful to the beautiful." That summarizes his central idea pretty well, I think. . . .

2. *What question does this idea answer?* Well, I suppose the question must be whether democracies are able to produce great art, or whether they are less able to do so than aristocracies. I guess this was interesting to de Toqueville because in his time democracy was a fairly new form of government (or was it?). People were interested in whether the quality of life would change in a democracy. Since I live in a democracy and de Toqueville didn't, I don't see the issue in quite the same way he does. I think we do have great art. Then again, when I think about the The Louvre or the cathedrals of Europe, I wonder whether America has an artistic heritage like that. Maybe de Toqueville has a point. We certainly do have a lot of mass-produced junk, and I sometimes have trouble deciding whether some of it is "art." I guess it's an interesting question, even if it might be sort of "academic". . . .

3. *Why does de Toqueville think this question is important?* Maybe there's more to it than I thought at first. When he talks about art, toward the end of the essay, he seems to make the issue much more than a matter of whether America has better art than Europe. His idea of what art does for people is pretty heavy: "glimpse of Divinity," "imagination an unbounded range." Maybe he thinks that if a democracy doesn't create great art, it loses something else that is much more important, like the ability of its people to aspire to perfection. He should have seen commercial TV! Anyway, de Toqueville takes the issue seriously, because he thinks that art is important. Perhaps if we can decide whether democracy changes our attitude toward art, we can learn something about ourselves. Yes, de Toqueville seems to be talking about the difference between "mediocrity," as he calls it, and excellence. . . .

4. *How persuadable am I?* My "untested reaction to the author's thesis" is that he is wrong. But I'm not a fanatic about believing that democracy cultivates great art, so I guess I'm open-minded on this question. I don't have any vested interest in coming out on one side or the other. The more I think about it, the more interested I am in trying to figure out where I *do* stand. So, I'm willing to consider de Toqueville's reasons. No problem. . . .

5. *What are de Toqueville's reasons?* Good question! He has a lot of them. Maybe I better try to find the most basic ones. De Toqueville's main reason for saying that democracies discourage great art is because he thinks that in democracies each person is able to get ahead, unlike the "class" system of aristocracies, so people will produce art for the sake of getting rich rather for the sake of making beautiful objects well. If you try to use art to make money, you will make it as cheaply and poorly as you can get away with—". . . the democratic principle . . . induces the artisan to produce with great

rapidity many imperfect commodities, and the consumer to content himself with these commodities." So, de Toqueville reasons that if bad art will satisfy people's basic need to get ahead, bad art is what we'll get; there is no motivation for doing better. We may get more art, but it will be worse. But why worse? What does de Toqueville think good art is? His reason for saying that this art will be worse is because it will "put the real in the place of the ideal." Is that a reason, though? . . .

6. *Where does his reasoning stop?* This seems to be what de Toqueville takes for granted and won't give reasons for: Art is worse to the degree that it is useful, better to the degree that it is beautiful only. So, that's why great art should be "ideal," and anything with a "realistic" side to it can't be great. But de Toqueville doesn't seem to have any reasons for saying that art *should* "aspire to surpass nature." He just says so. Do I believe this? Well, I guess I think that art should do *something* more than just be useful and that it should go beyond "nature." But I'm not sure I would use the same terms to describe it that de Toqueville does. So I do agree, sort of. . . .

7. *Are the reasons logical?* What connects the reasons to the conclusion? Well, let's see if I can work this out:

> Democracies make all citizens equal.
> Therefore, people in a democracy want to rise in social class.
> They will rise by selling commercial products.
> Therefore, they "habitually" seek what is useful over what is beautiful.
> Great art is not what is useful but what is beautiful.
> Therefore, they do not make great art.

There's more to it, I know, but this seems to be the "logic" as near as I can figure it. Do the conclusions follow? They seem to follow, if we take a few more ideas for granted and if these statements are true. I do think it follows that people who want to get rich will fit into the logic of Toqueville's argument. But I don't think it follows that in a democracy all people necessarily want to get rich. Of course, de Toqueville only says that there is "a large number" and "a multitude" of such persons, and he concludes that "the democratic principle *tends* to direct the human mind to the useful arts," so with these qualifications the logic seems to follow better than if it's put into absolutes. . . .

8. *What responsibility does the writer take for the verifiability of information?* Well, there isn't a lot of "information" here, but de Toqueville could be making everything up. What he says about particular artists at the end could be checked out, but it wouldn't matter

a whole lot, since de Toqueville is giving his interpretation of what these artists did. If art historians disagreed with him, these interpretations could still be supportable. De Toqueville also tells a story to illustrate his point about shabby American workmanship. Maybe he never did go to New York. That I could find out. But, again, it wouldn't change his argument much. I can think of hundreds of other examples that make the same point, so I'm not inclined to doubt his. I don't think de Toqueville has any reason to lie. If he weren't telling us what he really saw, his own writing would be shabby in the way he says democratic art is. If he's serious about what he says about art, and he seems to be, de Toqueville must be a careful writer. And he does write beautifully, even if the logic has a few holes in it. So, for someone writing the reasons for his beliefs, de Toqueville takes responsibility for what he says. He could have taken more, if he had. . . .

9. *What has de Toqueville done to put his reader in a receptive frame of mind?* Well, right at the beginning he tells us that he doesn't want to waste our time. Something tells me that de Toqueville was writing for a European audience, however, because he also starts right out flattering the reader for loving beauty, and he seems indirectly to refer to democracies as "them" and aristocracies as "us." The point of view in the essay seems to be an attempt to make the reader feel like "us." It's amazing that I can get this feeling when I am actually one of "them." I'm not sure how he does it, but his style is inviting: a little archaic (although he probably didn't think so!), maybe, but clear and not fancy. He doesn't overdo it. He has organized the ideas so that they are easy to follow. He talks about himself; that helps, too. And when he gets to the end, he manages to bring emotions into his writing. He also qualifies his ideas to make them more believable, but he isn't wishy-washy. That gives me confidence in him. He *sounds* intelligent. . . .

10. *What am I going to do about it?* Well, de Toqueville's essay isn't exactly a call to action! He doesn't necessarily want his reader to do anything other than to understand what kinds of attitudes may be created in people by their forms of government, and perhaps to examine their own attitudes. Do his ideas have relevance to my thinking? Yes. Not that I would have put it quite the way de Toqueville did, but he's made me interested in how our lives may be trivialized in ways we don't ordinarily think about, just because we do want to "rise above our means." Art is only one way this might be happening in our democracy. This doesn't make me want to live in a different form of government, but it does make me want to look at the kinds of values I have acquired because of accepting certain premises about what a democracy is. I certainly don't want to go

back to an aristocracy. But de Toqueville did teach me that art was important to people in a certain way that we may have lost. What else have we given up in our quest for the useful. . . ?

*   *   *   *

What have I accomplished by thinking about these things? I have read an essay, but its ideas have become my own, in a sense. This is active, as opposed to passive, reading. The critical reader makes reading an occasion for thinking more, and finishing an essay becomes the beginning of speculation. In the process, one learns not only what a writer thought, but what one thinks oneself, about the writer's ideas and one's own. Reading is a transaction between two active minds, and the critical reader produces as much thought as he or she consumes. But why do this? If thinking were a bad thing, there would be no reason to become an active reader. Of course, I think thinking is a good thing; that's where *my* reasoning stops! The process of coming up with *new* ideas, the active, creative thinking that takes us beyond what we already know, takes place when we are confronted by the ideas of others. It is when our ideas are in conflict with those of another that we expand our thoughts to take in more. Good reading is the means by which we bring this conflict about, since it is how we find and assess new ideas. Notice that I said good reading, not reading good books. You are *how* you read. Of course, the better you read, the more you may want to read good writing.

Implications for Research

The final chapter of this book is devoted to a full discussion of research, but the subject is so important to you as a critical reader and as a writer that you can think about it as we go along, in relation to other considerations. Thus, you'll find "implications for research" sections at the ends of the next two chapters also.

As a student—and as a voter, a consumer, a person who must decide things—you will often need to find out more than you already know about some subject before committing yourself to a conclusion or a course of action. Critical reading is necessary in order to know what to make of the knowledge that you discover when you look into some subject, but it will also help you to decide what needs looking into. When, in your further reading, you try to judge the conclusions you find against the adequacy of the reasons given for them, you will be able to isolate the particular areas in which your knowledge needs to be increased. By reading critically, you may find that you need not read further in one area, such as "anaesthesia," but do need to know more about some other, such as "sodium pentothal."

In formal research, you will be responsible for finding information to explain a phenomenon and evidence for arguing a reasonable conclusion about it. In informal research—the kind we do whenever we have unanswered questions, even if no writing will result from it—you will want to assure yourself that your ideas or actions are founded on reasons that you understand and trust. The goal of either kind of research is confidence in what you know. Critical reading will guide you in gaining that confidence, even though, as we see in this chapter, that confidence is not easy to come by.

If you are required to do formal research in connection with the writing you do while using this book in class, you should read the last chapter. But, even though no formal research is required, you will be doing a kind of informal research anyway, in the form of critical reading on subjects discussed in class. Discussion itself is like research, if it expands your understanding by confronting you with the ideas of others. Writing argumentative essays will require you to make up your own mind on issues that are open to speculation and inquiry. This involves assessing arguments that you encounter—in reading and discussion—and determining where you stand in relation to them. You may find, as you try to identify your position, that you are relying on information or reasons that you lack confidence in, or that are subject to challenge by others. You will have to inform yourself or adjust your reasoning until you have found the "best case." The "best case" available to you is relative to what you know. Critical reading informs argumentative writing; they are both part of the same process of making up your mind.

QUESTIONS FOR THOUGHT, DISCUSSION, AND WRITING

1. Have you ever had the experience of believing something you read and then discovering later that it was not true? What did this experience teach you about reading?
2. Have you ever read something that someone told you was bad for you? Was it? How do you know? How about something that someone said would be good for you?
3. Can you think of any ideas that you agree with only to a certain degree? What has your agreement to do with the quality of the reasons you have heard in support of these ideas?

4. Do you agree or disagree with H. L. Mencken's statement that "No normal human being wants to hear the truth"? Why?
5. In general, how would you define a "good reason"? Find some examples of good reasons and bad ones to illustrate what you mean. Does everyone agree with your examples?
6. Analyze an essay by thoughtfully considering the ten questions in this chapter. Choose an essay that you think is well argued.
7. Do you agree or disagree with de Toqueville's conclusions? What further reasons do you have to support or to refute them?

CHAPTER 3

How to Tell If
You're Having an Idea

An Idea Worth Writing About

As a critical reader, you know now that it's your obligation to ask "why?" when you encounter the assertions of others. As a writer, of course, you must expect your reader to ask the same question when you make assertions. You can't answer every "why?" question that might be asked, but you can at least keep in mind that a critical reader does not have to take your word for anything you say. You must try to provide good reasons.

What can you do, however, when faced with the possibility that this same critical reader might ask "so what?" The best way to answer this question is to make sure that you have something worth writing about. An idea is worth writing about when there's something of genuine interest in it for you *and* for those whom you wish to reach with it.

Argumentative writing is writing in which the writer takes a stance and offers reasons in support of it. A writer is in an "argumentative" situation—one that calls for a stance to be taken and reasons to be offered—when there is a problem at hand, a question that needs answering. You can best assure that your reader will not ask "so what?" if you think of yourself as writing about questions that you can expect your reader to share, problems that you have in common, even though you may not share the answers or the solutions. (If you shared the question *and* the answer with your reader, you'd have no reason to write at all. In writing, as in good conversation, when everybody agrees, somebody changes the subject!)

The word *argumentative* in this book does not mean the kinds of things one says when one is fighting mad. Let's call that kind of writing (for the sake of argument!) a rant. When we are in a contentious or perhaps angry mood, we are certainly moved to speak our minds, but we are less likely to be reasonable, because our purpose is generally to prevail by force of words rather than to inquire by using reason. *Argument* here means the kind of writing that attempts to present the *best case* that one is able to make. We are aided in our attempts to write arguments by being able to imagine a reader who is critical—the more critical the better, since what we want out of the writing process is to discover the best available basis for assent. The challenge of being reasonable is a better guide to good thinking than merely wanting to "win." If the process of argumentative writing is defined in this way, as **reasonable inquiry into the best grounds for agreement,** then we do not have to worry about losing the respect of critical readers, since they are readers who want to look for this basis with us.

Good writing by this definition is not confined to the academic essay, of course. You have probably written arguments in letters or other informal situations whenever you felt the need to explain or support one thought with another one. The argumentative *essay* (the word comes from the French word for "attempt") is no more than a composition that attempts to deal reasonably with significant ideas. It is the form that college writing usually takes simply because in an essay the writer encounters ideas directly, for the sake of coming to a new understanding. (This should be the case, of course, even if some college professors only care to read what they already believe!) By writing essays, a student can explore ideas for the sake of coming to an earned conclusion. But this process goes on in college for the sake of a larger aim: to prepare students to deal with ideas wherever they may encounter them. College is a place where ideas matter. So is an essay. Ideas matter in both because we all live a "life of the mind" and much depends on how well we live it.

What a Thesis Is and What It Does

A "significant idea" is not necessarily any idea that one happens to come up with. Some of our ideas are so conventional that they cannot be said to be "ours." Some are trivial. Some might seem like good ideas for a moment but turn out to be silly after a bit of thought. Ideas of these kinds occur to everyone. But when we set out to *write* about an idea, it is generally not one of these. We write because we have an idea that is worth writing about. Such an idea is one that the writer thinks should matter to other people and that the writer cares enough about to discuss. This means that the writer also thinks that others can be led to share the idea and that the writer, therefore, accepts the "burden of communication." If an idea is worth writing about, it must be worth communicating effectively. Having a significant idea confronts a writer with certain responsibilities: to be sure that sufficient reasons exist for believing the idea and to be sure that those reasons are able to be understood by others. These responsibilities are present throughout the writing process. They begin when one thinks about composing a "thesis."

I have already discussed what a thesis is and what its function is in writing. The first discussion, in Chapter 1, describes how a thesis represents the *end* for which the other elements of writing are *means*. The second discussion, in Chapter 2, makes use of this concept for the purpose of critically analysing the writing of others. I now discuss the thesis again in more detail for the purpose of helping you to write one. First, a definition:

> **A thesis is an idea, stated as an assertion, which represents a reasoned response to a question at issue and which will serve as the central idea of a unified composition.**

After the previous discussions, this definition should come as no surprise. Let's take a closer look at it, to determine what a writer needs to think about when trying to come up with a thesis that will provide the best basis for composing an essay. Each of the terms of this definition has special significance for the process of composing a useful thesis statement, on the way to composing a good argumentative essay.

A thesis is an idea. . . .   Fine, but what's an idea? Some people use the word *idea* to mean something like "topic" or "subject," phrases that indicate an *area* of potential interest, such as "economics," or "a cure for cancer," or "my first encounter with Professor Smith." These phrases might be said to be "broad" or "narrow" subjects, but they are not yet ideas because they do not say anything *about* economics or a cancer cure or the first time I met Smith. Perhaps you have had a teacher who was fond of telling you to "narrow your subject." Such advice misses the point, unless that teacher also pushed you to come up with an idea by saying something about your subject. The noun *economics* is not an idea. The narrowed (or "focused") noun phrase "economic conditions in South Africa in 1875" is still not an idea. "Economics is bull" *is* an idea—although, of course, not a very good one. The difference between noun phrases that are not ideas and statements that are ideas lies in the predication:

Ideas are sentences; they complete a thought by connecting a verb to the noun phrase. Saying something *about* a subject requires making some kind of connection between it and something else. It isn't the size of the noun phrase that matters; it's what you have to say about it—and this will be found in the verb that you connect to it. Any noun phrase, no matter how broad or narrow, might become the basis of many different ideas, even totally contradictory or incompatible ones. "Economics is my best class" is a very different idea from "Economics is bull," and yet both apparently share the same subject. The difference is in the predication; that's what makes them ideas.

A thesis is . . . stated as an assertion.   Not all ideas make good thesis statements. The difference between an idea and an assertion is more subtle than the difference between a subject and an idea, but no less important. Not all ideas are stated with the intention of asserting something to be the case. Even though an idea must be a complete sentence, not all sentences are uttered for the purpose of asserting a proposition. "Go away" is certainly a sentence that communicates, but it does not seem to be proposing anything as true. It expresses a desire but does not put forth a claim. "I guess I'll take a walk." "What a day for baseball!" "Please tell me how to get to the Geology building." "Gimme a break!" Sentences, ideas, can perform many other actions besides asserting.

To assert is to claim that some condition is the case. Each of the nonassertions above could be made into assertions by making them into such claims. "A walk would be good for me right now." "Sunny days are best for baseball." "Geology is to the left of Art." Assertions propose ideas to which one might respond, "No, that's not the case," or "Yes, that is the case." As you can see, making assertions implies that one believes in what one has just said. To seem to assert without belief would be a different kind of action: to lie or to joke. Assertions imply a willingness to defend an idea against the possibility that it might not be the case. An assertion, because it claims that something is a certain way, is an invitation to discuss the merits of an idea, as an idea. Still, not all assertions make the kind of claims that we are looking for in thesis statements, so let's consider the next part of my definition.

A thesis . . . represents a reasoned response to a question at issue.   This part of the definition points us backward, toward the situation from which a thesis is derived. What makes an assertion worth writing about? Where does it come from?

An assertion is worth writing about when not everyone already believes it and when people should care whether to believe it or not. A thesis answers a question, in other words, that people are really asking because they do not already share the answer. A question *at issue* is one that people might answer in different ways, the kind of question, that is, that calls for a reasoned response. All assertions answer a question of some kind. Not all assertions answer a question at issue. Consider these assertions and the questions to which they are answers:

It's raining.	Is it raining?
Today is election day.	Is today election day?
You should vote "no" on Measure 6.	Should I vote "yes" or "no" on Measure 6?
Measure 6 will violate your constitutional right to own a handgun.	Will Measure 6 violate my constitutional right to own a handgun?
The Constitution does not make handgun ownership a right.	Does the Constitution make handgun ownership a right?

Are the questions to which these assertions respond *at issue?* You're right if you answer "it depends." It depends on who is asking them and why. It depends on the context in which the question is asked. A thesis is a response to a *situation,* which includes an audience of people who, for their own reasons, are addressing certain questions by virtue of arguing on certain subjects in certain ways. There are situations in which these questions might constitute questions at issue, and there are different situations in which they would not. The difference is whether the answer calls for argumentation. Is there some doubt whether the answer should be believed? If I assert that "It's raining" in a situation where the question is not at issue—where no one cares whether it's raining or not or where everyone is satisfied by my mere assertion—then there is no issue to be argued. If I assert that "Today is election day" in a situation where everyone already knows it, then there is no issue. In this case, however, the question at issue might become "What, then, should we do about it?" and argument might ensue over whether it's worth going out in the rain to vote. Then, again, it might not, if that question is not at issue. If I am talking to some friends who have already decided to vote against Measure 6, then my statement that "You should vote 'no' on Measure 6" would not be at issue, although my statement that "Measure 6 would violate your constitutional right to own a handgun" might be at issue if those friends were divided on *why* Measure 6 should be defeated. If I were addressing an audience of uncommitted voters, my assertion that "Measure 6 will violate your constitutional right to own a handgun" might address a question at issue. But if that audience happened to believe that the Constitution does not provide citizens with such a right, then I would have missed them with my argument because I chose to address the wrong question. I would have to back up and address the question of whether there is, in fact, such a right. Only by finding the question at issue and arguing for an assertion that answers it, do I find my audience.

It is possible, then, to argue but to miss the point by failing to address a question that is, in fact, at issue for the audience addressed. The judgment of whether one has focused on such a question can be made only by inquiring into one's audience. What do they already believe? What answer do they share with me? On what issue are we divided? Such questions are necessary in the decision to argue one assertion rather than another, and the decision can change from situation to situation, depending on one's audience.

One significance of this for the writer of argumentation is that the decision to argue one idea rather than another is in part determined by the writer's audience. The intention of any piece of argumentative writing combines what the writer has to say and what the audience needs to hear: what is at issue for the audience. We are all free, of course, to choose to argue anything we like, but only when we "find our audience" with what we have to say do we really face the necessity of reasoning well. If I argue that "A moon colony should be used for the purpose of manufacturing perfect golf balls" to an audience that in no way cares whether I am right or wrong, then it hardly matters whether I base my case on good or bad reasons. (Remember Alice and the Cheshire Cat?) But if I argue it in a situation where some people believe that moon colonies should not be used for commercial purposes or who believe that perfect golf balls are a useless commodity, then the reasons I choose will make all the difference in whether my idea is believed or not.

Having asserted this relation between one's audience situation and the thesis that one chooses to argue, I must admit that knowledge of one's audience is never complete. Not only does an audience usually consist of more than one person, with many more than one set of interests and beliefs, but audiences may also consist of people who are entirely unknown to us. The question of who constitutes an audience is not a simple one, nor should it be made to seem simple. It is one of those matters about which a writer must make a judgment, using whatever knowledge there is to be used, without being able to arrive at certainty. But lack of complete knowledge of one's audience should not be an excuse to avoid thinking about it. Writers do not have to think about their audiences as particular people with particular, or peculiar, predispositions, and they do not have to invent imaginary readers—who often function as mere "straw men" to be blown over by incomplete reasoning. They write, instead, to a more general audience, imagined to be made up of people who *do* share their situation, who do view their assertions as at issue, and who are capable of reasoning in response to their assertions. Whether a writer thinks of this general audience as an extension of the point of view of a particular person or as a composite of possible points of view, the relevant characteristics of that audience are characteristics that a thinking person might possess. As I compose this book, for instance, I do not try to imagine a particular student reader and adjust what I have to say to that individual's peculiarities, such as red hair and a tendency to slouch in the back row. I do try, however, to think about those qualities that I know students have in common that may affect how they will understand and accept my meaning. I may misjudge this sometimes, for some readers, because I cannot take all of these unknown individuals into account. But I must consider what I do know as a basis for formulating my arguments. The issues that I write of here appear somewhat different when I write about this subject for an audience of other professors, even though I don't know all of them as individuals either. The issues that I address are in each case determined by what I know, and what I can surmise, about these general kinds of readers.

As a reasoned response to a question at issue, a thesis is determined by a process of inquiry. It is a response that one makes for certain reasons, but it is also a response that one makes because there is a real or potential audience for it. A thesis is an assertion, in other words, that cannot be taken for granted, but that needs to be argued because an audience exists to make argument necessary. Writers do not find themselves with assertions and then look around for an audience to fit them to. I do not decide to write a complaint about my bank account, for instance, and then look around for some likely person to whom to address it. Writer's find themselves with something to say because they discover themselves in situations in which something needs saying. If my banker created the trouble with my bank account, and if my purpose is to get my trouble fixed, then my banker is the actual audience for my argument. If my purpose is to argue about banking procedures in general, however, I might need to address a larger audience, one that shares some such question with me, but one that is less well defined. Or I might report my experience to a friend in a letter, because I think that she would be amused by it. But I would argue my case differently depending on which audience I addressed, because each possible audience changes my own understanding of what my case is. In each situation, I may even have a different thesis.

An argumentative situation is determined, then, by the existence of a writer with something to say and an audience to whom it needs saying. Neither alone will constitute a real argumentative situation, in which good reasons must be found. A writer who has a genuine thesis will be one who has responded to a question that is genuinely at issue, whether for a small audience that may be known well or a more general audience that can only be reasoned about.

Such a writer, in the interest of finding a thesis that addresses such an issue, has a further responsibility—to be sure that the idea is reasonable. A thesis is not something that one decides before thinking about it. It is something that one decides after a serious inquiry into the question. Whether this inquiry goes on wholly in one's head or whether it goes on in writing, it is such a process that *generates* a thesis. A stance that does not emerge from inquiry is sometimes called a "knee-jerk response," to indicate that it is an ill-considered or premature reaction. It is the responsibility of a writer to see to it that his or her thesis is not of this kind.

The *kind* of thesis that one composes depends on the *kind* of question that defines the reader-writer relationship. In composing a thesis, it helps to think about some of the different kinds of questions that readers are most likely to ask about the subject at hand. Here are some kinds of "questions at issue":

> *Questions of definition* arise from the reader's need to know "What is it?"
>
> *Questions of value* arise from the reader's need to know "Is it good?"
>
> *Questions of consequence* arise from the reader's need to know "What effect will it have?"
>
> *Questions of policy* arise from the reader's need to know "What should be done about it?"

In any argumentative situation, questions of one kind or another will be at issue while others will not be. The particular disputes that arise in a discussion may be said to focus on one or more of these types of issue. (There are other kinds, of course, but for now we need only consider that questions at issue differ from each other in such ways.) In a discussion of civil disobedience, for instance, controversy may arise over the meaning of the term itself—or it may not. A writer may misjudge the issue by choosing a definitional thesis (such as "Civil disobedience applies only to laws that are unjust," or "Any law is unjust that imposes the will of a minority on the actions of another minority") in a situation where a question of consequence is what, in fact, divides the audience. In his essay, "On the Duty of Civil Disobedience," for instance, Henry David Thoreau wrote:

> Unjust laws exist; shall we be content to obey them, or shall we endeavor to amend them, and obey them until we have succeeded, or shall we transgress them at once?

By putting the question in this way, Thoreau assumed that the question of definition (what makes a law unjust?) and the question of value (is an unjust law good?) were not at issue, but that the question of policy (what should we do about unjust laws?) is the one that needed his attention.

More than one kind of question may be at issue, of course, in a particular argumentative situation, and questions of one kind may have to be answered before one can ask questions of another. But the writer who wishes to make a genuine contribution to an inquiry may be aided by thinking about the kind of question that defines the situation. "What is really at issue here? Are we questioning how to *define* a concept, or whether an idea (or action) is *good,* or whether a certain consequence will *result,* or what we *should* do about it?" Trying to place the question in this way is one means by which the writer may "find the audience." Answering the wrong kind of question in any situation will lead to missing the audience—talking at cross purposes or saying the obvious. We don't want our readers to say "Yes, but what about . . .?" or "Sure, but so what?"

(I discuss kinds of questions at issue more fully in the last chapter, on research. If you're interested in thinking more about them at this point, you might want to read that discussion now. Look at pages 184–191.)

A thesis . . . will serve as the central idea of a unified composition.   This final part of the definition points us forward, toward the process of development by which a thesis becomes an essay. The last two parts of the definition, one pointing backward and one pointing forward, suggest that a thesis has two functions, which stand at the center of one's thinking about what one will write. It represents the result of a process of inquiry about an issue and it represents the beginning of a process of thinking about the kind of reasons that will do justice to one's position. As a beginning, a thesis provides a basis for the further thinking that one must do to produce a fully developed argument. If a thesis is reasonable in the sense that it emerges from the writer's considerations about what assertion to argue, it should also be reason-able in the sense of being able to be developed by reasons.

We have already seen that a thesis is the central idea of a whole composition, standing for that whole, in a way, and representing its overall intention. This means that the parts of a composition are, in some sense, the parts of its thesis. A thesis statement should suggest to a writer what the parts of the essay must be. As a predicated idea, a thesis will have several parts, and identifying them will become a basis for planning what the essay must say and how it must say it.

For example, suppose I have decided to argue that:

> Hydroelectric power is an acceptable alternative to nuclear energy in supplying present energy needs.

Assuming that this assertion satisfies the definition of a thesis in other ways (although it may not), consider how it might point forward to a unified essay. Its parts must become parts of that essay, since that essay would not be complete without satisfying certain demands that the thesis makes. The thesis calls for the essay to describe hydroelectric power and nuclear energy, and also to compare them according to how each satisfies "present energy needs," which must also be described. Finally, the essay must make the essential connection that is asserted in its predication: "is an acceptable alternative to." This will necessarily entail a discussion of *how* hydroelectric power is preferable to nuclear power, probably by showing that it has some benefit that nuclear power lacks or that it avoids some risk that nuclear power creates, or maybe both. There are further parts that this essay might contain, of course, but these constitute the essential elements that an essay written from *this* thesis must contain in order to be complete. The thesis itself demands that these elements be present. It acts as a kind of promise that I make to myself to *do* certain things in my composition.

Let's consider another example. Suppose I decide to make the following assertion my thesis:

> The use of calculators in basic math courses results in students lacking a fundamental understanding of number theory.

Once again, the thesis tells me that my essay must contain certain parts, without which it would not be a complete discussion of this thesis. It must describe "the use of calculators in basic math classes" and it must describe "fundamental understanding of number theory." It must also show that an understanding of number theory is somehow part of the purpose of a basic math course, because the thesis relies on this idea. Finally, my essay must somehow make the connection between the parts that is asserted in the predication "results in." I must demonstrate that one is the cause of the other. The *way* in which I demonstrate that connection will depend on the reasoning that I choose to develop. (This process is the subject of Chapter 4.) But the thesis itself tells me that whatever reasoning I choose must address this connection. Until I do all of these things in my essay. I have not kept a bargain I made with myself when I decided to make this assertion, and not some other, my thesis.

These examples illustrate that any thesis statement creates responsibilities for a writer and provides the basis for the fulfillment of those responsibilities. One is free to choose one's thesis, but having done so one becomes bound by its requirements, although there is still an incalculable range of choice that a writer has within those bounds. A writer becomes responsible for developing essential parts of a thesis and for earning its predication. There are limitless kinds of thesis statements possible, but all will have essential parts that must be developed and connections that must be earned. A writer must be able to see what all of these are. Without the ability to analyze one's own thesis in order to determine what responsibilities it creates for development, a writer risks producing an incomplete composition. An incomplete composition is a failure to assume all of the responsibilities that come with having an idea worth writing about.

This is why my definition of a thesis also contains the term *unified.* An essay is unified when all the parts that make it a whole are present. The creature lacks neither arms nor legs but has each part intact that makes it the kind of creature that it is. It also contains no parts that do not belong to it. A thesis, while it indicates those elements that an essay must have, also enables the writer to see clearly what elements it can or should do without. It is as much a guide to what the writer does not have to include in the essay as it is to what the writer must include.

In our two examples of thesis statements, for instance, we can see that there are certain discussions the essays do not need to contain. In the case of the thesis about hydroelectric power, for instance, there are potential facts about the subject that will not "belong' in the completed essay, because the thesis does not need them. For instance, it would not include a comparison of the different kinds of cement that are required to build nuclear and hydropower facilities, even though these details could be considered "part" of the subject. They are not relevant to the idea; the thesis does not need these details to be argued. In fact, they would be in the way. Other details might be included, such as the relative costs of constructing the two kinds facilities, but even this detail would probably be out of place. The decision of whether to include it would depend on one's consideration of the following question: Is this detail necessary to enable me to explain or establish my thesis? Knowing what one's thesis is enables one to answer this question positively or negatively, and thus to be thoughtful about what to include or what not to include in the essay. It helps one to distinguish between details that are necessary and those that are superfluous, and between details that are sufficient and those that are insufficient. Of course, no "rules" will tell a writer what details are necessary and sufficient to make a complete essay, because every thesis will make its own unique demands. But a precise thesis will make the choices clearer.

Finding and Testing a Thesis

A good thesis statement will function as a bridge between the writer's thoughts about the purpose of the argument and the task of actually composing an essay. We can now establish some criteria that a thesis ought to satisfy to have this function. When you compose a thesis statement, think about how it satisfies the following tests:

1. Is it an *idea?* Does it state, in a complete sentence, an *assertion?*
2. Does it answer a question that is really *at issue* for the audience? (What *kind* of question is it?)
3. Does the thesis say *exactly* what I want my essay to *conclude?* Are the terms I use precise and clear?
4. Has it developed out of a process of reasoning? Have I considered each side of the issue adequately?
5. Can it be developed reasonably?

A thesis that satisfies all of these criteria will enable you to see clearly what responsibilities must be met in the essay that you will write in support of it.

Such a thesis is frequently the result of rethinking and redrafting, for the first thesis sentence one writers will seldom satisfy all of these questions. The process of rethinking and redrafting a thesis is extremely important because it forces you to confront difficult questions in your thinking before you face them in the essay itself. It is much easier to rephrase a thesis statement until it works than it is to try to tinker with an essay that is well along but not working out. One cannot predict every feature of an essay before writing it out, of course, but one can at least have the advantage of thinking through potentially good or bad directions that an essay might take. Rewriting a thesis enables one to take advantage of the opportunity to think about potential aspects of an essay while they are still *potential* and not yet committed to essay form. Attending carefully to the thesis can help you avoid premature commitments to ideas that may not work out.

At this point, let's consider a hypothetical thesis in the making, to illustrate how these questions might be used in revising a thesis and how such a process might save a writer from premature commitments to unprofitable directions. If you follow the stages of my thinking in this example, you will see how you might go through something like them yourself. You won't, of course, go through an identical process, since you will have different ideas and they will have developed out of different situations. You might not be as methodical as I am in this illustration either, but you will nevertheless face similar questions, to be answered in your own way. What follows is not a model for your own thinking, but one of many possible mental stories.

Suppose I have just left a class in which we have had a good discussion on the subject of science and morality. In class, we read and analyzed some essays on different aspects of this subject, and in the process of discussing them the class began to argue whether scientists are morally responsible for the harmful effects of their research. My search for a thesis might go like this:

*   *   *   *

The discussion was always interesting, but it was also confusing, because, like all discussions, it seemed to develop in several different directions at once. It seemed as though different members of the class were discussing different things, simply because there were so many points of view. Sometimes we talked about examples, such as genetic research and nuclear weapons. One I never quite followed was experimental psychology as an example of harmful research. Sometimes we got into abstract subjects, such as the nature of objectivity and whether it is possible. Somebody said that the objectivity of science requires scientists to put their moral values aside, or else they could not search freely for the truth, but somebody else said that this is not possible because scientists make moral decisions whenever they decide what to study next. I was interested in that controversy, but I got a little lost when the class went off into the question of whether the research was sponsored by an agency that had direct application of the research as its aim.

Someone in class said that a scientist had to be paid, and if a scientist's employer intended to make weapons, for example, rather than to find a cure for cancer, that would be what determined whether the scientist had any responsibility. I could see his point, but I didn't think he was right. I even spoke up in class then and said something like, "Yes, but the same research that might lead to a cure for cancer might also get into the wrong hands and be applied later on as a weapon. Facts can be used for either good or bad. Shouldn't scientists be able to predict both kinds of applications?" Of course, after I said this someone else asked me, "Well, what would you do? Stop all research for good causes simply because someone might misuse the knowledge? We wouldn't get anywhere if we did that." Yes, I thought, that's true, too. But I still thought that maybe scientists should at least consider possible misuses. The so-called objective scientific method shouldn't stop them from thinking, after all.

At the end of class, I was somewhat frustrated; I thought that

I felt a certain way about the problem we had discussed, but I hadn't been very clear about what it was. I also wasn't sure I knew just what I was trying to say. At that point, I had only a vague sense of my own position. Other members of the class seemed more certain. But my problem isn't them. My problem is me. What do *I* think? I could, of course, decide to forget the whole thing. But I have a paper to write for that class, an argumentative essay based on our readings and discussions. Anyway, I also have a problem that I can't escape. The issue we discussed is clearly an important one, and I ought to know what I think about it. Maybe I won't solve it completely, but I ought to be able to figure out something to say about it that will at least satisfy some aspect of the problem. What *do* I think? To answer the question, I'd better start thinking about a potential thesis.

"Science and morality" is a huge subject and I can't possibly handle it. I tried narrowing it until it seemed manageable, but all the time I was nagged by the idea (I read it in the textbook!) that it isn't how broad or narrow my subject is that matters, but what I have to say *about* it. Okay, forget narrowing and get to the point. Grab a sheet of paper and try out some thesis statement. What do I think? Well. . .

> Scientists should be morally responsible for the results of their research.

That seems to satisfy criterion number one, but so would a lot of other sentences. Is this what I really want to assert? It seems a bit fuzzy, with a lot of "what ifs?" hanging off it. What about criterion number two? Certainly the class was divided on the general "policy" question of whether a scientist should be responsible, but it was never a matter of a simple yes or no answer. No one seemed to think that this responsibility was absolute; it always depended on something. I remember that one student said something like: "How can the person who invented fire be responsible for all the arsonists? That's ridiculous." She was right. I could just hear her hooting at my thesis. The issue was never in terms of unqualified responsibility. It was always a question of where the responsibility started and where it stopped. So, my thesis doesn't address a question at issue, since no one in class would agree that what we were really discussing was ultimate responsibility, as in my thesis. How can I change it?

Well, what kind of responsibility do I mean? I certainly don't think that every scientist who ever lived should be blamed for all the bad applications to which people have put their findings. But I do think that scientists ought to think about possibilities, as I said in class. Maybe my thesis ought to say . . .

> Scientists should be morally responsible for the results of their research if they are able to foresee those results.

Is this what I intend? Not quite. I don't think "results of their research" makes much sense any more. It isn't precise enough to say what I really mean. I'm already thinking about criterion number three, making the terms precise so they say just what I intend. Okay, then, I'll change it:

> Scientists should be morally responsible for the harmful applications of their research if they are able to foresee those applications.

I like that better because it answers a more specific policy question, one that really did concern the class. Harmful application was the issue, not just "results." I thought I knew what I meant by "harmful applications," since we talked about several examples. Maybe I'll use the one about cloning as a harmful effect of genetic research, especially since a scientist ought to be able to foresee this result. But, wait a minute, what do I mean by "foresee"? I can foresee a lot of things that might not happen. Scientists probably have better imaginations than I do. They might think cloning is right up there with antigravity machines. How should I know? Should their imaginations stop them from doing research? It doesn't seem like it. I remember something someone else said in class: "Don't scientists think that the risk of harmful effects is worth the potential benefit? They make a choice between probable good and improbable bad." I hadn't understood this at the time, but now I think I might. Scientists have to do more than just "foresee" effects; they must also think about how probable they are. What if a scientist can imagine a result but decides it isn't going to occur? If genetic research is needed to find a cure for some horrid disease, should the unlikely future of a cloned society stop the search for this cure? Well, that depends on the probability of that future occurring, as far as the scientist is able to determine it. It's a relatively sure thing against a relatively unsure one. I think I also may have to address the issue of "consequence" in my thesis. (I wonder if it's okay to talk about two kinds of questions at once? Why not?) Maybe now I'm getting somewhere:

> Scientists should be morally responsible for the harmful effects of their research only if those effects are highly probable in comparison to the potential good.

But, maybe this isn't right after all. I'm still bothered by the question I just asked myself. Yes, a cure for disease is important, but a cloned society would be horrible. What troubles me is that I don't think my thesis is what I really want to argue. I think I've been sneaking up on a different idea, but my original thesis statement has been keeping me from seeing it. Since I have been thinking, I have gotten away from the scientist's responsibility for *effects,* as such, and begun to think, instead, about a different kind of responsibility. I don't want to *blame* scientists for anything; I just want to make them more responsible for what they do. A cloned society will be the result of many more decisions than any single scientist's. It isn't a question of who's to blame, but of what a scientist's responsibility really is. If the problem is how to make scientists responsible, then maybe the issue is: responsible for what? Back to my page, this time to make a major change:

> Scientists should be responsible for making sure that they have considered the harmful effects of their research and weighed the probability of those effects against the potential good.

Hey, I like that. I think I'm having an idea. I think I'm contributing something to the discussion that answers part of the problem. The issue is not whether to blame scientists afterward, but to be sure that they think about what they're doing beforehand. In my essay I can talk about a genetic scientist's need to think about how probable cloning is, human cloning that is, the kind we don't want to see. I can begin to see my essay taking shape.

But, since I'm answering a different issue now, I should ask again whether I'm being precise enough. Well, not really. What do I mean by "responsible" now, if I don't mean "blame"? I don't mean that I want scientists to go to jail if they don't consider these things. I just think they ought to think about them as a necessary part of what they do. Aha! I know:

> Scientific education should include the issue of moral responsibility so that scientists will learn to consider the harmful effects of their research and weigh them against the potential good.

I think I'm still interested mainly in a "policy" kind of question, but it's a different policy! That's a good clear stance that I think I can argue, and one that I think might help the class to clarify the issue we struggled with. It doesn't answer all the questions, but it helps me to see what I think needs to be done in response to the problem.

Have I satisfied criterion number four for a good thesis? Of course, I have! Reasoning is what I've been doing all this time. Well, what about number five? Yes, I think I can develop it reasonably, because I know what I have to do to explain it. My essay will have to put the issue into a new light by explaining that scientific education might not address moral questions adequately. Then it will have to describe how a failure to address such questions can result in the failure of scientists to consider harmful effects. I think I'll have to say that this consideration cannot guarantee that those effects won't happen, to keep my reader from misunderstanding my purpose, but it might make the effects less likely since scientists would at least be weighing them against potential good effects. I'll argue that this kind of education will lead to scientific research that at least takes morality into consideration. And I'll have to make that connection. But what will I say to show that this will happen? Well, it will happen *because* . . . .

* * * *

I end this fictional mental narrative here because we've come upon the problem of what to develop as a major reason, the subject of Chapter 4. But at this point we can at least see how the result of testing an initial thesis against the five criteria can lead one from a loose, general, ill-considered thesis to the discovery of a thesis that has a much better potential to generate a good argument. Of course, I had to oversimplify and dramatize a process that will always be sloppy and unpredictable, with more roundabout thoughts and dead-ends than my fictional narrator experienced. Nothing can guarantee that you will come up with a good thesis, even by working at it. Some people can come up with good ideas without working at all, or going through such an elaborate process of questioning. Having good ideas is simply part of the intuitive mystery of the mind, and no rules can be written to account for it. But the point of this illustration is that *something* has to happen inside one's mind, some kind of serious consideration about one's ideas has to go on, if an argument is going to be at all reasonable. Trying out a thesis and then thinking about rewriting it—with the five criteria as a guide—is one way to keep this thinking alive and focused in a concrete direction.

Doing all this thinking without some kind of a draft of a thesis sentence on paper will be less likely to result in productive, useful effort. By writing a thesis down, and doing all revisions of it in writing, you can keep some of your thoughts from getting stringy and unproductive, the way some thinking often gets to be. You can also go back to a written thesis and pick up where you left off, or look back at an earlier form and reconsider it. Thinking that is done without writing it down can be easily lost. More importantly, however, the act of writing thoughts down creates the need for greater clarity than if they are left inside the head, subject to change or vagueness. Without writing down all the versions of your thesis statement, these advantages are lost.

What went on in my illustration was a dramatization of a thinking person rehearsing potential lines of reasoning, in response to a situation and based on his knowledge of an audience. The hypothetical student was thinking about what he thinks and why he thinks it, but he was aided in doing this by thinking about the discussion in which the issue arose; his knowledge of how his audience had and might respond provoked new ideas. He was thinking as a member of an audience that took the issue seriously and wouldn't let him get away with mental laziness. In the illustration, the student didn't know where he was going to come out when he took the first step into his inquiry, and that, of course, was the surest sign that he was really thinking, rather than just coasting along the road of least resistance. His ideas developed because he kept forcing himself to question. At some point, he had to call a halt to what is potentially an endless process of speculation, but at least he did it after, rather than before, doing some hard thinking.

When you go through something like this process in your own way, you will also have to stop sometime, in order to write an essay. But if you stop after doing your best thinking, and not until, it will all pay off in an essay that does justice to what you believe—rather than one that just does.

Implications for Research

It may seem from this discussion that coming up with a reasonable thesis is only a matter of thinking about what you already know; it does not require you to become well informed before jumping off into speculation. Not so. Coming up with a reasonable thesis is *primarily* a matter of thinking hard about what you know. You will not find your thesis by going to the library in search of what you think. But in the process of thinking about potential theses, you will encounter gaps in your knowledge of a subject, and if these gaps prevent you from thinking about that subject further, because you do not know something that is vital to your understanding, then you should attempt to fill those gaps. There is a difference between rash speculation and honest speculation, and if you are unsure of something that is crucial to your position, or if you are assuming that some part of your idea is true because you "heard it somewhere" or because "my sister told me," then you are being rash. An honest commitment to an idea should be based on your confidence that the knowledge that idea seems to assert is real knowledge.

The lesson here is simple. You must think hard about your ideas; there's no way around that, except to be irresponsible. But you might, by thinking hard, discover that you need to look something up, to find out or to verify the knowledge you want to claim. If that is the case, then "finding out" becomes your further responsibility.

QUESTIONS FOR THOUGHT, DISCUSSION, AND WRITING

1. Say whether you think the following statements fit the definition of a thesis. Why or why not? If they could be improved, what would the writer have to think about?
   a. I want to write my paper about sports and society and how it should be changed.
   b. Some people just don't know how to take a joke.
   c. I wish people would stop bugging me about what I'm going to do with my life, so I can find out.
   d. The escalation of defensive weapons into space will make a nuclear war more likely.
   e. The use of "he" and "man" to refer to both men and women is sexist.
   f. *The Federalist Papers* should be read by all students before they graduate from high school.
   g. All teaching will someday be done by computers, leading to a more effective education for all students.
2. What responsibilities does a writer accept in choosing any of these statements as a thesis? What parts would an essay about each of them have to contain to be complete?
   a. Legalization of marijuana would give young people greater confidence in government.
   b. Procrastination, more than any other cause, leads good students to perform badly on assignments.
   c. Belief in a CIA conspiracy to murder President Kennedy has led critics of the Warren Report to misinterpret its findings.
   d. Overpopulation is a greater threat to world peace than nuclear proliferation.
   e. Eradicating cigarette smoking by the year 2000 should be a priority of the U. S. government.
   f. A clear conscience is not necessary for happiness.
3. Having read an essay and discussed its ideas in class, construct a thesis that represents your own response to an issue you have discov-

ered. Test that thesis against the five criteria discussed in this chapter, and revise it until you think it will provide you with a good basis for writing an argumentative essay. Then discuss that thesis in class again, to see whether the responses of others suggest the need for further thought.

CHAPTER 4

Giving Reasons,
✌ *Taking Responsibility* **☙**

What a Reason Does

A reason is nothing more than the answer to the implicit question
"why?"; a reason is anything that one might say after "because" or
before "therefore." Reasons do not, of course, have to be connected
to conclusions by such phrases, but they nevertheless *function* in the
way that such phrases indicate. Reasons are also assertions. They are
ideas (complete with verbs) that connect to other ideas by offering
support. Words like *therefore* and *because* signify this kind of connection between one idea and another, but the connection is often implied when one sentence (or group of sentences) is set alongside another.

> The garbage has to be taken out tonight. It's Wednesday.

The second idea is easily understood as providing a reason to accept
the first one, even though no connecting word (such as *since* or *because*)
signifies this relationship. It isn't the idea itself that makes it either
a reason or a conclusion but its function in relation to another idea.
Any sentence might function in either way.

> I hope Molly gets home before dark. The garbage has to be taken out
> tonight.

In this example, the same sentence that functions as a conclusion in
the previous example is functioning here as a reason.

Because any idea can have either function, a sentence can be a reason and a conclusion simultaneously, if it supports any idea but is itself supported by another reason. Here is a paragraph in which some of the sentences seem to have this dual function:

> Ours is a paradoxical world. The achievements which are its glory threaten to destroy it. The nations with the highest standard of living, the greatest capacity to take care of their people economically, the broadest education, and the most enlightened morality and religion exhibit the least capacity to avoid mutual destruction in war. It would seem that the more civilized we become the more incapable of maintaining civilizations we are.*

This writer has made a series of assertions, without labeling them as reasons or conclusions by adding connective phrases. But we experience the sentences as functioning logically anyway, simply by understanding what one sentence has to do with another. After analyzing these relationships, we could make them explicit (at the expense, perhaps, of the dignity of the author's prose):

> Ours is a paradoxical world. *Why? Because* the achievements which are its glory threaten to destroy it. *I say this because* the nations with the highest standard of living, the greatest capacity to take care of their people economically, the broadest education, and the most enlightened morality and religion exhibit the least capacity to avoid mutual destruction in war. It would, *therefore,* seem that the more civilized we become the more incapable of maintaining civilization we are.

The first sentence is supported by a reason in sentence two, which in turn becomes the conclusion of another, more detailed reason in sentence three. The last sentence is a conclusion based on the reasons offered in sentences two and three, which is itself a reason explaining the general assertion in the first sentence. People often speak of writing as having a "line of reasoning" because the sentences of prose are often held together in this way; one reason gives rise to the need for another. Reasoning is the glue that holds the ideas together.

As this example also illustrates, any reason, because it is an assertion, can be supported by another. But a writer cannot keep supporting reasons with reasons forever. This passage comes at the beginning of a book that offers much more specific support for these general claims as it goes along. But, however much support is given,

---

*F. S. C. Northrop, *The Meeting of East and West* (New York: Macmillan Publishers, 1946), p. 1.

it must stop somewhere. At some point, the writer must decide to stop answering the question "why?" A line of reasoning must result from consideration of what assertions to support and what reasons to develop, since it cannot, obviously, support and develop all potential lines of reasoning that might be followed. Of all the potential reasons for asserting that "Ours is a paradoxical world," this writer had to choose those he thought best. Then he had to decide how far to pursue the line of reasoning he had chosen. Writers can make such decisions only by asking themselves what makes a good reason and how far it must be developed. In order to pursue one line of reasoning, we have to give up the pursuit of some other, and our problem is to decide which of many possible lines is worth pursuing and which is not. This consideration, in relation to a thesis, will be what determines the shape, or structure, of the composition.

Kinds of Appeal

We can begin to distinguish potentially good and potentially bad reasons by thinking about the *kinds* of reasons that are available to us. At the expense of oversimplification, I will begin by distinguishing three general kinds of reasons. After these categories are distinguished, I will discuss their logic. (It might seem that we should have some clear idea of what "logic" is at the outset, but I want to postpone that issue in order to show that "logic" is a natural activity and not a system of rules and regulations. The very mention of "logic" makes some people feel uneasy. They have encountered so many "don'ts"—perhaps in the form of the so-called fallacies—and so many formulas, that they view logic as nothing but a lot of traps set for the unwary. This is unfortunate. Logic is something we all do, all the time. It is as much a part of our ongoing mental activity as talking. We don't do it because we know the rules. We do it because we are human; but more about that later.)

What kinds of reasons are available to us? In general, reasons may be said to belong to one of these kinds of "appeal":

1. The appeal to authority.
2. The appeal to preference.
3. The appeal to the nature of the case.

The first kind of reason, the appeal to authority, seeks to establish belief in an assertion by referring the reader to the credibility of a source. Appeals of this kind range from the writer's establishment of his or her own expertise to citations from others who are assumed to be believable on a given subject. It is a common form of reasoning, and it takes its power from our willingness to grant superior credibility to others based on their "credentials." Such appeals depend on our willingness to accept an idea based on *who* says so.

The second kind of reason, the appeal to preference, seeks to establish belief in an assertion by referring somehow to the reader's desire that it be so. Appeals of this kind can range from the writer's outright manipulation of the reader's feelings to the construction of reasons out of shared moral principles such as justice or mercy. This is also a common form of reasoning, and it takes its power from our willingness to grant superior credibility to ideas that correspond to our preference for what ought to be true. Such appeals depend on our willingness to accept an idea based on our *desire* to believe it.

The third kind of reason, the appeal to the nature of the case, seeks to establish belief in an assertion by showing it to be a necessary consequence of belief in some other idea or ideas. Appeals of this kind can range from the use of proven experimental data to the suggestion that one idea "follows" directly from the acceptance of another one. This common form of reasoning takes its power from the sense of necessity that accompanies logical relations, and such appeals differ from the first and second kind in that the conclusion seems to follow, and to remain valid, no matter who says it or whether we wish it were true.

It might seem from this preliminary description that the third kind of reasoning is the best. To be sure, it is the "purest" kind of reasoning, insofar as it does not depend on the sometimes "irrelevant" considerations such as accepting authority or submitting to emotion. But these considerations often enter into our reasoning, to a greater or lesser degree depending on the kind of conclusion we are arguing. One could probably not persuade a mother and father that their love for a child is irrelevant to their reasoning about the child's education. An art critic could probably not be persuaded that emotion is irrelevant to his or her reasoning about the qualities of a painting. And you could not persuade me that the expertise of my accountant is irrelevant to my attempts to defend my income tax deductions. Even arguments that seem purely logical often seem to deserve more or less belief based on their source or on how well they accord with our desires. When it comes to reasoning, it is less important to try to do it "purely" than to try to do it well. Purely logical reasoning can lead one astray as readily as can appeals to authority and preference. All kinds of reasoning can be abused as well as used well. "Good" reasons come in all three kinds, depending on what we are reasoning about, who we are reasoning with, and who we are. It isn't always possible to separate our wishes and our sense of who is credible from our reasoning, and in real argumentative situations we rarely do.

It would not be wise, therefore, to try to prescribe some general rule about the choice of such appeals; they will always appear more or less appropriate depending on the issue, the writer, and the writer's audience. It is wise, however, to think about these differences in relation to those aspects of the argument and to try to balance one's use of these appeals accordingly. It is important to remember that any given reason may be an appeal in more than one of these senses. No logical reasoning is so "inhuman" that it neglects authority and preference altogether.

Perhaps the best way to demonstrate how these appeals work in relation to specific kinds of issues is to offer a few examples. Whether a reason is good or not in a given case will always, to some extent, be a matter of whether the issue calls for an appeal of a certain kind. These examples illustrate appropriate and inappropriate reasoning in each of these categories of appeal, but you must understand that no selection of examples can do justice to the enormous range of differences that is possible. For this reason, you should pay particular attention to *how* these examples work.*

Appeals to authority

Appeals to authority establish an idea based on the credibility of its source. Thus, each of these examples, in its own way, is an appeal of this sort:

> An exciting game of tennis relieves stress because it works for me.
>
> An exciting game of tennis relieves stress because it says so in Dr. Merit's *How to Relieve Stress*.
>
> An exciting game of tennis relieves stress because several studies have shown it.

Here are three reasons put forth in support of the same assertion. These lines of reasoning might be developed further; the reasons themselves could be developed and supported. The reasons are not convincing by themselves as written, but each might become the basis for a convincing discussion. Each suggests a different kind of discussion, however, and we must decide initially whether the basic

---

*To make the examples easier to follow, I put them all in a consistent *assertion–because clause* form. This form makes the reasoning more apparent, even though real writing will contain many examples of relationships between reasons and conclusions that do not take this form. For further discussion of this form, called an *enthymeme,* see pages 84–85.

reasoning underlying that potential development is sound. If we were to make this decision on the principle that appeals to authority are never sound, none of the examples could be said to provide a "good" reason for believing the conclusion. But, in fact, they provide quite adequate reasons for accepting the conclusion in certain circumstances.

If, for instance, the question at issue is whether tennis ever relieves stress, the testimony of a single individual that it does, as in the first example, would be one way of answering that question convincingly. Once that testimony had been given, who would dispute the fact that, for that individual, the claim holds true? This issue would be better supported by the reasoning in the first example than the reasoning established in the second example, because the best judge of whether one's own stress has been relieved is oneself, not the writer of a popular self-help book. But Dr. Merit's authority to make a general claim about the value of tennis for others may be greater than the authority of any single amateur based on a few Sundays on the court. So, if the issue is how best to relieve stress, the reasoning in the second example might be more adequate than in the first. This would depend, of course, on how credible Dr. Merit is. Why should I take his word for it? Because he signs himself "Dr."? Certainly not. I should only take his word for it based on what he has to say for himself. If all Merit has to say is that he has enjoyed many rousing tennis games and felt better afterward, then he could hardly be trusted as an authority on what other people ought to do. What worked for him won't necessarily work for others. But if Merit's reasoning proceeds along the lines suggested in the third example, his authority might become more credible—as credible, at least, as the authors of the "studies" he cites.

Anyone can *say* that something is true "because several studies have shown it," but the speaker's authority is then only as good as the authority of those studies, whatever they are. Sloppy studies, based on inconclusive samples or weighted by inappropriate assumptions, need not *show* any such thing, even if that is what they conclude. Here, then, is an appeal to authority that is only appropriate if the studies themselves are reliable, and such an argument would have to depart from its appeal to authority and talk about the nature of the studies themselves. "Studies" can be used as appeals to authority or they can be used as appeals to the nature of the case. As mere authorities, studies will generally provide weak support. As a context for discussing the reasons that the studies themselves offer in support of a conclusion, their use can be quite appropriate.

The appeal to authority provides appropriate or inappropriate reasons depending on whether someone's special knowledge, or testimony, is relevant to the issue. Some issues will call for such reasoning. It is important to consider, however, whether a conclusion would continue to be true no matter who asserted it—and if that is the case, authority might provide relevant reasons that are nevertheless insufficient. Suppose I were to argue, for instance, that

> U. S. foreign policy is inconsistent because my political science professor said so.

I could in that statement be said to have chosen a more appropriate appeal to authority than if I had chosen to argue the same conclusion by saying

> . . . because Bruce Springsteen said so.

My political science professor can probably be expected to know more about the subject than Bruce Springsteen does. But the appeal to authority is not my only choice, and probably not the best one. The issue underlying the assertion is not one that calls for anyone's testimony. It calls for an explanation of what it is *about* U. S. foreign policy that makes it inconsistent, independent of what my professor or anyone else might say. If I can read the newspaper, chances are I can offer this explanation without having to find an expert to agree with me. Although the assessment of an expert might be relevant, it would not be sufficient. Suppose, instead, I make some kind of appeal to the nature of the case, such as

> U. S. foreign policy is inconsistent because it does not uphold human rights when they are in conflict with the interests of U. S. investors.

With this statement, I invented a line of reasoning that is more appropriate than any appeal to authority. If I could develop that reason adequately, my logic would be more effective than if I merely quoted my professor's or anyone's authoritative pronouncements.

Appeals to preference

Appeals to preference can also provide appropriate reasons in certain circumstances. But, like appeals to authority, they do not generally offer the best support available unless the issue specifically makes the reader's desires relevant. Here are three examples of different reasons offered in support of a single conclusion:

> Students should support the clerical workers' strike by boycotting classes because only scabs will go to class during the strike.

> Students should support the clerical workers' strike by boycotting classes because joining just causes shows courage.
>
> Students should support the clerical workers' strike by boycotting classes because the clerical workers are underpaid.

In different ways, each of these reasons appeals to the reader's desire. The first example is a kind of threat, and it appeals to the reader's desire not to be thought a "scab." This kind of name calling would probably not be effective, but there is a power nonetheless in reasons that act on the fears of the audience.

> You should not go into Kasstle Park alone at night because if you do you may be a victim of a mugger.

This is not an unreasonable statement, even it if uses a strategy similar to the "scab" argument. What makes that argument seem inappropriate, however, is that the issue—whether students should boycott classes—is not answered by such a threat, the way the issue of whether one should venture alone into Kasstle Park at night is answered by noting the potential danger. "Victims" is a term applied to people who are mugged, while "scab" is a label that is used to denigrate people who disagree. No one would choose to be a victim, but people can decide for reasons of their own not to participate in the boycott. Thus, even though each appeal works on the basis of an implicit threat that we will become something we don't want to be, there is an essential difference between the two.

Just as the first example appeals to preference by threatening the reader with a derogatory label, the second example works by flattering the reader with a positive image. Because people can be expected to desire to be thought courageous, the reasoning connects a desired image on the part of the reader with a desired action on the part of the writer. Taken as a reason for believing that students should join a boycott of classes, however, the appeal is weak. It may flatter the reader into thinking that he or she can be a courageous defender of a just cause, but it does not provide support for the justice of the cause itself. The reader is asked to take part in a cause to be courageous, as if any cause would do. This answers the question of why students might *want* to join the clerical workers, but it does so in a way that serves the appearance of the students more than the cause itself.

In the third example, unlike the second, the reasoning answers the issue by referring to the needs of the workers. Hence, the third example seems to contain reasoning that is more relevant to the issue.

The justness of the cause, not the reader's desire to escape or to ac-
quire a particular image, is the basis of the appeal. However, that
reasoning is also, in a way, based on an appeal to preference, since it
arouses the reader's sympathy. Why, in other words, is the fact that
the workers are underpaid a good reason to support them? It is a
good reason because we desire that people should not be underpaid;
we want fairness. Thus, although the reasoning seems more logical,
it nevertheless depends on the reader's sense of compassion and a
preference for fair treatment of the clerical workers. It may not be as
blatant an appeal for sympathy as arguing that the workers cannot
afford to feed their families, but it is the same kind of appeal.

The emotional appeal is often ridiculed as illogical—as in the
joke about the man accused of killing his mother and father who asks
the court for mercy because he is an orphan—but it is nevertheless a
frequent form of reasoning, and justly so since emotion rightly affects
our beliefs. The appeal can be abused, but it is not illogical for that
reason. In the case of issues having to do with what is right and just,
such appeals are unavoidable, since our feelings inevitably, and prop-
erly, enter into our sense of what we *should* believe and do. In the
example, the reason "because the workers are underpaid" is an evaluative statement that functions to arouse our consciences. Some emotional appeals attempt to play on our feelings at the expense of reason, but others result from attempts to find reasons that are not "cold
and objective," or devoid of human feeling.

That third example suggests that the earlier distinctions between types of appeals are not as clear-cut as they might have seemed
at first, since it is at once an appeal to the nature of the case and an
appeal to sympathy. This is because the nature of the case is one that
calls for some kind of sympathetic commitment as well as an intellectual choice. The argument is a call to action. The issue asks what
should be done. If the line of reasoning in the example were extended,
however, we would enter into the need for reasons that appeal more
directly to the nature of the case. To answer the question of why I
believe these workers to be underpaid, for instance, I would have to
develop a reason that makes no necessary appeal to sympathy, such
as

> These workers are underpaid because their earnings are 18 percent
> below those of comparable workers at other colleges in the state.

This reason makes its appeal based on the accuracy of the facts and
the validity of the reasoning. Such a reason does not require sympathy
to be believed.

Appeals to the nature of the case

Appeals to the nature of the case derive one idea from another independent of the writer's authority and the reader's sympathy. The use of this kind of reason does not guarantee that the specific reason chosen will be appropriate, of course. Here are some examples of appeals to the nature of the case in which the reasoning is not always well chosen:

> Commercial television threatens to diminish the intellectual standards of American society because most people would rather watch television than read.
>
> Commercial television threatens to diminish the intellectual standards of American society because it portrays people who only value money and status.
>
> Commercial television threatens to diminish the intellectual standards of American society because it demands no thought from the viewer.

These lines of reasoning all in some way appeal to the nature of television and its threat to intellectual standards, but they provide more or less adequate answers to the question of why we should believe that threat exists. In the first example, even if it may be the case that many people would rather watch television than read, this in itself does not seem to address the question of why commercial television threatens intellectual standards. The reason seems somewhat remote from the conclusion. That reason is certainly *related to the topic* (as, for instance, "because dog biscuits contain oatmeal" would not be), but it does not seem directly *relevant to the issue.* After all, if these same people read nothing but trashy magazines, their intellectual standards might be as low or lower than if they watched television. It is the sort of reason that makes us want to respond with a "so what?" There is nothing in the reason that directly addresses the nature of television's threat, and so it seems to lack sufficient connection for us to see it as an answer to the question "why is it true?"

The second example does address the nature of television and, therefore, has more relevance to the issue. But the way in which it attempts to make that connection is nevertheless inadequate. If it is the case that television portrays people who value only money and status, (and, of course, such a generalization is itself too sweeping), this by itself has little relevance to television's threat to intellectual standards, unless viewers are assumed to hold the same values as the characters portrayed. It seems that the reasoning, although less remote, still is not complete.

Of the three examples, the third uses a line of reasoning that has the most potential to explain why the effect of television on the viewer is a threat to intellectual standards; it seeks to connect the conclusion not only to the nature of television but also to the nature of television's audience. It thus provides a better reason than the first two because its relevance is direct and apparent. If it were to be developed by showing *how* television places no demand on thought (which would not be an easy task, but possible), and by showing how this affects intellectual standards (whatever they are), then this reason might provide the basis for a fairly good, although not airtight, argument about the effects of television on society. It is an argument that you may have heard in one form or another. It is one that a few authorities have used to convince people, emotionally, of television's dangerous qualities. It may be an argument that contributes to making television better. At any rate, although it may have all of these functions, it is an argument based on the nature of the case, independent of who says it or whether we want to believe it. This argument will be convincing or not depending on how well each of the aspects of its logic can be supported. It will be convincing, to use the term I introduced in Chapter 1, if its assertions are *earned*. But before the necessary support can be mustered, the reasoning itself must have the logical relevance that we saw in this example, but failed to find in the first two.

Logical Relevance

If you followed the discussion of these three general types of appeal, you went through a certain mental process each time. You may not have been conscious of all the stages of that process; if you agreed that some of the reasons were more appropriate or more relevant to the conclusions, you probably made intuitive judgments, sensing the appropriateness or relevance rather than deriving it by systematic procedure. I have not been very systematic in my discussion of these examples on purpose, in order to emphasize, as I said before, that logic is a natural process that we all undergo whether we are conscious of being logical or not. Before the examples, I asked you to pay attention to *how* they worked, and you might have been aware as you went through them that the process by which you were able to think about each reason's appropriateness was similar in each case. I will now be somewhat more systematic about what that process is, because a fully conscious understanding of how reasoning works can help you in your search for good reasons to support your ideas in writing.

In each of the above examples, we perceived a greater or lesser degree of connectedness between the conclusion and the reason based on our intuitive assessment of an *assumption,* which we were required by the reasoning to accept. By accepting certain assumptions, we were able to follow the reasoning. By rejecting certain assumptions, we were prevented from following. Logical assumptions are always present when two ideas are linked in a "because" or a "therefore" relationship. It is the particular assumption underlying such a connection that will make the reason seem like a reason.

Let's illustrate this last statement with a nonsense example. Suppose I met you on the street and said, "Say, I happen to know that Mary's lamb was at the movies last night." If you didn't already believe what I was telling you, you might respond by asking me, "How do you know?" You want me to give some kind of a reason, in other words, to believe that Mary's lamb was at the movies. Then suppose I said, "Well, I know it because I saw Mary there." Now you would have to decide whether to accept my reason as a reason. Of course, you have no cause to doubt my credibility; I wouldn't lie to you. You have to decide based on the logical connection between my two assertions. Your decision would be based on whether you were able to accept the assumption that I had implied by my choice of a reason, and it will be this that will determine whether you think I am being logical or whether you think I'm crazy. That assumption is, of course: "Everywhere that Mary went, her lamb was sure to follow." If you accept this assumption—which I never stated, even though I relied on it for my reasoning—then you will accept my reasoning. But if you reject this assumption, then it would seem that I responded to your request for a reason with an irrelevance. You do accept this assumption, of course, so you say "I see," and change the subject.

This obvious example illustrates a universal principle of reasoning: **Any reason offered to support a conclusion will imply the existence of another reason that must be assumed in order for the stated reason to function as a reason.** Assumptions (sometimes more than one) are always present when reasons are given. If the logical assumption is not believed, the stated reason will not seem to support the conclusion. No reason that seems to support a conclusion is without its attendant logical assumption. How does one know what this assumption is?

Logical assumptions are present and understood because of the nature of deductive reasoning, which follows the form of the *syllogism.* If you already know what a syllogism is, the following discussion will seem very basic. But even if you know what a syllogism is, you may have been taught it as a scary formula that you had better adhere to or else. A syllogism is nothing more than the normal and inevitable shape that thought takes, whether we are aware of it or not. We cannot help but think in this logical form, so it is useless to demand that we must do so. It's the very essence of reasoning. It's only scary because some textbooks or teachers make it seem difficult or unnatural. It's not difficult at all; it's something you already know how to do, even if you may not recognize that you do it. When you accepted or rejected reasons in the previous discussion of reasons, you did so by reconstructing syllogisms in your mind.

The nonsense dialogue we just imagined is based on the following syllogism:

> *Premise one:* Everywhere that Mary went, her lamb was sure to follow.
> *Premise two:* Mary went to the movies.
> *Conclusion:* Mary's lamb followed Mary to the movies.

This syllogism is said to be "valid" because it derives a conclusion as the inevitable consequence of two linked premises. (Notice that just because a syllogism is valid, that does not make it true.) Syllogisms always have these three parts: a major and minor premise and a conclusion.

Here is another syllogism, one that should clearly show how the premises result in an inevitable conclusion:

> *Major premise:* All sports have rules.
> *Minor premise:* Baseball is a sport.
> *Conclusion:* Baseball has rules.

The conclusion here states a specific instance of the general principle asserted in the major premise, and it is connected to that premise by a minor premise, which states that the specific subject is a member of the class referred to by the generalization in the major premise. That's a complicated way of saying a fairly simple thing—the mental process is easier to do than to describe. Why does the conclusion seem inescapable? Let's analyze this simple syllogism another way. The premises establish categorical conditions, which can be shown in the graphic form at the top of page 79. What these circles picture are categories defined by certain qualities. The category "sports" is shown to be a subcategory of "things with rules," and "baseball" is shown to be a subcategory of "sports." If these relations apply, then baseball is also necessarily a subcategory of "things with rules." Now, all that a syllogism does is to put these relations into words, by asserting the conditions that apply to the categories. The major premise asserts the relationship between the category "things with rules" and the category "sports." The minor premise asserts the relationship be-

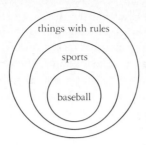

tween the category "sports" and the category "baseball." The conclusion asserts the relationship between the category "baseball" and the category "things with rules," a relationship that follows from those already established in the major and minor premises. In other words, any relations between "sports" and "things with rules" must be a relationship shared by "baseball" and "things with rules."

The three circles contain three "terms," as I call them, which the statements of the syllogism relate in different ways. A syllogism will always distribute three terms into six positions, as the accompanying diagram shows. Each of the three statements of a syllogism

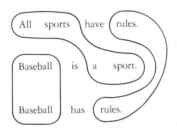

shares two of the three terms, and no two statements share the same two terms. These facts about the syllogism make it possible to reconstruct a complete syllogism from any two of its parts. On the basis of the conclusion and one of the premises, one can easily recreate the missing premise, since that premise must relate the two terms that are unshared by the conclusion and the stated reason. (See the following diagram.) This shows why any one reason and a conclusion im-

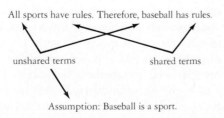

plies the presence of another reason (the logical assumption). In actual discourse, logical assumptions may be fully stated, but if not, they are implied. Implied or unstated assumptions may be reconstructed easily because they assert relationships between the terms that are unshared by the conclusion and the stated reason. Thus, if I were to reason that "Soccer must have rules because it is a sport," my reason would seem like a reason only because it depends on an implied assumption that is accepted as true.

Valid syllogisms do not, as I have already hinted, require true premises. The following syllogism is valid, even though its premises are not true:

> All sports require a catcher's mitt.
> Embroidery is a sport.
> Therefore, embroidery requires a catcher's mitt.

The fact that valid reasoning is not necessarily true reasoning means that reasoning is always *conditional;* acceptable conclusions follow from premises only *if* the premises are accepted. The premises of syllogisms assert conditions about the nature of things, and if the conditions are not acceptable, the conclusions are not acceptable, even though they may result from valid syllogistic relationships. Thus, logical assumptions, those premises that are implied when reasons are given, must constitute acceptable conditions, or else the reasons will not support the conclusions. Suppose, for instance, that I assert

> The use of biological warfare is moral because it is an effective means of defeating an enemy.

You might respond that I am being logical or that I am being irrational. The difference will be whether you accept the assumption I have relied on as an appropriate condition. Whether I am aware of it or not, if I make that argument I necessarily commit myself to the implied condition that

> Anything that effectively defeats an enemy is moral.

It is the acceptability of this condition, this major premise, that will determine how good my stated reason seems. Those who accept this assumption will be inclined to see my reason as supportive of the conclusion. Those who refuse to accept that assumption will not accept the reason as offering support. Many arguments fail because they depend on assumptions that the audience rejects. It is the responsibility of a writer to know the assumptions behind his or her reasoning. Exercising this responsibility often means exploring *why* the assumptions are true. Anyone facing a real audience with the above argument, for instance, would benefit from giving that major premise a good deal of careful thought.

Reasoning depends on the acceptance of givens. It makes assumptions simply because reasons cannot be given in an endless chain. *Something* has to be assumed as a basis from which to start a line of reasoning. The nature of implied assumptions will enter into our determination of whether the stated reasons are good or bad.

Based on this analysis of the logic of the syllogism, we can return briefly to some of our earlier examples and see how our knowledge of assumptions affected our acceptance or rejection of various kinds of reasons. Whether we were systematic or whether we simply perceived the assumptions unconsciously, our acceptance or rejection of assumptions helped us to determine whether our choice of reasons was appropriate.

Appeals to authority, such as those discussed earlier, rely on assumptions about the credibility of sources. Thus, when we discussed the weakness of this argument,

> An exciting game of tennis relieves stress because it says so in Dr. Merit's *How to Relieve Stress,*

we were demonstrating an unwillingness to accept the implied assumption. That assumption is understood by the process described above: It must assert a relationship between the terms that are unshared by the reason and the conclusion. These terms are not easy to find; this reason doesn't seem to follow the form of the syllogism very closely. We can understand the underlying logic better, if we paraphrase the statement:

> *Minor premise:* Dr. Merit's book says that tennis relieves stress.
> *Conclusion:* Therefore, it is true that tennis relieves stress.

Now the assumption is easier to reconstruct. It is:

> *Major premise:* Whatever is said in Dr. Merit's book is true.

It is on the basis of this assumption that the conclusion follows— *because* Dr. Merit says so. This is simply another way of saying what we already noted about the reasoning, that it requires faith in Merit's credibility. That faith is expressed in the logical assumption that underlies the reasoning. But it may or may not be acceptable to an audience as a precondition. That would depend on who Dr. Merit is and how prepared the audience is to accept whatever he says. Appeals to authority are generally weaker than appeals to the nature of the case, we can now conclude, because they require a reader to accept logical assumptions about the universal credibility of sources that go against common sense; no one is universally credible. Thus, another earlier example can be stated as a syllogism:

> Whatever my political science professor says about U. S. foreign policy must be true.
> My political science professor says that U. S. foreign policy is inconsistent.
> Therefore, U. S. foreign policy is inconsistent.

Put that way, the reasoning clearly depends on an assumption that is not probable.

Similarly, we can reconstruct the logical assumption underlying the reasoning in the examples of appeals to preference. For instance, when we rejected this reason,

> Students should support the clerical workers' strike by boycotting classes because joining just causes shows courage,

we were actually rejecting the truth of the implied assumption. Even if we agreed that the stated reason is true, we found it unacceptable that

> Students should do anything that shows courage.

(This major premise is reconstructed by realizing that the "shared term" of the original reason and conclusion is "just cause." There is, therefore, another underlying assumption in this reasoning and that is the equation "the clerical workers' strike = a just cause." We might also reject the reasoning by rejecting this assumed redefinition.) In deciding that the reasoning was unacceptable, we were rejecting the general condition required by the assumption. Similarly, when we thought about whether this reason might be adequate,

> because the clerical workers are underpaid,

we were involved (somehow) in measuring our agreement to the logical assumption that makes this reason work:

> Students should do whatever supports underpaid workers.

Should they or shouldn't they? Our answer will determine how we respond to the logic.

When we looked at an example that seemed to provide an adequate basis for reasoning, our decision was also based on our understanding of the underlying assumption. Thus, in the example that argued

> Commercial television threatens to diminish the intellectual standards of American society because it demands no thought from the viewer,

we recognized the relevance of the reason based on the connectedness it derives from the implied assumption:

> Anything that demands no thought from viewers threatens to diminish intellectual standards.

This assumption may not, of course, be true, and in an argument it would no doubt require explanation and support. Nor need we accept the further assumption left out of the paraphrase, that "American society is made of up television viewers." But these are nevertheless the kind of general assumptions many of us would accept as probable. If a reader could be brought to understand that major premise, if it could be explained how the lack of intellectual challenges diminishes intellectual expectations, for instance, then the idea that television demands no thought provides a good reason for arguing that this threat exists. This reason would, of course, have to be explained also, and perhaps it would have to be admitted that it does not hold true for every single program on the tube. But such an argument would at least have the advantage of depending on an assumption that is *potentially* shareable, so that the reasoning can proceed from that beginning.

The kind of practical reasoning that goes on in the examples, and that goes on whenever we offer reasons for our assertions, is much less precise and tidy than the purely logical statements found in examples of syllogisms. This often makes it hard to see how syllogistic form underlies our reasoning. Rephrasing and a certain amount of reduction of meaning may have to take place to make the syllogisms behind our thoughts apparent, but this is only necessary if we do not readily perceive the logical relationships that syllogisms make plain. Reconstruct the syllogisms underlying your reasons if you need to in order to test their validity and the assumability of their implied premises. It is one way to force yourself to be precise, and it occasionally helps to shake the cobwebs out of your head.

Enthymemes

At this point we need a name for the construct illustrated and discussed in this chapter. Statements that relate a reason and a conclusion, thereby implying an assumption that the audience is expected to accept as a precondition to accepting the conclusion, are called enthymemes. **An enthymeme is any combination of a conclusion and a reason, connected by the assumed beliefs of the audience in order to establish a line of reasoning that will appear probable and by that means achieve agreement with a conclusion that is otherwise in doubt.** Enthymemes, like syllogisms, arrive at conclusions based on premises. Enthymemes differ from syllogisms, however, in two ways:

1. Although valid syllogisms may be constructed by using any kind of statement, whether believable or not (such as "All sports use a catcher's mitt"), enthymemes derive premises from beliefs that the particular audience is assumed to accept as given. They seek to establish, for that audience, a doubtful assertion by linking it to an acceptable assertion—one that will require no further argument. Thus, if a reason is found that assumes a major premise an audience will accept, that reason establishes the "burden of proof," or the central focus of the writer's attention.

2. Although syllogisms are complete logical structures, enthymemes need only imply all of the statements that a complete syllogism might contain. Thus, the earlier examples of reasons in this chapter were all expressed as enthymemes, since they did not contain the major premises that would have made them (more or less) into syllogisms. Syllogisms are rarely found completely written out in common discourse. Enthymemes occur frequently in writing, whenever the parts of a syllogism are suggested, whenever, that is, a reason is given.

Enthymemes provide the basis of the informal reasoning that goes on in all kinds of argumentative writing. Here is a brief passage from Machiavelli's *The Prince,* a "handbook" on government written in 1513:

> Cruelties should be committed all at once, as in that way each separate one is less felt, and gives less offense; benefits, on the other hand, should be conferred one at a time, for in that way they will be more appreciated. But above all a prince should live upon such terms with his subjects that no accident, either for good or for evil, should make him vary his conduct toward them. For when adverse times bring upon you the necessity for action,

you will no longer be in time to do evil; and the good you may
do will not profit you.*

Each of the enthymemes by which Machiavelli argues depends on
assumptions that he expects his readers to accept in order for them
to accept the reasoning offered. A paraphrase of these enthymemes
makes this clearer:

> Cruelties should be committed all at once because if committed all at
> once each one will be felt less and give less offense.
> > *Assumption:* Cruelties should be felt as little and give as little
> > offense as possible.
>
> Benefits should be given one at a time because if given one at a time
> they will be appreciated.
> > *Assumption:* Benefits should be done so as to be appreciated.
>
> A prince should treat his subjects consistently because if he varies his
> conduct toward them he will not be able to do good or evil when the
> time requires.
> > *Assumption:* A prince should be able to do good or evil when the
> > time requires.

These are not syllogisms in the logician's sense, and in Machiavelli's
prose they appear even less like syllogisms. They are informal reasons.
Enthymemes like this depend on the reader's ability to infer consequences from probable assumptions. They take many forms and are
not always easily reduced to logical propositions. (See what my par-
aphrases leave unexplained about Machiavelli's appeal.) Enthymemes
make up the practical logic of our thinking whenever we attempt to
support a claim in ordinary language. We can't escape using enthymemes, so we ought to try to make them reasonable. Which of Machiavelli's assumptions do you share with him? Is your sense of how
reasonable he is based on your answer? Enthymemes are the bridge
between the writer's believability and the reader's beliefs.

The Logical Thesis Statement

If it is the writer's responsibility to develop a line of reasoning that
attempts to earn a conclusion, the enthymeme can provide the writer
with a way to think about the argument in advance. The thesis represents the conclusion of an argument, a response to a question at

*Niccolo Machiavelli, *The Prince,* trans. Christian E. Detmold (New York:
Washington Square Press, 1963), p. 39.

issue. Making that thesis into an enthymeme is a means by which a writer may discover an adequate line of reasoning to develop in support of that thesis, one that will be based on an assumption that a reader may be expected to accept. By this means a writer might achieve not only a fair shot at successful persuasion, but also—and more importantly—the satisfaction of knowing that the conclusion is founded on a fully rational and shareable basis. By attempting to make a good thesis into a good enthymeme, the writer gains a greater understanding of his or her own ideas. As I said earlier in this book, writing can be a way of learning not only *what* one believes, but also *why* one believes it. The composition of an enthymeme that will represent the central logic of an essay—in the way that a thesis represents the central idea—is a powerful way of learning whether one's reasons are, in fact, adequate to support one's beliefs. By this means, it is possible to test one's best ideas by trial of reason.

The remainder of this chapter deals with the process of making a thesis into an enthymeme. In Chapter 5, I discuss the advantages of such a two-part thesis statement in determining the essential structure of the argumentative essay.

Once you have discovered a thesis that represents the conclusion of your essay, you can begin to think about potential reasons. Obviously, many reasons are possible. What we seek at this stage is a reason that might function as the central or main rational basis for arriving at the conclusion. Putting that reason together with the thesis will make the thesis statement into an enthymeme. This means that the reason you choose will be derived in part from the potential assumptions that you expect your reader to accept without further argument. You will be searching, in other words, for a line of reasoning that can be used to establish your conclusion, by starting with an assumable condition.

The thesis statement, or enthymeme, that we now seek will have the following basic form:

assertion 1 *because* assertion 2
  (thesis)   (reason)

Each assertion is a complete idea. The first one will be your thesis and the second will be the main reason you will choose in defense of that thesis. For this new thesis statement to be an enthymeme, these assertions must share one logical term, in the way that we talked about "shared terms" earlier in this chapter. This is necessary so the reasoning will have the quality of logical relevance that we also discussed. If a thesis statement is in this form, you can reconstruct the assumption that completes the syllogism, and by that means ensure

that you have thought about the potential connection that your reasoning makes to the beliefs of your readers. It isn't necessary for
you to write that assumption out as a part of your thesis statement.
As we have seen, it will be there anyway, whether you write it out
or not. But it is necessary for you to know what it is. Otherwise,
you will not be assured that the reason you have chosen is adequate,
both to the issue addressed in your thesis and the audience for whom
you write.

The task, simply stated, is to find the best reason you can for
supporting your idea. Chances are, then, that this reason will be one
that appeals to the nature of the case rather than one that depends on
appeals to authority or preference. I say this not because appeals to
authority or preference necessarily provide bad reasons—they don't
always, as we have seen. I say it because in composing a thesis statement, you want to be assured that you do not avoid the issue but
confront it directly. The because clause should provide a direct answer to the question "Why is it true?" (Of course, the honest search
for such an answer might result in the need to rethink the thesis
itself. In fact, it often does. The weaknesses of our ideas appear to us
most readily when we carry out a search for adequate reasons.)

This task can be guided by some criteria for an adequate because
clause. Once you have decided on a thesis that meets all of the criteria
discussed in Chapter 3, the following considerations should guide
your search for a because clause:

1. Is the because clause a complete, precisely stated idea?
2. Does it represent a central reason for answering the question "What
   makes the thesis true?"
3. Does it share one logical term with the thesis?
4. Is the implied assumption one that the audience can be expected
   to accept without further argument? (This means, of course, the
   same audience for whom the question answered by the thesis is at
   issue.)
5. Do the "unshared terms" mean the same thing? (This will result
   in "circular reasoning.")

If these five criteria are satisfied, the thesis statement as a whole will
be an enthymeme that one can rely on to provide an adequate line of
reasoning for a good argumentative essay. Enthymemes provide the
logical "backbone" for such compositions.

To illustrate how the search for an adequate enthymeme will
entail a process of discovery, guided—but not governed—by these
criteria, let us return again to the anecdotal narrative of the student-
in-search-of-a-thesis from the preceding chapter. That student, you
recall, had just arrived at what he considered to be a pretty good idea

for an essay, in response to a class discussion about science and morality. Once he had found this thesis, however, he faced the question of how to earn it.

*   *   *   *

Well, it will happen because. . . . Let's see, I'm going to make a case for the idea that

> Scientific education should include the issue of moral responsibility so that scientists will learn to consider the harmful effects of their research and weigh them against the potential good.

I have to decide on a reason. Why is this class always making me think? Oh, well. I got this far, didn't I? I guess I can keep going. Anyway, why should I bother to think so hard about my position if I'm not willing to think about why I hold it? Some classes will let a person get away with just reporting what other people think. I suppose I could write an essay based on all the sources that agree with me—but I've found an idea of my own and I don't know if I can find anyone else who has argued it. "Because Einstein said so"— wouldn't that be great? But the appeal to authority won't work in this case and I know it. I have to think about why it's true.

Why, then, should scientific education include the issue of moral responsibility? Well, if it didn't, we all know what might happen. Scientists could get so caught up in their experiments and their data that they may not stop and think how horrible their ideas might be in the hands of immoral—or even amoral—technocrats. Look what happened at Los Alamos. So, what if I tried to make an enthymeme by adding

> because harmful effects are always possible.

Anyone who is concerned about the possibility of harmful effects should be willing to accept that reason for making scientists think about them. And we're all concerned with that possibility; we live in fear of what might be done with scientific knowledge. Of course, I'd be appealing to the reader's fears, but so what? Okay. Now, what's the assumption? Let's see, the shared terms must be "harmful effects of science," so the assumption must relate the unshared terms. I think it must be something like this:

> Education should prepare one for whatever is possible.

That seems to be assumable. Or is it? It sounds a little dumb, now that I write it out. Something bothers me about my reasoning, but I don't know what. My enthymeme is this:

> Scientific education should include the issue of moral responsibility so that scientists will learn to consider the harmful effects of their research and weigh them against the potential good, because harmful effects are always possible.

I wonder if it fulfills all the criteria? The because clause is a complete idea. Does it answer the question "What makes it true?" I think that's my problem. My appeal to the reader's fears that something might go wrong have directed my attention away from the real issue. Sure, that's a reason that scientific education *should* include ethics, but my reasoning has nothing to do with why such an education would make scientists "weigh" potential effects, and so on. When I asked myself for a reason earlier, I asked, "Why will it happen?" What I need is a reason that addresses the point that moral education will do what I say it will. But that means that my thesis itself may not say what I want it to. It seems to contain two ideas: one is what should happen, the other is what will happen as a result. My because clause only addressed the "should" statement, not the other one. I think I'm going to have to make the thesis more precise after all:

> Ethics classes for scientists will teach them to weigh the potentially harmful effects of their research against the potential good, because
> . . .

Yes, that's better. The "should" part of my thesis really isn't necessary, since what I need to address is the reason that such an education will have this result. If I can say that, well, the "should" part ought to take care of itself. The central problem here is really to say what such an education is good for. What seemed to be a question of policy turns out to be a question of consequence. But where does that leave me for a reason? I know one thing, I can't appeal to fear any more. I've stated the issue now in such a way that I have to appeal to the nature of the case.

   Why, then, will ethics classes teach scientists to weigh harmful effects? Hey, that's easy:

> _because such classes would raise questions of right and wrong about science, which a purely scientific education would ignore.

Now I can sneak in that "pure science" definition after all. But maybe that's too easy. It seems that I may have just repeated what an ethics class *is* and made a circular argument. What's my implied assumption? Something like:

> Weighing harmful effects against potential good is a question of right and wrong

Sure, but that *is* a circular syllogism. It just says the same thing over again. Ethics is ethics. I can do better than that. Scrap that because clause and try again. Let's see:

> because raising questions of right and wrong in relation to science will provide a new perspective.

I like that a little better. But what's my assumption now? Let's see, do I have a shared term? Well, if my reasoning was circular before because "ethics" and "questions of right and wrong" were really the same thing, then I guess that those are my shared terms now. They don't have the same words, but the concept is the same: "Ethics classes for scientists" is simply redefined as "raising questions of right and wrong about science." So, my assumption must be

> Learning to weigh harmful effects against potential good effects requires a new perspective.

That sounds assumable to me, and it seems to make a good syllogism. But have I satisfied all the criteria? That because clause is a complete idea, but is it precise? I guess not, since "new perspective" could mean a lot of different things. There I go again, thinking that something clear to me is clear in the words I use! Since I'm going to have to say what this "new perspective" is anyway, I ought to be able to say it here. What *do* I mean by it?

I guess I must be thinking about the perspective of the scientist as being restricted to empirical proofs, while the perspective of morality allows for human feeling. Didn't one of our readings say something like this? Scientists can study the phenomenon of pain, somebody wrote, but they won't understand it until they feel it. I guess I mean that the new perspective will be one of feeling. But is that precise? Do I really mean something like "compassion?" Let me try it out in my because clause:

> because raising questions of right and wrong in relation to science will require compassion.

Not quite. Maybe it would be better if I said

because raising questions of right and wrong in relation to science requires actively confronting one's compassionate feelings for other people.

That seems precise, and it also seems to say something that supports the thesis well. "Actively confronting" seemed necessary because everybody has feelings, but not everyone bothers to think about them. I still have to test the implied assumption, which now is something like this:

> Weighing potentially harmful effects of scientific research against potentially good effects requires one to actively confront one's compassionate feelings for other people.

Is that assumable? Well, maybe not, since it's very general. But I think I can explain what I mean by it, and if I can make it clear I don't think I will have to argue for it. It seems assumable in that sense. Yes. I think I can do that. And I think the syllogism is valid:

> *Major premise:* Learning to weigh potentially harmful effects of scientific research against potentially good effects requires one to actively confront one's compassionate feelings for other people.
> *Minor premise:* Ethics classes for scientists (that is, raising questions of right and wrong in relation to science) will confront them with their compassionate feelings for other people.
> *Conclusion:* Ethics classes for scientists will teach them to weigh the potential effects of their research against the potential good.

Well, that may not be the best syllogism in the world, (I think there may be an extra assumption in there), but at least it's a case I can make reasonably. And I think it's worth making. It helps me to understand what I think we can learn from the issue of science and morality and maybe even what we can do about it. So, now maybe I'm ready to write the essay. I've got a lot of ideas to develop and a line of reasoning to hang them on as I go along. But where do I start?

*   *   *   *

Once more, we leave this student in midthought. (We will return to his problem of structure in Chapter 5.) Let me stress again that the process just portrayed is only an illustration of the need for thinking and not a model of exactly the steps that you or anyone must or will follow. The point is not that the fictional student does everything systematically and comes up with a good result (you may have thought the resulting enthymeme was not logical or not worth arguing), but that the *task* of finding a thesis and a because clause that satisfies the criteria placed on them will be a stimulus to thought. These criteria can't guarantee any result; they can merely keep you from being too easily satisfied with your thinking, if you take them seriously, until you have taken that thinking through some active stages to a conclusion. If this student seems to you to be too simple-minded or too abstract, remember that the same general process of discovery must go on no matter how simple or complex, abstract or concrete, the ideas are. The general process need follow no prescribed order. It won't be a conscious process at every stage. But it must contain, as this student's thinking did, certain considerations that are prompted by the five criteria. Once again, such considerations are more likely to be serious if you *write down* successive drafts of the because clause.

A thesis statement, in the form of a well thought out enthymeme, provides you with the line of reasoning that a unified argumentative essay can develop. It thus provides you with the major parts that will need to be present in your essay, and the connections between them that will hold the structure of your composition together. By thinking through the enthymeme, you will have given yourself a basis for thinking about structure. The shape that your essay will take on will, therefore, be the shape of your reasoning, a structure that you have generated to fit the argument that you have chosen to develop as a response to your confrontation with an issue. You need rely on no "model" essay form to find that shape. Your reasoning will generate a structure of its own. How to recognize and build on that structure is the subject of the next chapter.

Implications for Research

Reasons, since they are also assertions, are subject to verification if they rely on information that the writer is not absolutely confident about. In that case, everything I said at the end of Chapter 3 about the possible need to inform yourself before making "rash" statements in your thesis applies to the claims you decide to use as reasons. Your reasoning does not depend solely on the validity of your logic. It depends equally on the dependability of your information. Hence, my advice now as before is: When in doubt, look it up. Think about how our student might have profited by following that advice. Would it have changed his conclusion, altered his reasoning, or simply given him a better basis for making his case, to have informed himself about any particular aspect of his subject? At what point?

You know by now that "looking it up" is not sufficient. How do you know whether to trust what you find? By thinking about logic in this chapter, you have refined the kinds of critical questions you can apply to the information you might discover as you seek to inform yourself. The considerations raised for you to apply to your own reasoning in this chapter can be used to assess the reasoning of others. Thus, as you do any "further reading" that may seem necessary to your own case, you can determine its trustworthiness, in part, by applying some of the ideas in this chapter. As you read, for instance, consider the *kind of appeal* that the writer is making. Does this give you more or less confidence in the source? As you read, isolate the enthymemes and reconstruct the assumptions that you are expected to accept as self-evident. What does this say about the writer's view of his or her reader? How does this affect your understanding of the subject?

You may also find it helpful to try to reconstruct the *main* enthymeme underlying the whole argument of the source. This enthymeme will probably not appear in the writer's prose, but something like it will be implied by the conclusion the writer has chosen to develop and the line of reasoning by which it is argued. Uncovering this implicit enthymeme will enable you to think about the relationships that prevail among the writer's reasons; some of the reasons will be necessary to develop other reasons and some will function to provide the essential "burden of proof" of the argument. By distinguishing the main reasons from the writer's subordinate reasons, you can focus your attention on the most essential features of the case. But no matter how you apply the ideas in this chapter to your reading, you will be doing research of the best kind—not perfunctory research that consists of merely copying down what you find for the purpose of quoting it later, but an honest search for reliable knowledge. Of course, everything I said about that search as a *reading* process applies equally to information you encounter in other ways. Research is not restricted to reading; I discuss other kinds of research in Chapter 8.

QUESTIONS FOR THOUGHT, DISCUSSION, AND WRITING

1. In the following passages, describe which sentences are reasons and which are conclusions. Do some sentences have both functions? How do you know?

a. I like reading detective novels. They keep me looking for interesting possibilities, like a game of chess. I never can guess the right solution, though. The writers are clever. I'm also too gullible. But it's fun to be fooled. It wouldn't be a challenge if I always knew "whodunnit."

b. The narrator of "The Turn of the Screw" is unreliable. It isn't possible to tell whether to trust what we are told. Henry James seems to want his reader to wonder whether the events really happened or whether they occur only in the minds of the characters. But which characters? The reader must be meant to wonder which of the characters can trust their own impressions. I think it's a story about the ambiguity of appearance and reality.

c. Sixty-seven per cent of the people surveyed said that they are not influenced by advertising with irrelevant sexual content. This does not, however, mean that such an influence is not more common. If we accept the possibility that there is a "subliminal" appeal in advertising, some of those who say that they are not influenced might be influenced without knowing it. Survey techniques alone cannot test hypotheses about subconscious knowledge.

2. What kinds of appeal are being made in each of the reasons offered here? How appropriate is the choice of each kind of appeal? Why?

a. Salaries for state employees should be based on "comparable worth," since women workers on the average earn lower wages than men.

b. A recent study showed that cocaine users are no more likely than anyone else to experiment with heroin. But only a fool would accept this as a "green light" to use coke.

c. When you consider the extent to which the computer will be used in all parts of our lives in the near future, it becomes obvious that computer literacy should be taught in elementary grades.

d. We need leaders who are not afraid to tell the truth. Without them, this country is doomed.

e. The newspaper decided to print pictures of men who went into adult bookstores in our town, hoping to humiliate them into staying away and by this means force the stores to close. The question is whether the newspaper is guilty of invasion of privacy, or whether freedom of the press can include this kind of action. I think the paper has the right but would be wise not to use it. The public's trust in the press is undermined when it abuses its freedoms, just as the booksellers lose respect when they take the First Amendment too far. In both cases, the First Amendment is pushed far enough to risk a backlash that could destroy it.

3. Reconstruct the logical assumptions that connect these reasons and conclusions.

a. The student union should be allowed to sell beer because this would create more revenue to support student activities.

b. Boxers frequently suffer permanent injury as a result of the impact of brain tissue hitting the inside of the skull. Yet some people continue to call this a "sport." It's not a sport, it's a brutal entertainment spectacle. It should be outlawed.

c. As long as the nation's laws are written and voted on by a majority of whites, the laws that send minorities to prison in greater numbers than whites are political laws. This makes political prisoners out of people who have done no more than follow their consciences in matters that they have not been able to change with their votes.

d. The only way a politician can get elected is by telling people what they want to hear. No honest person can win enough votes to get into office.

e. If the Constitution hadn't guaranteed people the right to pursue happiness, Americans might not be as selfish as they are.

4. Having decided on a thesis for your next essay, construct an enthymeme by adding a "because clause" that satisfies the five criteria discussed in this chapter. (If in the process you discover the need to revise the thesis itself, go ahead.) Bring this enthymeme to class for further discussion.

CHAPTER 5

✑ *Controlling Structure* ๛

In Chapter 1, I defined structure as the relations among the parts of a composition that give meaning to the whole discourse because they are determined by the writer's need to earn a thesis. Structure, therefore, is generated by a search for the best means of support. By now, these have become familiar concepts. In the attempt to write an enthymeme, one searches for the best means of supporting a thesis. The thesis itself represents the whole intention of the essay: its conclusion. The logic of the enthymeme represents the means of arguing that thesis. The most basic units of the structure of a whole composition, then, are contained in the enthymeme. The relations that will hold the parts of the composition together—to give it that sense of progress that one feels in the presence of structural coherence—are implicit in the enthymeme. The process of discovering these relationships in an enthymeme and constructing a coherent structure is the subject of this chapter. But first: What *is* a coherent structure?

Structure and the Reader's Experience

Structure is a quality of writing that enables a reader to focus attention on the ideas themselves, without being distracted by gaps in the presentation or by digressions into seemingly irrelevant material. A good structure seems to a reader to contain the right idea in the right place, so a structure that works may not be noticed by a reader, since the relations among the parts will seem to arise naturally from the ideas themselves. Although readers may not be conscious of structure when it is working well, writers must be conscious of structure in order to be sure that readers are not distracted by structural problems. The apparently natural connection among the ideas from the reader's point of view is the result of careful artfulness from the writer's. The writer who neglects to consider how a reader will respond to the structure is taking a big chance that the reader will respond badly.

Here, for instance, is an example of student writing that fails to achieve structural coherence:

STUDENT CASSANDRAS

1. Last month, the gallery in the student union had a controversial exhibit of photographs depicting students as drunken partiers. It featured pictures of fraternity bashes, the local bar scene, and ads for beer that put down the idea of studying. Of course, the exhibit sparked a lot of letters to the editor, some condemning the students and some condemning the exhibit. One called for the exhibit to be removed because it was "harmful to the image of the university."

2. The dean wrote a letter praising the photos and the gallery for showing them. He wrote that "the exhibit does *not* fairly represent the student body, but it wasn't meant to. It was meant to make a statement by drawing attention to a problem. The university is a place where all points of view can be freely expressed."

3. This isn't the first time the dean has expressed such an idea. One is reminded of his letter several months ago in which he said that the students who picketed the CIA recruiters were advocating violating the CIA's right of free speech. Is the dean being consistent here?

4. That was a rather strange episode: the picketers carried signs protesting the CIA's covert intelligence operations. They made lots of claims. It was hard to tell which of them were true.

5. One of those claims was that the CIA had tapped the telephones of student members of the Marxist Youth Organization. Come on! Why would the CIA care what a few disorganized undergraduate radicals talk about on the phone? Did they think they'd get some juicy details?

6. The MYO is harmless, really. They say a lot of radical things but nobody listens to them. They're like Cassandra in the Greek myth, fated to be disbelieved. Maybe if the members of the MYO dressed a little neater people would take them more seriously. Maybe not, though. The dean buys his suits at Brooks Brothers, but who listens to him?

Is there any principle of structure holding the parts of this essay together? You might say that it is held together by a vaguely defined topic, such as "campus conflicts" or "student opinions." The parts of the composition relate *somehow* to some such general, but undefined, topic in the writer's mind. Furthermore, the title attempts to assert some kind of connection among the details by suggesting a thematic unity: students not being believed. But these topical and thematic categories nevertheless fail to account for the selection of details and the connections among them. The topic is too diffuse to tell us why *these* parts are necessary. The title seems to be an obvious attempt to assert coherence after the fact. As readers, we can't excuse the randomness by which we are taken from part to part.

There is a principle of structure, however: the principle of free association. It is not hard to imagine how this essay got written. We've all done the same thing at one time or another. This writer began with an idea that sounded promising and decided to "take it from there," letting the connections follow from whatever associations occurred as each new sentence was written. The structure of the writing follows the association of ideas in the order in which the writer happened to think of them, without considering what relevance they might have to an overall purpose. It is not surprising, then, that as readers we do not follow those connections.

It is not just that we do not follow each leap in the essay's progress. We are also aware, as we read, that the new directions in which we are being taken are not what we expected. The essay takes the reader by surprise in some passages simply because those passages defy expectations that have been created by earlier ones. At the beginning of the essay, for two paragraphs, we are introduced to a controversy. We expect that the essay is going to deal with this controversy. We are led to expect a certain kind of discussion only to discover that we were wrong. In the third paragraph we get a new idea of what to expect; we have to readjust our sense of what is at issue in the essay. Then, just as we get adjusted to this new sense of where the essay is going, it shifts again. The effect is dizzying. By paragraph five, we are muttering, "How did I get here?" What, in other words, does the content of paragraph five have to do with the content of paragraph one? The answer is: nothing at all. Both paragraphs do not *belong* in the same essay. Yet, we got from one to the other by a process of connecting thoughts.

The essay has transitions. Notice that each of the paragraphs connects to the one that goes before. The problem is not that the paragraphs fail to connect. It is that they fail to connect in the service of any obvious purpose; they fail to make progress *toward* any obvious destination. These paragraphs are like elephants in a circus parade, each one hooking its trunk to the tail of the one in front. But in this case, the elephants aren't following the parade route; they are meandering aimlessly. Each idea relates somehow to the next one, but together they do not relate to any considered end. The essay is inconclusive because it has no conclusion to give it a sense of wholeness. To create conclusiveness, more than transitions is required.

The beginning of an essay functions as an implicit promise that a certain kind of discussion will follow. The writer creates that promise and the reader accepts it as a basis for understanding subsequent transitions. In this essay, the writer prepares us for a discussion in which a particular problem will be somehow resolved. That is, as we read its first two paragraphs, we are introduced to an issue created by the incident described. We feel it to be a real issue because there are good reasons for viewing the controversy in different ways: The photo exhibit is not justified because it portrays students unfairly; it is justified because it represents a point of view. By introducing such a problem, the writer promises a solution of some kind. But this writer does not make good on that promise, and the essay—no matter how interesting the rest of its details might be—is a disappointment. Does this essay have a beginning, a middle, and an end? "Yes" in the empirical sense; it starts, it continues, it ends. But "no" in the functional sense; its middle paragraphs do not develop its beginning, and its ending paragraph does not bring anything to a satisfactory conclusion. The writer is simply out of control of the structure and thus has failed to take responsibility for the experience of the reader as it unfolds.

There is another kind of structural failure, which results from control that is faked rather than genuine. The following essay illustrates this:

URBAN ECONOMIC PROBLEMS

1.   The study of urban problems provides many topics of interest. Understanding the economic problems of urban areas involves the examination of different aspects of this general subject. This essay will examine three such aspects: the problem of urban growth and land use, the problem of race and poverty in the city, and the problem of environmental quality. Together, these show us the inter-relatedness of urban problems, which cannot be solved by focusing on one area alone.

2.   Land use problems develop during periods of economic growth. The land available for urban expansion is always limited, but during economic prosperity there is a greater demand for each available parcel. Industrial vs. residential, privately owned vs. designated for public use, zoned for mixed uses vs. a single purpose—these are examples of some of the decisions that must be weighed against economic conditions.

3.   As urban growth occurs, the gap between the haves and the have nots frequently widens. Those who benefit most from sudden prosperity tend to be the white middle class, while the fortunes of minority residents of the inner city may decline. The depopulation of the inner city in favor of the suburbs, where new jobs are to be found, results in ghetto conditions for the poor. And the racial tensions that are found in schools and the workplace increase.

4.   Growth also presents problems in environmental quality. As industry expands into unpopulated areas, bringing along residential sprawl, problems of pollution and of the destruction of natural lands arise. The values of economic prosperity—more jobs, a higher standard of living—come into conflict with the less tangible but deeply felt values of quality of life. Political turmoil can result, since each of these values will have staunch advocates who will refuse to compromise with the other side.

5.   As you can see, a growing economy is not all good. Solving the problems that come with urban prosperity requires an understanding that there
is an inter-relatedness to all aspects of the urban economy. Land use and
environmental problems bring racial tensions and a conflict of values over
the environment. A wise public policy will look at all factors and how they
relate to each other before urban growth is permitted to go forward unre-
gulated.

Of course, this essay fails for many reasons. It fails to say anything
that isn't obvious. It fails to hold our attention because it is boring.
It is written in a style that is flat and impersonal, like a textbook.
Its statements are too general and its assertions are not supported. It
contradicts itself. These criticisms are all valid, but they do not get
at the most fundamental problem in this essay, which is structural.
The dullness of the ideas and the prose is inseparable from the dullness of the structure. Having nothing of his own to communicate,
this writer adopts an arbitrary structure from a formulaic model and
then fills up this empty, prefabricated form with content. The flat,
uncaring tone of the essay is simply the surface manifestation of a
failure to be committed to an idea, so that filling in the form is all
that matters. One can just hear this student complaining under his
breath as he writes: "Teacher asks for a paper on urban economic
problems, I'll give her a paper on urban economic problems." But
that's all. The structure lends itself to this limited intention very
well. This student has allowed it to do his thinking for him.
    The trouble with the structure of this essay is not that we do
not know how we moved from part to part, as in the case of the first
example. The trouble here is that we know all too well. We can
predict the next part before we get to it, and we are bored in advance. Its structure is phoney, and the reader knows that the writer
knows it. The writer has taken the easy way out of fulfilling a writing
assignment, by producing the "standard five paragraph theme." We
all know what this formula looks like: "In the five paragraph theme,
first state the general topic and then narrow it. End the first paragraph by stating three aspects of the topic in a thesis statement. In
paragraph 2, expand on aspect 1. In paragraph 3, expand on aspect
2. In paragraph 4, expand on aspect 3. In the conclusion, summarize
and state significance." This is what is sometimes called the "keyhole
format." Perhaps some ideas lend themselves to this approach, but
falling back on such an all-purpose, empty format can be numbing
to thought—for the writer and the reader. Yet, the temptation to
fall back on it is always with us. After all, it is easier to fill in such
a form than it is to discover the inherent structure of one's ideas.
    Although such a formal model seems to guarantee that an essay
will have structural unity and that the reader will follow the transi-

tions without wondering how they relate to the whole, the unity and the transitions that it fosters are fake. The choice of three (or any number of) aspects to be discussed as subtopics of a general topic guarantees no necessary connection among those aspects. The form *seems* to assert such a connection without the writer having to show it. The writing seems to be making connections, but, in fact, there is no good reason why *this* aspect is chosen over *that* one. To deal with all potential "urban economic problems" would, of course, require many more paragraphs, so the writer has to choose. Why these choices? Because they are convenient for filling up the demands of the form ("I know I can get one paragraph out of each of them") and no other reason. This being the case, the conclusion must attempt to create a connection where none really exists, and the phoniness of that conclusion—its vapid self-evidence—results. Here is writing by a person who has given up on independent thought, at least in this essay, and the surrender is made all the more tempting by the semblance of structure created by the empty formal model.

These two examples represent extremes of structural incoherence. The first is underdetermined; the writer has no reliable structural principle to hold the parts together, and the result is chaos. The second is overdetermined; the writer has a too-reliable structural format to hold the parts together, one that has nothing to do with the specific content, and the result is form for form's sake. Both extremes find their way into student essays, but both are avoidable. They have their origin in the student's failure to decide on an idea that is worth writing about and then to take responsibility for having that idea. After having thought about an issue, taken a stance, and developed a line of reasoning, *creating* structure should become the writer's next task. An adequate structure, one that is neither underdetermined or overdetermined, arises out of the connections that are inherent in one's reasoning. It cannot, therefore, be created except by careful thought about the necessary and sufficient parts that one's particular argument requires. Such thought will produce, not chaos and not form for form's sake, but form for the sake of the writer's reasons and the reader's assent. Neither of the essays we have seen could have been written by a student who valued his or her own ideas and who cared about the reader's agreement.

From Enthymeme to Structure

In the broadest sense, the parts of the enthymeme can be thought of as the largest units of an essay's structure. They can be diagrammed as follows:

Enthymeme		*Structure*
(question at issue)	→	beginning
(assumption) ⎱ because clause ⎰	→	middle
assertion	→	end

The enthymeme, which has heretofore been the product of thinking about one's ideas and one's reasons, can now be looked at as the source for the specific functions of these large structural parts—"specific" because each enthymeme will have its own requirements. But these requirements can be understood nevertheless by thinking of the structure of an essay as the fulfillment of the logical relationships in the enthymeme:

> *Beginning:* The reader is introduced to a problem that is of interest because it requires a solution. *The question at issue.*
>
> *Middle:* The solution to the problem depends on the reader and writer sharing a common understanding. *The assumption.*
> Given this understanding, an answer to the problem can be developed if a condition can be shown to be the case. *The because clause;* the "burden of proof."*
>
> *End:* Given the assumption and the condition just developed, the solution follows. *The assertion.*

Needless to say, these parts can be as long or as short as the specific case requires. They do not correspond to paragraphs; this could be the structure of an essay, a chapter, or a book. And within these parts, many kinds of sentences and transitions can occur, as they are called for. But these basic functions are common to essays that *take a reader through a developing line of reasoning toward an earned conclusion.* The well-constructed enthymeme, then, contains the basic elements that a structure needs if it is to be held together by progress of thought. An essay moves from problem to solution, linking them by reason, just as thought itself does.

Having come up with an enthymeme does not signify that one's thinking is over and the writing simply follows without adding new considerations. The process of moving from enthymeme to essay involves rethinking the logical steps in such a way that they can be

---

* "Burden of proof," here, means simply that the because clause will be that part of the logic most fully demonstrated in order for the conclusion to be earned, *if* the assumption is, in fact, assumable.

clearly and effectively communicated. This means that the writing continues to require thought about one's argument, and this thought will be even more focused than before, since the composition must include the detailed explanations that the enthymeme itself necessarily overlooks for the sake of logical coherence. It is a process, therefore, of examining the implications of the enthymeme itself, which means going over some thoughts again *and* taking some thoughts further into more fully developed ideas. The enthymeme represents the undifferentiated logic of the whole essay, which must now be differentiated into the parts of the essay.

This act of differentiation, leading to a developed structure, requires intuitive judgments about what to include in the essay and what to exclude, as well as where the chosen details should go. The enthymeme is a guide to such intuitions, but it doesn't guarantee that they will happen. There are intuitive leaps involved in fleshing out an essay, just as there are in coming up with a thesis and reasons to support it. The process of structuring can begin with an analysis of the enthymeme itself, since its terms and their relations will be the basic elements of the essay.

To show how such an analysis might take place, let's return to the enthymeme generated by the fictional student in the previous two chapters. That enthymeme turned out like this:

> Ethics classes for scientists will teach them to weigh the potential harmful effects of their research against the potential good, because raising questions of right and wrong in relation to science will confront them with their compassionate feelings for other people.

The structure of the essay will arise from the terms of this logic and their relationships. The terms are the noun phrases; the relationships are the predications (verbs) linking them. These parts of this enthymeme may be diagrammed as follows:

A	verb^1	B
Ethics classes for scientists	will teach them	to weigh potential harmful effects against potential good

because

A' (A redefined)	verb^2	C
raising questions of right and wrong about science	will confront them	with their compassionate feelings for others.

The purpose of this diagram is no more than to isolate the parts of the logic for consideration. The labels are simply for convenience. Based on this analysis of the significant terms of the logic, we can begin to construct the line of reasoning that the essay will follow, the linear progression of ideas that will introduce and connect these terms.

An essay structured according to the logic of this enthymeme might begin by conveying to the reader that there is a problem to be solved. The question at issue is implicit in the thesis, but it requires explanation nonetheless. What makes the issue an issue? Such a consideration seems to provide the best place to start. Thus, the first thing the essay might do is to state the problem in such terms:

> The problem of whether scientists should be ethically responsible for the harmful applications of their research is one that concerns us all.
>
> Even if someone else makes the application, the scientist is responsible to some degree if he or she is aware of the possibility of harmful effects. Thus, one aspect of the problem is to find a way for scientists to consider their options by weighing harmful effects against beneficial ones.   (B term introduced)
>
> It should not be assumed that scientists, schooled in objective methods of research, necessarily know how to do this.
>
> Thus, it may be a question of how scientists are taught.   (verb[1])
> Might the addition of ethics classes for scientists enable them to learn how to weigh harmful and good   (A term effects, as a way of thinking about their responsibilities?   introduced)

Here—in undeveloped form—is the beginning of a line of reasoning. As part of the introduction to an essay (we don't know yet how many sentences or even paragraphs that introduction might take), these ideas function to develop the need for the writer's thesis and to promise an answer. To continue, this line of reasoning might next develop a connection to the terms of the because clause:

> The answer depends on understanding what kind of knowledge is required to be able to weigh harmful effects against good ones.
>
> What does "harmful" mean in this case? It means effects that hurt people.

Thus, if scientists are to weigh the harm done to other
human beings, they must be able to feel compassion   (*C* term
for others' suffering. Feeling compassion is what makes   introduced)
it possible for one to know how harmful an effect
might be.

At this point, the assumption implicit in the enthymeme has been
proposed (by asserting the connection between the *B* and *C* terms).
The structure now requires linking this assumption with the remaining terms of the because clause (verb^1 and *A'*). The essay's structure
now enters the crucial "burden of proof" phase of the reasoning in
the enthymeme:

How do people become aware of their compassionate
feelings for others? By confrontation. In other words,
if people are confronted with their feelings about the   (verb^2)
welfare of others, they cannot help but think about
the extent of their compassion. What kind of activities bring about this confrontation?

Asking questions of right and wrong. Questions that   (*A'*)
require a choice between a right course of action and
a wrong one will involve one in examining compassionate interest in the welfare of others.

At this point, the major and minor premises of the logic have both
been asserted, but the "redefinition" of the *A* term has not yet brought
the logic of the enthymeme to its conclusion. This is now an easy
matter:

Raising such questions of right and wrong about   (*A* = *A'*)
matters of science would be the aim of an ethics class
for scientists.

Such a class would, therefore, enable scientists to learn   (*A* → *B*)
to weigh potential harmful effects against potential
benefits of their research, and help to make them see
their responsibilities.

The logic of the enthymeme has now resulted in a linear progression
of ideas, from problem to solution. This basic line of reasoning resulted from introducing the terms of the logic of the enthymeme and

making connections between them, in an order that the reader might be expected to follow.

These statements do not yet constitute the prose of an essay. They merely represent the rational backbone of the essay. We have been concerned only with finding a structure that will unfold according to the logic of the case as we have worked it out, so that the parts of the essay will follow each other and progress toward the conclusion. The statements constitute an outline that has yet to be fleshed out with further connections, further development, even further support. This is not the sort of outline that you may be used to, the kind that proceeds by subdividing categories and that subordinates them under headings, all neatly labeled with roman and arabic numerals and capital and lowercase letters. Rather, it is an *outline of ideas,* each one standing for a major link in the progress of the essay's thought. It has not resulted from trying to fill in blank spaces labeled *II* or *D* or *4,* but from trying to rethink the ideas in the enthymeme in the order that one will use to present them to a reader. To produce such an outline is not always necessary, but it can be an effective way of ensuring that the essay will follow the logic carefully and thoroughly, and not stray from the point. Writing such an idea outline is a way to think about structure, after having thought about the logic of the case and before undertaking to compose the actual sentences of the essay. Having developed such a structure of ideas, a writer can use it as a guide for the composition, to help define the specific responsibilities the writer will face at each point in the essay's progress.

Notice that the outline of ideas just produced necessarily contains some statements that were not part of the enthymeme itself. The enthymeme was written in an attempt to boil the logic of the case down to its most precise form, in response to many considerations about the issue and the audience. Generating a structure *from* the enthymeme necessarily requires bringing some of those considerations back into consciousness, so that the precision of the enthymeme can now be expanded into an understandable line of reasoning. An enthymeme serves the writer in thinking concretely about the argument, but the reader will require much more than the bare bones logic to be able to follow and accept the reasoning. Readers will need to be taken through the steps of the reasoning more completely, to understand the need for moving from one part of the logic to the next. The outline of ideas that is generated by the enthymeme must now generate an even more thorough treatment, in the actual prose of the essay, according to the needs of the reader.

Each of the ideas contained in such a linear structure may be developed in many ways. Intuition and judgment are again required; no rules are available to tell you exactly how to develop each of these major structural parts of the essay. But considering the potential experience of the reader can again help you to discover what is needed. What does the reader need to know at each point in order to understand, to follow, and to agree? The writer must provide the answers —by guessing, of course, since the actual responses of readers can't be predicted with much certainty. The answers might come in many forms. In order to develop such a structure of ideas, a writer might decide to provide a definition, or to explain a concept, to provide an illustrative example, to cite the writing of others, or to bring in additional reasons in support of some claim. All such additions to the basic structure might be provided in response to a reader's potential needs, at points where the reader might be imagined to ask "What's that mean?" or "Can you show me an example?" or "Why should I believe that?" Anticipating such questions, when they are reasonable, is one way in which the writer can decide whether any of the innumerable "things to be said" should be said in *this* essay, and if so, where those things should go. The advantage of having created such a structure of ideas is that it can be used as a basis for deciding which of those many potential "things to be said" are relevant to advance the argument and where in the progress of the reasoning the need for them arises. With such a structure laid down, the writer can think most effectively about the specific points that will enable the reader to follow and to assent to the writer's ideas.

In this process of deciding what to say to develop each part of the essay's structure, one more consideration is crucial. In addition to making the argument progress clearly, the writer must also be responsible for acknowledging counterarguments that a reader might make to the unfolding logic of the writer's case. In developing the structure, the writer will make many assertions, and these, like the thesis itself, are subject to a critical reader's potential doubt. Thus, a writer must be able to anticipate where a reader might object, because there are also reasons for arguing otherwise. Counterarguments may arise at any point, but this doesn't mean that the writer must refute every possible objection. That would not be possible, nor would it result in an essay that confidently developed its thesis. Remember that the purpose of argumentation is not to guarantee a victory for one's position, but to present that position as reasonably as possible. Argument is a process of inquiry into the best available reasons, not a contest of skeptical nay-saying. Thus, a writer need not anticipate every possible objection while taking responsibility for those that might nevertheless be raised by a critical reader.

A writer can acknowledge potential counterarguments in a variety of ways. Some counterarguments might result in the writer changing his or her mind and require a return to an earlier phase of thinking. A revised thesis may be needed. But other counterarguments can be acknowledged without changing the overall logic of the case, except to introduce conditions or qualifications. Other counterarguments might be shown to be irrelevant to the circumstances of the present logic, or they might be shown to be invalid by refuting them. How the writer handles the reader's potential counterarguments will depend entirely on the nature of the specific case being made and what the writer really thinks about those counterarguments. An honest, thoughtful writer will not simply skip over possible, and reasonable, counterarguments, however, in hopes that no one will notice. A critical reader *will* notice. The writer is responsible to try to see his or her own argument from the point of view of a reader who may not already agree with it and to consider whether good reasons may also be found to support opposing ideas. This consideration helped the writer to develop a reasonable thesis in the first place. It can now help the writer to develop a better essay, by enabling him or her to deal with objections as they arise within the essay's developing structure. A good argument is never completely one-sided, in the sense that it ignores a reader's capacity to disagree. Arguments that take seriously questions that are genuinely at issue must credit their readers with the power of responding with thoughts of their own.

We have moved from the design of an enthymeme to the design of a structure by rethinking the logic of the case in linear order. We have also considered that such a structure may be developed by responding to the needs of a reader. We are now ready to produce the actual prose of the essay. Chances are, of course, that some of this prose already has been written, since the process of making an enthymeme and of generating a structure from it will have resulted in many ideas that were written down—perhaps in notes on scratch paper, in trial paragraphs, or in attempts to write parts of the essay that may have seemed premature. At any rate, so much thinking has gone into the process thus far that the actual writing is made somewhat easier; one cannot go through the process of composing an enthymeme and of finding a structure of ideas in it without having thought about many potential ways for the essay to develop. The actual writing, although it will present new challenges of its own, will seem like going over familiar ground. The mental work that one has undergone should result now in confidence, for writing is always easier when it is approached with a sense that one has an idea worth communicating, an audience that cares enough to want to think about it, and a strategy in mind that will bring the two together. This sense does not come to writers as a gift from the gods; it must be forged by the writer's commitment to keep thinking.

From Structure to Essay: An Analysis

We have already discussed the kinds of considerations that a writer must attend to in the process of composing an essay structured according to the logic of the case. Remember that there are no rules for producing the sentence-by-sentence prose that this essay will contain. Apart from the previous "considerations," therefore, I have no further advice to give. Let's look at an example of an essay and try to analyze the process by which it took shape. Since we have followed our fictional student with the "ethics classes for scientists" thesis, let's see an essay that this same student might write, based on the structure we have already examined. This won't be a perfect essay, nor will it be the only kind of essay that might be written using the same structure. Since it could only have been written by making many choices—at each sentence, at each word—it is by no means intended as a model. There are no model essays. Each one is different, depending on what it says, who is writing it, and for whom it is written. Even these "variables'" will yield a vast number of equally "right" choices. So, here is the essay that our student wrote:

THE NEED FOR AN ETHICAL EDUCATION FOR SCIENTISTS

1.   Scientists are taught to discover "truth" by conducting experiments in an objective manner, without allowing personal feelings to affect the outcome. Yet this view of science has often come under attack, when the possibility exists that objectivity may do more harm than good. The "truth" that scientists regard as the product of their research will eventually become available to others to use. When the application of scientific knowledge creates harm, many are willing to blame the scientists, or at least to argue that the scientist shares in the ethical responsibility for these applications.

2.   It would be ridiculous to assume that all scientists share in this responsibility equally. Sir Isaac Newton, for instance, cannot be blamed for the applications that the scientists and technicians who developed the first atomic weapon made of his basic laws of physics. It is interesting, though, that Albert Einstein, who built his theories on the basis of Newton's, expressed regret about his contribution to the atomic age. The scientists who worked on the Manhattan project have recently expressed even more sense of responsibility for their more direct contributions to atomic weaponry. Thus, the question of responsibility seems to be a matter of degree, depending on the closeness of the scientist to the application itself. It seems reasonable to think that scientists share a greater burden of ethical responsibility if they are more able to predict the specific harmful application and its likelihood. Newton thought he was disclosing the wonders of God's creation. But the Los Alamos scientists were fully aware that they were working on a bomb.

3.   These scientists, who were motivated to end World War II but who nevertheless knew that the knowledge of atomic weapons would continue to exist after that war, faced a choice. They could contribute their knowl-

edge to uncovering the secrets of the atom, or they could withhold their support for this project. Some chose to participate because, as scientists, they desired to increase knowledge, while others were motivated by the patriotic goal of winning the war by any means. Some chose to stay home, or even to protest the activities of the Los Alamos scientists. These scientists all made ethical decisions because they knew that their research could lead to specific harmful applications.

4.   Although responsibility must be shared with those who choose to make the application, it does seem that scientists who make a choice to conduct research in full knowledge of the potential beneficial and harmful applications have accepted some ethical responsibility for themselves. They have made their choice by weighing the beneficial applications against the harmful ones, by deciding to risk the possibility of one outcome against the likelihood of another. This kind of decision does not depend on how much one understands about science—although scientific knowledge does help one to predict the likelihood of a result—as much as it depends on being able to determine right and wrong. Scientists have ethical responsibility not as scientists, but as human beings with consciences. They are no more or less able to know what is morally right than anyone else. Yet, because of the power given to scientists by virtue of their ability to create knowledge, they seem to have a special obligation to choose whether to conduct certain kinds of research.

5.   Modern society invests scientists with this power, yet it does not seem to do anything special to teach them how to exercise it conscientiously. That is, an education in science is ordinarily understood to mean technical and theoretical training in one or more scientific discipline. Enormous resources are used to ensure that scientists are good at practicing science, but very little is done to ensure that they become better at making ethical choices. In a world in which the impact of science on the quality of people's lives is enormous, and especially after recent history has shown us how scientists do make ethical choices, it seems obvious that thought should be given to how a scientific education might prepare future scientists for making ethical decisions.

6.   Although ethics classes for scientists seems like a good idea—it's hard to imagine anyone arguing that scientists should not learn about ethics—it isn't necessarily clear how such classes might actually make scientists better able to weigh their options, to decide whether or not to conduct research based on weighing potentially harmful effects against beneficial ones. A commitment to the idea of adding ethics classes to the scientific curriculum would be easier to make if we were sure that such classes would succeed in making future scientists more capable than otherwise of thinking about their ethical responsibilities. The question then becomes how such classes would make a difference: Would ethics classes for scientists teach them to make ethical choices?

7.   To answer this question, we might consider what kind of knowledge is required by anyone who is able to weigh harmful effects against beneficial ones. This is the kind of question that any ethics class must address, whether for scientists or anyone else. How does one learn to think about the relative importance of good and bad outcomes, when both might result? This is a difficult problem, and I cannot solve it to my own complete satisfaction. I think there is a way to begin thinking about it, however, by asking what we mean in this case by harmful and beneficial.

8.   "Harmful" and "beneficial" must refer to effects that hurt or benefit people. They are terms that designate qualities of life, and they therefore refer to what people feel about their own conditions. Now, it may be possible to try to measure these conditions by some scientific means, but such efforts will always impose an outside view on feelings that only an individual can really know. What I mean is that "harmful" and "beneficial" could be defined so that they refer to statistical conditions: Society is harmed if unemployment rates rise, or society is benefited if the gypsy moth is eradicated. These are ways of thinking about harm and benefit as objectively measured characteristics, and by using such definitions, people's actual feelings are abstracted out of the picture. But another way of approaching "harm" and "benefit" is to see them as a matter of personal suffering or personal satisfaction. Each person's actual suffering as a result of unemployment will be different; each person's actual benefit as a result of employment will be different, too. Eradicating the gypsy moth may save an industry, but the degree of actual suffering caused by the elimination of that industry is different from the amount of money gained or lost in the process.

9.   This distinction is helpful, I think, because it enables us to see that scientific methods, such as the study of gains and loss in statistical terms, might provide one way of weighing harm and benefit, but that this way does not necessarily produce the ability to measure harm in terms of human suffering. The way in which suffering is really known, the way in which people can come to understand what it means in human terms, is not through statistics and balance sheets, but through compassion. Compassion—perhaps an old-fashioned sounding word to some—is the ability to feel another's hurt or pleasure and to understand it from the inside. If an action results in suffering for individuals, the actual degree of its harmfulness will be unknown to anyone who cannot feel that suffering by empathizing compassionately with the victim.

10.   If scientists are to learn to weigh the harm done to other human beings as a foreseeable result of the application of their research, they must be able to feel other's suffering compassionately. This sounds self-evident, but it is easy to forget that scientists may be more inclined than others to view suffering from the objective, "bottom line" perspective. But they need not be. Scientists can become aware of their compassionate feelings for others in the same way other people do, by being confronted directly with their feelings for others. Science education doesn't necessarily create this kind of confrontation, but other kinds of learning situations do. This sort of confrontation exists whenever students are asked to choose between right and wrong actions in particular situations where harm and benefit would result. In such situations, more than the likelihood of a specific outcome is at stake; one must also determine how much suffering one is willing to tolerate in exchange for how much benefit.

11.   Consider this example: If I am invited to go cycling with a friend, I might object to her refusal to wear a protective helmet. I would face an ethical decision. Should I refuse to go along unless she agrees to wear one? It's her own business to make up her mind, but it's my business whether to encourage her to risk hurting herself. She might say that the risk of having an accident is very slight. That's true, but the suffering that might result for her could be horrible. I have read about such accidents. My ethical responsibility, if that suffering were to result, would be great, I feel, because the suffering would be great. Thus, my decision would be based on three

factors: my ability to foresee the possibility of an accident, the likelihood of that possibility, *and* my compassionate understanding of the potential suffering. We all face similar decisions all the time—whether to let a friend drive drunk, for example, or whether to insist that passengers use seat belts.

12.   An education in science would presumably enable scientists to consider the first two factors, since scientific thinking can be applied to predicting effects and their likelihood. But an ethical education of some kind is necessary to enable one to consider the third.

13.   Ethics classes for scientists could present such choices in relation to actual kinds of research. Issues in medicine, for instance, such as whether certain kinds of human experimentation should be used, or issues in genetic engineering, would present students with the kinds of confrontation that I have described. Presented with a choice of actions, students would have to examine their own compassionate feelings in order to answer the question of whether the suffering would be worth the benefits. Scientists would not learn that the answers are easy, but they might come to a greater understanding of the kinds of ethical choices they will face in their research careers. This may not prevent harmful effects from occurring, but it might enable scientists to recognize their individual ethical responsibilities. In a society in which scientific knowledge is necessary to solve problems created by science, this is the least that we must hope for.

You may think this is a good argument or a poor one, but at this point let's suspend that judgment for a while and ask *how* this student got from the sketchy structure generated earlier to this more fully developed essay.

What we see here is the result of a process of *drafting,* which consisted of thinking about what to say next, about how to phrase it, and about whether to leave it phrased that way or to change it. The actual pages that this student worked on may have contained sentences and paragraphs that, for one reason or another, were changed or excluded from this essay. Words, sentences, paragraphs get tried out in this process as possibilities, but then get crossed out because they aren't right. Drafting is always a messy process. It takes place in spurts of fast writing and in slow, word-by-word plodding—in brilliantly perfect moments of insight and in false starts and awkward hesitations. All writers have the experience of writing some sentences that seem promising but that turn out not to work. They all have the experience of crossing out words and substituting others. They have all felt amazed that the right word just popped into their heads, but they have all agonized over choosing one word from many possibilities. The process of drafting is one of letting the thoughts flow and of simultaneously exercising critical evaluation of those thoughts. Once the words are found and committed to paper, they may be eliminated or changed or moved around. Thus, the process of drafting combines spontaneity and deliberation, in unpredictable combinations. The writer's *draft* might appear chaotic and confused, but only because the writer is fully engaged in composing thoughts.*

Writing is a process of discovery, and discovery happens within constraints. Writing combines freedom and control. The draft essay above illustrates this, even though we do not see what actually went on as the drafting progressed. As the student's thinking developed from enthymeme to structure and from structure to essay, new discoveries resulted at each stage, and they were prompted by the new kinds of questions that each new task presented. In the process of trying to develop the smaller units of the composition out of a clear understanding of the larger units (what I earlier called moving from "whole to parts"), the writer discovers new possibilities, new requirements, and new challenges. This is inevitable, since a writer cannot conceive of a complete, fully developed essay all at once; an essay must be built up part-by-part. The process of determining the logic and the structure before drafting is not meant to reduce the writer's freedom. Nothing could do that; there are always new possibilities to be discovered. It is meant to direct the necessary choices toward a consistent and intelligent end. Control is only possible when the freedoms of composition can be harnessed productively. Freedom is only possible when there are controls that provide the kinds of challenges that motivate discovery.

In going over the essay, in comparison with the student's structural plan, we can see where some of these challenges occurred and how the student responded to them. I will discuss only a few places in the essay where the student faced new considerations brought on by the need to fulfill the demands of the structure. These will be enough to illustrate how "discovery by constraint" may work during the process of composing, but you might find more examples on your own.

Notice first of all that the student takes four paragraphs at the beginning to get through the first two structural steps, introducing the problem of whether scientists should be ethically responsible as a subject for inquiry. Why? The writer probably had to back up so far because the *nature* of that problem has to be understood in a certain way in order to prepare for later elements of the essay. The first paragraph not only introduces and explains the general problem, but

---

*You might think that if you write on a word processor, the messiness of composing is eliminated. It isn't. The only difference is that the erasures and scratchings out, words written in the margins and between the lines, are consumed and realigned by the machine as the writer drafts and redrafts, rather than remaining on the page where the writer put them. *Retyping,* of course, is made much easier by the machine. But *drafting* isn't.

also speaks of it in terms of what the scientist is "taught," which will be a matter of concern later in the essay, as will the idea of "objectivity." The second paragraph attempts to clarify the kind of responsibility under discussion by using examples that also serve to introduce the need to solve the general problem. A new idea is introduced into this paragraph, one the "outline" had not specifically required, but that the progression of the prose now seems to call for: Not only is responsibility said to be a matter of degree, as in the second step of the structural plan, but degree itself is determined by the scientist's "closeness" to the application. This detail occurs, we presume, to explain why the writer thinks it is a matter of degree, but also to answer a potential objection, which the writer has anticipated: How can a scientist like Newton be responsible at all, even if he could imagine some kinds of application?

Certain details of these paragraphs are included to anticipate what the essay will later need in the way of distinctions or qualifications. Other details are included to clarify the writer's purpose to the reader. The whole of the third paragraph seems to have resulted from the writer's sense that the idea of ethical choice may not be clear to the reader. Thus, the writer feels a need to expand on the example of scientists who did know what the consequences of their research might be. This example demonstrates for the reader that the problem is not a simple one of choosing between good and evil, since it involves scientists who had to weigh their choice between conflicting "goods." Thus, the writer has prepared the reader to accept the next part of the structure, the idea that a way must be found for scientists to "consider their options by weighing harmful effects against beneficial ones." This idea is made explicit in paragraph five, but is implicit nonetheless in three and four. The writer has, in fact, departed from the order of the ideas in the outline, because new relationships among thoughts developed as the writing unfolded. The outline would call for saying at this point that "objective methods of research" do not necessarily teach scientists how to make this choice, but the writer has already made us aware of this and, in paragraph four, the writer goes into a variation on this idea, one that again was not part of the plan but is nevertheless relevant:

> This kind of decision does not depend on how much one understands about science—although scientific knowledge does help one to predict the likelihood of a result—as much as it depends on being able to determine right and wrong. Scientists have ethical responsibility not as scientists, but as human beings with consciences. . . . Yet, because of the power given to scientists by virtue of their ability to create knowledge, they seem to have a special obligation to choose whether to conduct certain kinds of research.

Here, the writer has developed new ideas, within the structure as planned and even *because* of the demands created by that structure. The writer is still thinking about the argument, and these new ideas emerge as a result. The distinction between using scientific knowledge to determine the likelihood of a result and using some other kind of knowledge to weigh good and harmful results is one that this writer had not previously thought about. It is not part of the logic of the enthymeme, and it is not an element in the idea outline. But it is to become a major feature of the essay as it progresses, one that supports the line of reasoning.

In the fifth paragraph, the idea of the scientist's "power" becomes a transition to the need for education, returning to the structure of the idea outline. This helps the writer make a transition from the question at issue to the writer's initial discussion of the thesis, but it also functions to add an appeal to the reader's preferences. Note the special appeal to the quality of our lives and how that appeal is strengthened by the writer's understated return to the earlier example of "recent history," reminding us of the nuclear threat without hitting us over the heads with it.

The sixth and seventh paragraphs follow the structural outline and move the argument forward. In explaining the next stages of the line of reasoning, these paragraphs also attempt to respond to a critical reader's potential doubts. They are functional paragraphs, leading the reader to the next crucial step in the logic, but they also defend the need for going on to that step. "A commitment to the idea of adding ethics classes to the scientific curriculum would be easier to make if . . ." This prepares the reader for an answer at the same time that it asks the reader to speculate along with the writer before rejecting the possibility. In the seventh paragraph, the writer sees a need to make a confession:

> This is a difficult problem, and I cannot solve it to my own complete satisfaction. I think there is a way to begin thinking about it, however, by. . . .

The writer has become aware of the possibility that a reader might say something like this: "Who are you to be answering a question that has confused people for centuries? It's not as simple as you think." And the writer wants the reader to know that he is speculating, not trying to cram his belief down anyone's throat.

It is in paragraphs eight and nine that the new distinction between what can and cannot be known by scientific means becomes part of the writer's logic. (A reader of the essay would be surprised to learn that this distinction was not planned, but emerged during the composition, as the necessity for it arose.) The distinction works within the writer's logic by helping to explain what "harmful" and "beneficial" mean—a predetermined move of the writer's part, but not fully thought out when the structural outline was written. It also smooths the way for the introduction of an important term in the logic: "compassion." The structural outline introduced this term abruptly; the essay makes its introduction seem more natural. The distinction between what scientific methods can teach and what they cannot is brought forward again, in paragraph ten, as a way of returning to the question of education, and the next term in the logical structure, "confrontation," is addressed.

When paragraph ten ends, the writer seems to sense the reader's potential confusion. "Confrontation" is a pretty abstract word here, and the reader may feel that it needs clarification. The writer might also sense that the essay has gone on in an abstract way for a while, possibly to a reader's annoyance. Paragraph eleven attempts to bring the essay back down to earth a bit and to make the meaning of "confrontation" come alive. The writer creates a believable example of everyday confrontation with a question of right and wrong. The bicycle example also clarifies the writer's earlier distinction between scientific and ethical ways of knowing:

> Thus, my decision would be based on three factors: my ability to foresee the possibility of an accident, the likelihood of that possibility, *and* my compassionate understanding of the potential suffering.

The example also takes us back to earlier parts of the essay. It reminds us that in being able to predict the outcome, we are more like the Los Alamos scientists than we are like Newton—"closer" to the outcome and hence responsible to a greater degree. In being able to calculate the likelihood of an accident, we are thinking like a scientist. In having compassion, we are able to confront the ethical nature of the decision most fully. Paragraph twelve explicitly connects the example with these principles. Thus, the writer's case has been well served by an example at this point. It adds reality to the logic. It was not invented, however—nor could it have been—until the writer attempted a fully developed essay out of the logic and structural materials he had already brought under control.

The last paragraph completes the logic of the enthymeme and the structure of the argument. Further examples are brought in to show the reader that the thesis is applicable to a variety of specific issues. The logic is summarized, but in the process the writer introduces a qualification that is once again not present in the structural outline. The writer is again reminding readers of the complexity of the issue and putting the thesis into that context: This is not the final solution, it seems to say, but a path to follow. The writer has not set out to save the world, but to deal with one controllable aspect of the complex issue of science and morality. To prevent the reader from leaving the essay with a false impression, the writer adds a final sentence that goes beyond the thesis and yet shows how the thesis might apply to our thinking about the issue. Don't get me wrong, it seems to say, I don't think science is bad. We need science. But we need ethics, too, if we are to make science succeed. The writer's final idea—once again, thought up in the process of composing—helps to make the thesis believable, not by continuing to give reasons for believing it, but by relating it to the hope for a better future that the writer and the reader are assumed to share.

This analysis leaves much out of account. It isn't meant to explain why the writer included every sentence or every word. No analysis could explain how a writer makes such decisions. Sometimes the answer to why a writer has done it one way and not another is simply "because it felt right." But that does not mean that as a writer you can use that reason for an excuse; a decision, after it is made, will either work together with all other elements of the writing or it won't, and this will always be a matter for you to determine on some basis. The best basis for making such a judgment, as this book has argued, is your own clear sense of your intention: what you want to say and how you plan to support it, what you want the reader to understand and how you plan to take the reader there. These considerations, in advance of actually composing the essay, will provide you with the best means of knowing, at any point in the essay, whether to proceed with a given word or sentence or whether to try another. The thesis and the enthymeme and the structure that you work out for this purpose will not guarantee answers or make composing easier. But they will bring the process under greater control than would otherwise be the case.

One serious matter that this analysis has not addressed is in what ways this essay may fail to earn its conclusion. It is not a perfect argument, nor is it written in perfectly eloquent style. The analysis postponed such questions and sought instead to focus on the essay *as if* it did everything right. (You might wish to undertake an analysis of this essay's faults, or of your own agreement or disagreement with its ideas.) To the extent that the writer thought and thought again, the essay did do everything right, since the writer's thinking progressed to a stage it had not before reached, and that is a significant achievement. It leaves room for further growth, of course. But without the attempt to make the argument as good as possible, this writer would not have achieved this much. So, although we could measure the success of this essay according to some absolute scale of quality and find it lacking, we can also see it as the result of a writer's struggle to come to a significant understanding and to structure and clarify that understanding for others. We can only measure what the writer achieved in that sense in relative terms, according to what level of thinking and composing he was capable of before and is now capable of as a result of making this "attempt." From here, two directions are possible: The writer might reconsider the issue, rethink the thesis, restructure the argument, or simply revise the prose, and produce a better essay on the same subject; or, the writer might use everything learned in the process of writing this essay—much of it unconsciously—to face the challenges of a new one.

   How, then, does one go from a structural plan, a line of reasoning, to a completely developed essay? No one knows the answer. One thing is for sure, however, and that is that no set of rules will suffice to generate prose. But a sense of responsibility to one's own ideas and to one's audience can keep one asking the right questions, and those questions will stimulate the intuitive capacities of the mind to come up with the ideas and sentences that are required. Frustrating? Yes. Worth it? You bet.

QUESTIONS FOR THOUGHT, DISCUSSION, AND WRITING

1. Analyze the parts of the enthymeme that you have finally decided to use as the basis for your argumentative essay. (Use the method of analysis illustrated on p. 103 if you are comfortable with it. Otherwise, use any other way of isolating its parts that you wish.)
2. Having analyzed the enthymeme, write sentences for each of the logical stages in the line of reasoning developed by these parts and the relationships that hold them together. You should try to have a complete idea to represent every major logical step, from "question at issue," through "because clause" and "assumption" (not necessarily in that order), to "conclusion."
3. Where in the developing line of reasoning might your argument require, or be enhanced by, any of the following kinds of parts?
   a. further premises
   b. examples/illustrations
   c. acknowledgement of counterarguments
   d. analogies
   e. description
   f. anything else?
4. Based on this work, write the essay. Don't be afraid to change any

part of your plan if you discover some better way while you are composing. Don't be afraid to try out anything that seems right; you can scratch out, tear up, or rewrite anything you want to—nobody will know. Think about your thesis as you write. *Tell* your readers about it.

CHAPTER 6

Style: Who Are You
When You Write?

What Is "Style?"

In thinking about writing the argumentative essay as a process of moving from "whole to parts," we have so far not been directly concerned with style. For many people the word *style* is practically synonymous with *writing*. When they think of writing, style is what first comes to mind. This is understandable if you consider that a writer's style may be the first thing that you notice when you read, because the style is there in the beginning, whereas the structure and the reasoning will not reveal themselves to you until you have read further. Some people associate style with good writing. Some have been taught that to write well they must "find their own style." They may have learned to write in different styles, as a kind of exercise, or they may have sought to make stylistic effects to dazzle their teachers with nicely turned phrases. Maybe you have done this, too. I know that I have. All writers probably strive for stylistic effects to a greater or lesser degree, even when they may not necessarily be clear in their own minds what purpose is served by such flourishes. It's only human.

Style does not have to mean the kind of fancy or eloquent devices that call attention to themselves. It refers just as much to writing that seems most invisible, in the sense that you don't notice the writing as writing but see through it to the content. Style may be "ornate" or "plain," personal or conventional, straightforward or roundabout. Every piece of writing is composed in a style of some kind, even if it is not the kind of writing that we would associate with "stylistic" effects.

Confusion over the meaning of style and its role in composing sometimes arises because of the ambiguity of word itself. Consider these two sentences:

> She really has style.
> She tries for an elegant style.

In the first sentence, *style* refers to some quality that people are said to have or not to have. Given this meaning, some other person might be said to lack style, as in "The trouble with him is that he has no style." (The word *style* may thus be applied in an evaluative sense; to have style, in this sense, is presumably a good thing.) In the second sentence, it is assumed that she might try for an elegant style, or some other style. The word *style* here does not refer to a quality that is either present or absent, but to one's manner of writing. One must always have a manner; one cannot write without doing so in *some* way. Style, in this sense, is choice.

This same difference in meaning is illustrated in the following two questions:

> Does this writing have style?
> What style is this writing in?

In the first case, a piece of writing, like a person, may or may not have this special quality of style. In the second case, it isn't a question of *whether* style is present but of *what* style is chosen. The first question implies that some pieces of writing have style and some do not. The second question implies that all pieces of writing have a style of some sort.

When I said above that "Every piece of writing is composed in a style of some kind," I used *style* in the second sense. This is the way I will use it throughout this chapter, to refer to the manner in which a piece of writing is composed. It is important not to confuse this meaning of style with the other one. But this is not the end of this word's ambiguities. Even if style is said to refer to the manner of composing, it may be used to refer to many different ways of writing that are subject to choice. Consider the following sentences:

> She writes in a journalistic style.
> She writes in a classical style.
> She writes in a philosophic style.

Your style is fresh.
Your style is distracting.
His style is elegant.
Please make corrections according to your handbook of style.

In none of these sentences does the word *style* necessarily refer to the same kind of characteristic in the writing. Each of them might refer to significantly different kinds of features. "Journalistic," for instance, may refer to the length of the paragraphs or sentences, or to the objectivity of the writer's perspective. "Classical" might be taken to mean that the sentences contain long, balanced clauses or that they contain many latinate words. "Philosophic" might indicate that the writing expresses profound thoughts, or that it is written from an abstract point of view. "Fresh" could mean a wide variety of things— possibly indicating originality of word choice or even originality of topic. "Distracting," similarly, could refer to word choice or organization, or to some peculiar habit the writer has, such as beginning most sentences with dependent clauses. "Elegant" could refer to any specific characteristic of words or sentences, or to their total effect on the reader. And "style" in the last example seems to refer to matters of correct usage or mechanics, since those are what a "handbook of style" generally describes. What seems to be a feature of style in one case may not be labeled as such in another. The word *style* by itself doesn't indicate what features of the writing are being pointed out. Even naming a kind of style does not necessarily indicate clearly what features are meant. Those features have to be described so that the kind of choices referred to by *style* can be understood.

One further ambiguity makes the word *style* potentially confusing. Style refers to choice. It, therefore, assumes that a writer is conscious of and in control of the stylistic options he or she uses. Style is not always used to mean this, but to mean instead those ways of writing that the writer is unable to choose. In the eighteenth century, a French critic, George Louis Leclerc, comte de Buffon, coined a phrase that is still sometimes quoted as a definition of style: "Le style c'est l'homme, meme," he wrote, or "Style is the man, himself." Of course, modern nonsexist usage requires us to say "style is the person," but Buffon's definition is not thereby changed.* What

---

*Avoiding the use of "man" or "he" as generic terms for "person," and all other language that excludes women when humans in general are being discussed, is expected of careful writers now. Buffon's sentence illustrates, however, that this expectation did not always apply to writers. It results from our present culture's awareness that language can perpetuate sexist attitudes that may be taken for granted in society. The use of

he meant is that a writer's style results from who the writer is. A particular personality characteristic is assumed to give rise to a particular style, one that is unique to an individual. This definition seems to make style something other than a matter of free choice. Style is assumed to be determined by personality and is thus not under the writer's control. Thus, one's style could be said to be present despite one's attempts to write in a different way. Style, like handwriting, is thus considered to be a sign of personal difference. This definition is not wrong, necessarily, but it can give rise to misunderstanding if one is not clear to indicate that "style" is being used in this way.

Thus, the word *style* is easily misunderstood, simply because an enormous range of meanings is given to the term in common usage. Would it be better to avoid the word altogether, then? No, but it is necessary to qualify what it means in every new context. I have discussed the possible meanings of style so that I can create a working definition for this book, without bringing along a lot of extra baggage from those other meanings. Style, for our present purposes, may be defined as **the surface features of the prose that are controlled for the purpose of making the sentences readable and the voice of the writer appropriately reasonable.**

What does this definition mean, and what does it mean to us as we compose the kind of argumentative essay this book describes?

Style is the surface features of the prose . . . In saying this, I obviously refer to a distinction between what is on the surface and what is beneath the surface of the writing, but that distinction is not necessarily self-evident. Consider writing, for the moment, as analogous to a woven carpet or a tapestry. The weaving contains designs and patterns within its borders. These shapes are visible on the surface of the weaving, yet they are defined by the complete pattern of organization that makes up the design; it may be an abstract pattern, or it may be a symmetrical design, or a representational picture. Whatever this pattern is, however, it could be woven in many different ways. That is, the same pattern could be repeated in a weaving

---

exclusively male terms to refer to all people was not always thought to be sexist. But when many people in contemporary society became conscious of other forms of sexual discrimination, the subtle linguistic forms that this stereotyping took began to appear obvious. Some people resisted the pressure to change usage, as if the language were innocent, but most people now agree that the language will change to reflect changing attitudes, new linguistic norms will evolve, and the sensible course is to avoid language that may offend readers unnecessarily. As nonsexist usage becomes the norm, the use of old conventions will seem deliberately sexist, the same ones that in different times carried no such connotation for readers or writers. Styles change to reflect cultural standards, but changes in style can influence cultural standards as well.

that used coarse woolen yarn, or it could appear in a weaving made of smooth silk, which would give a different visual effect. Thus, the structure of the design can stay the same while the "texture" of the surface changes.

Style is like "texture." This is a metaphor, of course, but it is meant to clarify the distinction between style and structure. A piece of writing has certain structural features—this part comes first, the next part follows by means of a certain kind of transition—but these features may be rendered in a variety of different kinds of sentences, in a variety of different words, that will change the effect of the writing without changing its structural shape. Thus, the "texture" of a piece of writing emerges from choices that are made within a given structure. It results from decisions about the shape of sentences, the choice of words, and the tonal qualities that come from these.

Style is . . . controlled . . . In the previous chapter, I discussed the role of intuition in composition and how writing sometimes moves along without effort or without knowing where the choices come from. "Controlled" here does not imply any contradiction of this discussion. It means simply this: The textural features of writing are *subject to* the writer's deliberation. The writer can choose them, in the sense of thinking about this possible way versus this one. I do not mean that writers always do choose their sentence structures and words consciously, but that they nevertheless exercise the freedom to change any sentence or word that happens to occur to them. I don't mean control in the sense of positive deliberation over every choice. I mean it to signify that writers are not victims of whatever happens to flow out of their minds, but are able to select and alter anything about the writing that they wish, for a reason. The next two clauses in the definition describe two possible reasons that stylistic choices can be controlled.

Style . . . is controlled for the purpose of making the sentences readable . . . What good is a sentence unless it is readable? Perhaps this seems too obvious to need saying. Yet this clause of the definition introduces an important consideration about style— it exists, not for the writer's sake, but for the reader's. If it is the writer's intention to communicate an argument, to offer a reader the best possible reasons for accepting the writer's ideas, then the writer accepts the responsibility for making sure that the prose communicates that argument in an efficient way. The reader should not be expected to decipher imprecisely worded meanings, or to slog through circumlocutious sentences, or to put up with inappropriate departures from normal word order. A piece of writing that is difficult to read for such reasons usually earns the reader's distrust, and a reader who does not trust and respect a writer is not in a receptive state of mind. Thus, a writer must understand that a primary function of style is to make the reading as effortless as possible, so that nothing about the writing inhibits the communication of the writer's thought.

"Effortless as possible" does not mean simple-minded. We are talking now about style, not about ideas. Prose that is effortless to read may not be easy to understand, if the ideas are complex or unusual. But there should be nothing about the writing that makes the ideas harder to understand than necessary. One does not achieve a readable style by trying to simplify the ideas. One achieves it by trying to find the most efficient way in which to phrase them. Prose that is effortless to read is not necessarily easy to write. Nor is it necessarily hard. It is prose that is written with ease of understanding in mind, however, and this requires the writer to be aware of the ways in which stylistic choices may inhibit understanding. (I will illustrate a few of these ways shortly.)

. . . and the voice of the writer appropriately reasonable. Qualities of style contribute to the "tone" of a piece of writing, which refers to the mood or attitude that the reader *hears* in the words. Behind the silent words on a page, we are able to hear a voice, not necessarily the real voice of the flesh and blood writer, whom we may not know, but that of a possible or apparent speaker of the words. When we read, we may not vocalize the words, but we are nevertheless aware of qualities with which those words might be spoken. Those qualities give us our sense of the writer's attitude toward us and toward the subject. If we judge a writer to be condescending or patronizing, angry or deeply moved, open-minded or intolerant, sincere or hypocritical, we do so in part because the writer *sounds* that way. Sometimes these impressions result from the writer's ideas, but they often come from the way the "texture" of the writing is controlled.

Style and Attitudes

If style communicates the writer's attitude to the reader, then a consideration of attitude might be a useful place for the writer to begin thinking about stylistic choices. Attitude is hard to talk about; it is a combination of the writer's feelings toward the subject, toward the intended audience, and toward the writer's self. These feelings change from situation to situation, and even from time to time as the writer works on a composition. To discuss them requires oversimplification, but the purpose of this discussion is not to provide definitions of all possible attitudes. It is to give you some basis for thinking about your own attitudes and how they are reflected in the stylistic choices that you make.

The first consideration is that the "self" reflected in your writing is not necessarily the same "self" that you reflect in other situations. Even in different pieces of writing, depending on their purpose, you construct an image of yourself that may be different. The aspect of our personalities that we present to others at different times reflect the circumstances within which we act and the purposes behind our actions. There are times when it is appropriate for us to emphasize one aspect of ourselves while making certain to de-emphasize other aspects. We do this not because we are dishonest, but because we are adaptable. We are not bound so tightly to one side of ourselves that we cannot act in a way that seems called for by the situation. In writing, this means that we choose how we wish to appear to our reader, based on who the reader is and what we wish our writing to accomplish. I may come across as an entirely different sort of person when I write a letter to my parents, or to my former professor, or to my senator. I may seem like an angry person if I am writing to complain about something, or a tolerant person if I am writing to defend someone, or a serious-minded person if I am writing to express my concern over an injustice, or a clown if I am writing to get people to see something in a comical light. All of these are aspects of my true self, but I may choose from them to fit my purpose and my reader. Human personalities contain within them a wide range of possible "selves," which add up to who we are, even if some of them might seem contradictory. It is a sign of health, not of inconsistency, to be able to respond with different sides of ourselves to different situations.

Thus, who we are controls who we seem to be in our writing only to the extent that we respond to each writing situation with some part of ourselves while we may have to suppress other parts. How well you are able to do this depends on how well you judge the situation, how clearly you understand your own purposes, how you view the subject, and how you wish the reader to view it. As you think about the ideas you wish to present to the reader, and the reasons you wish to offer in support of those ideas, you are engaged in defining all of these attitudes at once, and if you have been conscientious in this thinking, you will already have done most of the work of adapting the right style. That is, writing that follows from serious thinking about good reasons and the shape that they should take in an essay will naturally come from the part of yourself that you have exercised in this thinking process. It is not necessary to do all the thinking first, and then to make all of the decisions about how to present yourself, since by doing the thinking you will have already been working on this presentation. You have been adjusting your attitude to fit the subject simply by giving it your best thinking in the first place.

All of us have probably encountered writing that we thought was somehow flawed in its tone, and have judged it accordingly. Whether we accepted the ideas in spite of this or not, we could characterize our response to the writer's way of presenting himself or herself to us by using adjectives that otherwise would apply to personality: This writer is childish, we might say, or self-indulgent, or selfish, or dishonest, or conceited, or petty, or condescending, or closed-minded. All such adjectives, when applied to writing, are responses to the writer's failure to control the tone of the writing in relation to its purposes. They reflect our judgment of the writer's attitude toward the subject, toward us, or toward himself or herself. Thus, the writer's tone is determined by how well these attitudes are shaped in the writing and kept in harmony with one another. Let's take a closer look at these attitudes and see how they may work for or against the writer's purpose.

One's attitude toward a subject is important, but it can take on so much importance that it eclipses all other considerations, and so reduces the importance of one's attitude toward the audience and the self. When we are led to characterize a writer's style by using adjectives such as pedantic, or lifeless, or monotonous, or even trivial, we are probably responding to our feeling that the writer has taken the subject more seriously than it deserves, by neglecting to consider the needs of the reader who must be helped to understand it.

Here, for instance, is a paragraph of prose that is no doubt serious about its subject but contains inappropriate stylistic choices:

> It is often contended that the citizens who protested this nation's involvement in the conflict in Vietnam during the anti-Vietnam demonstrations of the 1960s did so out of an abiding sense of patriotism for the country. Indeed, it is so often said by those who have not thoroughly analyzed the conflict that to suggest otherwise is to make one vulnerable to the charge that one believes in the slogan "My Country Right or Wrong." It is the case, however, that one can come to the inevitable conclusion that the protesters acted out of treasonous motives, in sufficient numbers of cases to warrant a skeptical attitude toward the protest movement in general, without becoming guilty oneself of any rashly suspect form of blind patriotic fervor . . .

If this were the beginning of an essay, would you want to read further? My guess is that your answer is "no," because the writer has somehow managed to put you off. What about this writing gives us the impression that the writer has neglected to consider the needs of the reader? It is enough, perhaps, to hear the writer's sneering tone and to conclude that he has no respect for the opinions of any reader who does not already agree with his stance. He is so convinced of his own rightness that he credits the reader with having no ability to come to any other conclusion but the one he wants to bully the reader into. This blindness to other potential points of view emerges as disrespect; any reader who might entertain another opinion has been labeled as someone who has "not thoroughly analyzed the conflict." The writer sees himself as one who has thoroughly analyzed the conflict, of course, and his attitude of superiority makes the prose sound pompous. The writer takes the subject seriously, but so much so that he forgets who he is writing for. His contempt for the audience is evident also in the kind of appeal he makes in his reasoning; he asserts his own invulnerability to emotional stereotyping while engaging in the same tactic himself. He calls others names while attempting to defend himself against name calling used against his own position.

The style of the paragraph contributes to this impression. Notice that the writer has tried to stay aloof from the discussion by making the prose impersonal. Perhaps he feels that he sounds more objective if he does not use the first person, but instead hides behind passive and infinitive verbs ("it is contended that," "to suggest"). Notice too that the paragraph contains three long sentences, each of which starts with the vague "it is" construction. The structures of these sentences make them unnecessarily difficult to read. The first one contains wordy repetitions ("who protested this nation's involvement in the conflict in Vietnam during the anti-Vietnam demonstrations of the 1960s," "patriotism for the country"), which bog the reader down in redundant information. The second one has an awkward word order, forcing the reader to have to reconstruct its meaning after reaching the conclusion. The third is interrupted by a distracting subordinate clause, one that makes a new point worth a sentence of its own. The three sentences are made even longer by unnecessary adjectives ("abiding," "thoroughly," "inevitable," "blind") and by phrases that could be rewritten using fewer words ("make one vulnerable to the charge," "come to the conclusion that," "in sufficient numbers of cases"). Notice too that the writer's diction is inflated. He uses "citizens" because it seems to sound more high-toned than "people," and it may seem to the writer that he is being scornfully ironic to call them "citizens" rather than "protesters." Likewise, the words "involvement" and "conflict" are chosen to make the role of the United States sound innocent; they are euphemisms. Some of the language is loaded; the writer uses "inevitable" and "treasonous" in ways that implicitly threaten the reader who might not accept them. The phrase "rashly suspect" is simply a clumsy oratorical flourish that makes no sense, and "blind patriotic fervor" is a bumbled cliché.

These stylistic choices help to give the passage its off-putting tone: by making the sentences harder to read than necessary and by making the writer sound like a pompous, narrow-minded quack. Even someone who agreed with his conclusions would be likely to be offended by such a style, since it finally makes the ideas sound foolish, whether they are or not. This writer may or may not have a good thesis, but until that thesis comes to us in carefully controlled prose, we cannot give it the credit it might deserve.

The writer of this paragraph had no excuse for turning out clumsy and careless writing; the subject matter is not so unfamiliar or complex that it can't be communicated in a plain, unoffending style. There are subjects, however, that may seem to call for writing that the reader will find difficult, simply because they are complex or unfamiliar. If the writer has a specialized knowledge that the reader is assumed to lack, the writing may contain concepts or vocabulary that make the reader's task difficult. If the ideas a writer is trying to communicate are especially complicated, it won't help to try to translate them into baby talk just to satisfy the reader's need for simplicity. The writer must use his or her best judgment about the appropriateness of stylistic choices; it is as easy to insult the reader's intelligence by condescending as it is by obfuscating simple concepts.

There are many times when the line separating these effects is not obvious, and a writer must learn to live with certain risks. Here is an example from my own writing earlier in this chapter:

> In the eighteenth century, a French critic, George Louis Leclerc, comte de Buffon, coined a phrase that is still sometimes quoted as a definition of style: "Le style c'est l'homme, meme," he wrote, or "Style is the man, himself."

When I wrote this sentence, I was aware of taking a risk. I faced the stylistic decision of whether to include the full name of the critic and, furthermore, whether to include the French phrase or the English translation, and I knew that my choices might affect the tone of my writing in ways that I might not want. Would I sound pedantic if I gave the critic's full name, or would I sound careless if I called him simply "Buffon"? I could have left his name out altogether—but would I then be insulting my readers by assuming that they wouldn't care who had coined the phrase? Would I seem to be parading my knowledge by including the information at all, rather than saying something like "Perhaps you have heard the phrase 'Style is the man'?" If I left out the English translation, would I be assuming too much about the reader and thereby making my point unintelligible, or would I insult the reader by including the translation? These are the kinds of considerations I faced when I chose to write the sentence in the way in which I did. I am not sure that I chose correctly. The sentence may have distracted you, or it may have insulted you, or it may have caused you to judge me as one who is too picky about details. I took the risk, however, because I made certain judgments about my intended audience in relation to my purpose. I decided that my readers might find this information interesting, and if I included the critic's name they could pursue it further. It's a name they may encounter again in other contexts. I decided to include the French and the English translation, because it enabled me to digress a bit in order to make a point about the cultural effects of style and how they change, in a footnote. It also occurred to me that if the reader had gotten this far, he or she was used to some of my other stylistic quirks and may forgive me this one. At any rate, my reservations about the potentially negative effects of these choices were overcome by the potential positive effects I might achieve by them, and I made them with the risks in mind. There are many times in writing when we must choose without being certain that we are making the right choice. The differences between the potentially pompous style of my sentence and that of the writer of the passage on Vietnam protesters is that I was conscious of my choices, considered my reasons, and was therefore in control of my style. The other passage, unfortunately, sounds as if the writer had no idea why he chose to write as he did.

When I wrote my Buffon sentence, I was also aware that I was probably including information that was not already known to my intended readers. I would have had no reason to discuss the concept of style at all if I thought that my audience already knew all about it. This is a textbook, and I must therefore assume that part of my purpose is to convey my understanding to readers who do not already share it. I was trying to convey some of the complexity of the concept of style in a clear and effective manner, so while I did choose to include a bit of arcane detail about Buffon, I chose not to introduce many terms that professional stylesticians use when they talk to each other about such matters. I tried, in other words, to avoid using "jargon," to keep the discussion from being more difficult than necessary—even though some of the terms I used may not have been completely familiar. I had to find a middle way between necessary technical terms that I thought my readers should know (or could look up if they didn't already know them) and those that might confuse my readers or complicate the discussion unnecessarily.

A writer who knows something that he or she assumes is unfamiliar to the audience always risks the appearance of an inflated style, because some new vocabulary always accompanies new areas of knowledge. The term *jargon* applies to the specialized vocabulary of any field of endeavor, and all fields have such terms that must be shared by those who would understand the basic concepts. (Certain terms, such as *syllogism* and *enthymeme,* were simply unavoidable during my earlier discussion of logic and composition, for instance, because they refer to concepts that must be understood, even if the terms themselves may be unfamiliar to most readers. I couldn't have written that discussion without them, and I would have underestimated my readers—you—by trying.) The question of when to use jargon and when not to must be faced by every writer whose purpose includes sharing information—and that's nearly every writer. This question, too, calls for a judgment.

Consider this paragraph, which contains several kinds of jargon, taken from an essay analyzing Robert Frost's "After Apple-Picking":

> The effect of distortion is enhanced by the use of hyperbole in line 18, which gives way to metonymy in 19 and 20 as we move quickly from a distant to a micro perspective. The use of the antithesis "not only" in line 21 makes the residual sensation of the "pressure of the ladder-round" seem extraordinary because it is contrasted to the "ache" as if an ache would be expected in such circumstances but not the sensation of a haunting pressure. We are made to feel the unbalanced sway of the ladder in the sudden irregularity of the rhythm, when the spondees in line 23 interrupt the building regularity of the preceding iambic pentameters. We are lulled, in addition, by the sounds repeated within this variable rhythm: the last two words of line 23 catch the echo of the sounds of loading, which rumbles in the consonance and assonance of lines 24 and 25 and the onomatopoeia in line 15.

Here is writing that would be virtually incomprehensible to some readers, yet is not necessarily unclear for its intended audience. The writer must have assumed that the readers for whom the analysis was intended would not stumble over the technical literary terms (*hyperbole, metonymy, spondees, iambic pentameters, consonance, assonance, onomatopoeia*) because those terms would be part of a vocabulary that they share. An audience of literary critics would not find the vocabulary alien, any more than an audience of doctors would need translations of medical terms, even though readers not sharing such terms would find them obscure. This is an example of jargon used appropriately, but only because the writer's assumptions about the audience are correct.

Style, in this sense, is like logic: its clarity and effectiveness depend not only on what is said, but on what assumptions about the reader are appealed to in the saying. Stylistic choices, like logical connections, are often neither good nor bad in an absolute sense, but only in their appropriateness to the knowledge shared by the reader and the writer. What appears obscure to one reader is clear to another. It is the writer's task to adjust the style, as well as the reasoning, to the audience. But just as reasoning cannot be reduced to saying always what the reader wants to hear, styles cannot always be chosen for their simplicity, when the ideas call for a certain degree of sophistication.

Thus, styles can be challenging to readers without being inappropriate, but the writer must be careful not to tax the reader unnecessarily. Jargon, therefore, should be used sparingly, only when it is a necessary and efficient way to convey the idea, and not when its function is to translate a simple concept into lofty language so that the reader will be impressed. Readers are generally not impressed by lofty language, unless they understand its purpose. The writer who tries to sound intelligent or educated by adding stylistic flourishes— complex sentences and inflated diction—will not fool the careful reader. But the writer whose style makes appropriate assumptions about the reader's knowledge and reflects a shared understanding and respect for the subject will have earned the reader's goodwill.

Writers who believe that they can improve their image by inflating their diction sometimes turn to a thesaurus in search of synonyms. This is a misuse of an otherwise useful resource and generally results in stylistic problems. The writer who tries to substitute a high-falutin' word for a simple one, consulting the thesaurus for a better-sounding word, risks two undesirable effects. The first is the possibility of misusing a word that sounds better but that doesn't quite mean what the writer wishes the word to say. If a word is not part of a writer's working vocabulary, if he or she never would have thought of it without looking in a thesaurus, then chances are the writer doesn't really understand what the word means. It is better to let the meaning choose the word for you than to let some unfamiliar word alter your meaning, just because it sounds more official. The second potential effect is that the writer's tone will become pompous as a result of putting long or fancy words in place of simple, direct ones.

Sometimes student writers consult the thesaurus because they have been taught not to repeat the same word. They search for suitable replacements to avoid repetition, which they assume is a fault. A writer who wishes to avoid repetition by using synonyms risks confusing the reader, since different words, no matter how close they are in meaning, convey slight differences, and the reader will assume that differences are intended when in fact they aren't.

Here's a passage of prose in which the words are all common and simple, even though the meaning is sophisticated:

> Because commercial television is intended to make a profit for its investors, programs that portray women in typically subordinate roles continue to be more common than those that portray independent women. The sponsors apparently think that the public favors such programming. If the shows are popular, then people must like to watch them. But it might be said that the popularity of the shows contributes to the perception of women that makes the shows popular in the first place. The shows, defended as an effect of the sexism in society, may also be part of the cause.

If the writer of this passage thought that her vocabulary was too commonplace or repetitious and that she could impress a reader with a lot of synonyms, she might go to the thesaurus, make some substitutions, and come up with something like this:

> Because capitalistic television is intended to fabricate a profit for its investors, programs that depict women in characteristically subordinate functions persist in being more prevalent than those representing independent females. The sponsors apparently cerebrate that the public favors such programming. If the shows are popular, then the populace must relish observing them. But it might be opined that the popularity of the performances contributes to the perception of women that makes the shows popular in the initial instance. The shows, protected as a consequence of sexism in society, may also be a component of the antecedent.

Not only has the sound of the passage become ugly, as a result of combinations of words that are not euphonious, but the tone is no longer reasonable. What we hear now is a pretentious speaker, inebriated by the sound of her own voice—to the extent that her original meaning has become muddled. The passage now is sheer hokum. This result does not come from the careful use of synonyms but from their thoughtless overuse. When Mark Twain said, "I never use *metropolis* when I can get the same price for *city*," he was exaggerating. *Metropolis* has some appropriate uses, or it wouldn't be in the language. But *city* will do in most situations where *metropolis* would be phony. So the principle behind Twain's rule is a good one.

A writer's language can become inflated in a variety of ways when the desire to create an "educated" or an "official" image for the writer's self overwhelms all other concerns. The needs of the subject and the needs of the reader are both sacrificed to this desire. It isn't always easy to know when one is sounding pompous, but at least one can resist the impulse to raise the level of the diction above that of one's own natural voice. A reliable guide, although not an infallible one, is to ask this question: If I were *saying* my ideas out loud to my audience, would I be embarrassed or uncomfortable to say them this way? If so, then the style is probably too elevated for the situation.

Writers may pay too much attention to the reader and too little to the subject, producing styles that are inappropriate because they suggest an attitude of someone who would rather conform to the reader's tastes than tell the truth. If a writer's tone sounds condescending or patronizing, it is because the style is out of control somehow; the balance between respect for the subject, respect for the reader, and respect for the self has somehow been lost. Student writers who first become conscious of the need to "consider the audience" often make the mistake of trying to bring the reader into the writing and end up producing sentences that are as much about the reader as anything else. Here is an extreme example of this sort of mistake:

> In this essay, I will try to persuade you that college athletic programs benefit all students. As a fellow student at this college, you are aware of this controversy, so I need not explain to you why it is important. You have heard that the college pays too much attention to sports, and perhaps you agree that the college could pay more attention to your education if sports programs were eliminated or cut back. As I discuss this issue, I will begin by describing the sports programs and their relation to academics and then I will list the benefits that you receive as a student from the existence of these programs. I will also attempt to refute whatever objections you may have to my reasoning, as I argue that athletics is indeed a benefit to you, whether you realize it or not.

All this talk addressed to the reader is not only unnecessary, it is insulting. It seems to imply, although inadvertently, that the writer thinks the reader is unable to understand the writer's purpose without this "hand-holding," and, in consequence, the reader is portrayed as an idiot. The writer also makes assumptions about the reader's beliefs that may or may not be shared with actual readers, and the essay further insults the reader's intelligence, therefore, by pretending that the writing is only addressed to those readers who need the writer's superior guidance. Even though there is nothing wrong with refuting potential objections in a persuasive essay, this writer gives the reader no credit for having any objections that are valid.

The paragraph actually says very little. It announces its stance and refers to a controversy. The first three sentences contain information that could be communicated quite efficiently in a single sentence introducing the issue. Then the last two sentences explain what the essay will proceed to do. These are also unnecessary; if the essay is well organized, there is no reason to provide the reader with these advance clues to the transitions that will come later. Sentences of this sort often find their way into writing, unnecessarily.

> "I am now going to take up the second part of my topic . . . "
> "At this point, let us look at the related question of . . . "
> "I will now begin the discussion of my reasons . . . "

Such road signs are seldom necessary, but writers often include them out of a sense that the reader needs help. These transitional markers do not make the structure easier to follow, as they may intend, but in fact bring unnecessary attention to the structure and distract the reader's attention from the content. If the writer constructs a clear transition from a given discussion to a related question, showing what the relation is, there should be no need to say "At this point, let us look at the related question of . . ." It will go without saying. Too many such phrases, meant to help the reader through the structure, can seem like condescension. They should be used sparingly. (Sparingly does not mean never. Do you think I have overused such phrases in this book?)

An inappropriate kind of attention to the reader may also result when the writer is tempted to define words that do not really require definition. In some situations an initial definition of a technical term will prevent the reader from being confused, or an operational definition—a special use of a common term—may prevent misunderstanding. In this book, I often define words that I think the reader needs to be familiar with in order to understand my use of them. I also include definitions where I think precision requires them, as in my above definition of "operational definition." Earlier, I provided lengthy operational definitions of *thesis* and of *style* because I did not necessarily use these words in ways that they might be used in other contexts. But I did not include many definitions of many other words that I used, although I could have. I had to decide when including a definition would contribute to the clarity of my prose or when it might get in the way or insult the reader.

Here's an opening passage that is typical of a kind of writing that many students, understandably, create:

> A society that remains ignorant of the government's foreign policy can find itself embroiled in conflicts that are not in the nation's interest. The dictionary defines "society" as "the totality of social relations among human beings." From this definition we see that what affects some members of the society must affect all. . . .

The essay is off to a bad start, mainly because the writer has thought it necessary to define a word that most readers would be unlikely to misunderstand, a word that in this case does not matter as much to the writer's argument as the meaning of "foreign policy" or "conflict." The impulse to begin an argument by referring to the authority of the dictionary for the meaning of some supposedly key term is a frequent one. Perhaps students have been told that it is helpful to the reader to have such definitions. But the problem is that the "according to Webster's . . ." opening gambit becomes habitual, gets used when there is no reason for it, and signifies the writer's lack of control. This is the sort of stylistic reflex that tells the careful reader that the writer is not sure of his or her own purpose and is stalling. It is as much a sign of the writer's inattention to purpose as the frequently abused opening, "Throughout history . . . ." What it really communicates to the reader is: "I don't know how to begin my essay." Because the opening dictionary definition is so arbitrary and so conventional that readers are wise to it, it is better to avoid it altogether. If there are times when "According to the dictionary . . ." is appropriate, they are rare.

One further result of paying too much attention to the needs of the reader is the impression that the writer cares more about pleasing the reader than about telling the truth. In other words, a writer's failure to find a stance—to write from a point of view that does justice to the writer's thoughts on an issue—can result in a desire to entertain that overwhelms any desire to find good reasons. Thus, the writing can take the form of an elaborate bluff. This is likely to be the case if we detect in the writer's style some attempt to use language to draw attention away from the subject and to the style itself. Here's how one student accomplished this feat in an essay on evolution:

> What's all the trouble about anyway? If our grand-daddies and grand-mommies got created in one big bang (no pun intended), or if they crawled out of the water, shook off their feathers and said, "where's the exit of this zoo?", it really can't make much difference to us. We all have to get born, whether the chicken came first or the egg. But,

you know, some people are never satisfied with not knowing something, so they feel like they have to invent an answer or bust. So the scientists, who could be trying to cure cancer, put their big brains to work theorizing about "evil-lution," while the glory brigade sing halleluja to a creator who didn't have to make cancer in the first place.

This writer is clever. The style features some interesting and original turns of phrase, and even some sophisticated uses of sentence structure (such as the parallel clauses about cancer in the last sentence). But are we amused, as the writer clearly intends that we should be? Maybe, but also puzzled. What's the point of this glib talk? There's nothing wrong with a sense of humor, and most of us would like to see a spark of wit in the things we read rather than an unremitting glumness. But wit can be purposeful or it can be a way of thumbing one's nose at ideas in order to avoid having to think about them. That's the impression I get from this writer, who clowns at the expense of confronting the questions that his own writing raises. Clowning can be a way of answering questions sometimes, but it can also be a way of avoiding having to come up with something to say about them. Thus, the impulse to keep the reader reading by being entertaining alone can become an excuse for not thinking. This writer obviously has talent. The more the loss, then, when he refuses to use his ability to do anything beyond keeping us entertained. (I wouldn't necessarily say this about a writer of popular fiction, you understand.) There is something insulting, too, about writing that carries on this way. Although it seems to want to give the reader credit for having a sense of humor (and that's good), it does so at the expense of portraying the reader as someone who prefers not to think.

The issue of whether to use humor, like other stylistic questions, cannot be answered with a rule. The only rule is: It depends. It would be as mistaken to take everything more seriously than it deserves to be taken as it would be to take nothing seriously enough. A balance, some kind of golden mean, is the best answer, and it is found when the writer is conscious of having a choice and of making it on the basis of careful considerations. How do I want to sound in this essay? What attitude do I want to reflect, given my stance and my readers' attitudes? What kind of style does my subject and my audience deserve? These considerations do not guarantee that the style will be appropriate in every case, but without them the writer will fall back on convenient habit, sheer clumsiness, or bluff. The trouble with our humorist about evolution is that he thought about the impression he wanted to make on the reader first, and then found ideas that would satisfy that need: "Look at me, aren't I clever?" His is the kind of writing that will sacrifice ideas to "self," in the sense that the writing is more about the writer, finally, than about the supposed thesis.

Should writing draw attention to the personality of the writer? It depends. (There's that answer again.) If the writer's ideas depend for their credibility on the quality of the reasoning used to support them, then those ideas need not depend on the personality of the writer for their power. On the other hand, writers whose prose has clarity, efficiency, *and* personality will make the best use of style in support of their ideas. The problem is to prevent "personality" from taking over and overwhelming the ideas, which should be capable of standing on their own.

Style and Clear Thinking

We have seen that it is important to pay attention to style in order to be sure that your writing says what you want it to say, that it is readable, and that it conveys an attitude that is appropriate to the reasoning. There is another reason that paying attention to style is important. We not only write in words and sentences, but we think in them as well. The thoughts we think can be affected by any habits that we may have in the use of words. Thus, style, when we lose control of it, can influence how we think. This is not a reason to use any particular style in a particular piece of writing. It is a reason to remain conscious of the possibility of being controlled by stylistic habits.

The potential effect of stylistic habits on mental habits is discussed in a famous essay by George Orwell, the British author whose novels include *Animal Farm* and *Nineteen Eighty-Four*. As you know if you have read these novels, Orwell was keenly interested in "group think," or the control of how and what people think by totalitarian regimes. He showed how language can be a powerful tool to suppress freedom of thought, open-mindedness, and independent judgment. The control of language by the state, he believed, was the same as the power to control thinking. Similarly, he believed that control of language by the individual was the same as freedom of thought, and that consciousness of style could, therefore, help the individual remain free of the unwarranted power of others' uncritical ideas.

Orwell's argument, in his essay "Politics and the English Language," goes something like this: It is easy for people to imitate stylistic habits that become conventional in the language they hear all around them. Some of these habits have their origin in uses of language that are deceptive, such as the euphemisms, half-truths, or misleading expressions that may be found in some political writing, advertising, or journalism. Some may be caused by simple neglect: Sloppy and inaccurate thinking has given rise to sloppy and inaccurate expressions. Whatever the origin of such habits, they can in turn become the cause of poor thinking. The English language, Orwell wrote, "becomes ugly and inaccurate because our thoughts are foolish, but the slovenliness of our language makes it easier for us to have foolish thoughts." Thus, failure to pay attention to style can produce unclear thinking, without our being aware of it. But, Orwell believed, "if one gets rid of these habits one can think more clearly."

Thus, although Orwell believed that language can have an insidious effect on our thinking, we can prevent this effect by taking the trouble to choose our manner of expression carefully. In what is to me the most powerful part of his essay, Orwell put it this way:

> A scrupulous writer, in every sentence that he writes, will ask himself at least four questions, thus: What am I trying to say? What words will express it? What image or idiom will make it clear? Is the image fresh enough to have an effect? And he will probably ask himself two more: Can I put it more shortly? Have I said anything that is avoidably ugly? But you are not obliged to go to all this trouble. You can shirk it simply by throwing your mind open and letting the ready-made phrases come crowding in. They will construct your sentences for you—even think your thoughts for you, to a certain extent—and at need they will perform the important service of partially concealing your meaning even from yourself.

It is that closing irony that makes this passage most effective, I think. Orwell has reminded us that life would be simpler if we did not have to think for ourselves, and we are often ready to give up freedom of thought for the comfort of conformity. But the price we pay for this comfort is self-deception. In another passage in the essay, Orwell summarized his principles for scrupulous writing:

> If you simplify your English, you are freed from the worst follies of orthodoxy. You cannot speak any of the necessary dialects, and when you make a stupid remark its stupidity will be obvious, even to yourself.

To add to our ability to judge our own thoughts, then, we can try to avoid habitual modes of expression and to strive for simplicity.

Orwell supported his argument with many examples drawn from contemporary writing. It is amazing how many of his examples continue to be found in popular language habits of today. Language, like other fashions, has fads and trends, some of which last longer than others. If you read Orwell's essay, you will be able to think of many expressions in fashion today that could be added to his list of examples. Many language habits may change over time, but the principles that Orwell argued have stayed valid. Based on his examples, Orwell devised six general rules of style, which he said could be relied on "when instinct fails." His rules are:

1. Never use a metaphor, simile or other figure of speech which you are used to seeing in print.
2. Never use a long word when a short one will do.
3. If it is possible to cut a word out, always cut it out.
4. Never use the passive when you can use the active.
5. Never use a foreign phrase, a scientific word or a jargon word if you can think of an everyday English equivalent.
6. Break any of these rules sooner than say anything outright barbarous.

Do these rules seem consistent with some of the advice I have already given about style? They are another way of saying some of the same things that I have discussed, without Orwell's gift for precision. His rule number six is another reminder that when it comes to style there are no real "rules," in the sense of laws that cannot be broken. Style serves a purpose. The purpose must determine the validity of the rule. It depends.

As a writer, you could probably not keep these rules in mind all of the time while you are composing. Worrying too much about rules, whether they are grammar rules or stylistic rules or rules for organization, can distract you from the most important consideration, which is the careful scrutiny of what you believe about an issue and why you believe it. The point at which one ought to think about such rules consciously is during revision (a subject I discuss in the next chapter). Rules, as Orwell said, are at our service when instinct fails. Applying them thoughtfully, as a means of revising, can help to make them instinctive. If you revise carefully, with such principles in mind, it will eventually mean that you will not have to revise as much as before, because the old, sloppy habits of composition will be replaced by new, sound habits. But habits of any kind are potentially dangerous in writing, and so it always helps to remember the importance of being in control of the stylistic choices faced at every phase of writing, from the drafting of a thesis statement, through the structuring of an argument, to the editing and proofreading of the final draft.

QUESTIONS FOR THOUGHT, DISCUSSION, AND WRITING

1. Analyze the style of a piece of argumentative writing that you think is effectively written. What stylistic choices seem to be present in order to make the sentences more readable? What choices seem to be present in order to make the writer should more reasonable? More credible, honest, sincere? What choices may hinder the writer's credibility?

2. Analyze a piece of your own writing in this same way.

3. After looking carefully for features that characterize the "texture" of your prose, make a list of any stylistic *habits* that you find in it.

4. Read George Orwell's "Politics and the English Language," and discuss these questions:

   a. Orwell admits that he has violated his own rules in his essay. Can you find some examples? Why does Orwell do so, and what does this tell you about the nature of language and rules for its use?

   b. Find examples from present-day political language that illustrate Orwell's principles, and say how you think their use has affected political thinking.

   c. Look carefully at an example of your own previous writing to find usages of which Orwell would disapprove. How might you change them? Do the same kind of analysis of the writing of a friend, a political columnist, or other writer.

5. A literary critic once said that "Every change in style is a change in meaning." Do you agree with this claim? Why or why not?

CHAPTER 7

❧ *Revision* ❧

Taking Responsibility, Again

It is probably misleading to think of revision as the last stage of the writing process, since writers revise continuously. Revision takes place whenever a writer replaces one phrase or sentence with another, adds a word or phrase or sentence or paragraph, cuts out some part of a composition, or moves writing from one part of an essay to another. These actions can take place at any time during composing, or as a separate activity after a draft is completed. Revision is recomposing, and as such it is simply a matter of changing one's mind about any aspect of the writing. There is no "right" time for changing one's mind; it can happen at any time the writer discovers a better way.

Rethinking one's choices may lead to the discovery of new ones. If writing is an act of taking responsibility for one's ideas, then revising acknowledges that responsibility as an ongoing obligation. It does not end when the first commitment is made. One commitment leads to another. Once a word, or sentence, or whole essay is committed to paper, a writer assumes the responsibility of reassessing, and changing if necessary, what is written.

When is writing ever finished? A time must come when a deadline is reached, an assignment is due, a final draft is abandoned. In that sense, writing is finished when it is submitted to its intended audience. Often, someone other than the writer has imposed a deadline or a due date. Of course, the final product ought to be as good as one can make it, given the time available, but this does not mean that the final product is finished, in the sense of no longer having "room for improvement." Writing may never reach that mythical point of perfection, simply because it is always subject to change. Thus, the decision to stop revising may be somewhat arbitrary, based on one's sense that further change would not substantially improve the writing. There comes a time when it is more important to get the writing into the hands of its audience than to continue to tinker with it.

Since any aspect of writing can be revised, a full discussion of revision would take us back to the beginning of this book. It is possible to reconsider one's thesis statement, to change one's mind not only about the way in which one has phrased it but also about the stance one takes or the question at issue that one decides to address. In the earlier example of a student composing a thesis statement, we saw revision taking place at this early stage. It is even possible to revise one's attitude toward a writing situation—to decide to take it as a serious challenge, for instance, after having started to approach it as a perfunctory exercise. It is possible to revise one's reasoning—to change one's mind about the kinds of premises one will develop—or to revise one's structure—to decide that an idea should go earlier or later, or that there should be a new transition between two parts of an argument. Even though revision applies to every decision a writer makes—to rethinking, constantly, what one is doing—it is most systematic and deliberate when a writer rereads his or her own writing and tries to make changes in it that are designed to make the whole writing better.

Even though a precise, well thought out thesis statement provides a writer with a conceptual goal, the act of composing frequently leads a writer to a clearer vision of his or her intention. This happens because all of the parts of an argument cannot be held fully in the mind from the beginning. As I said earlier, writing itself encourages discoveries. This means that revision is necessary to be sure that all parts of a composition continue to work together, to satisfy the writer's purpose, as that purpose refines itself during writing. Writers frequently discover that after they have finished a draft of a composition, they must return to the beginning, to change aspects of the writing to fit a new sense of purpose that has evolved. This does not necessarily mean that the thesis itself has changed, but that the writer's attitude, or even degree of conviction, may have changed the writer's approach to that thesis. Revision enables a writer to consider whether the whole essay, as written, consistently satisfies the needs of its thesis.

Obstacles to Revision

Students sometimes do not revise as fully, or as well, as they might because of certain obstacles, which deserve our attention initially, before we get into some specific techniques for effective revision.

1. Revision is difficult without "critical distance," a metaphor for the perspective required to see writing *as writing* and separate from one's self. Revising may sometimes seem harder than writing because we cannot separate ourselves from our thoughts enough to know whether they would be clear to someone who encounters them only through the words that we have written. Our own words seem clear to us because they are intimately related to the thoughts we had while composing them. We may miss many faults of our own writing simply because as we reread it we are engaged in the same mental process we went through as we wrote it. Yet a reader lacks this intimacy with the mental process that led to those words. Therefore, it is necessary for a writer to achieve distance from the writing, somehow, to see it *as if* for the first time. Of course, our own words can never be entirely new to us as we reread them. What, then, can a writer do to achieve as much distance as possible?

The best source of distance is time. If it is possible to return to a piece of writing after a long period of time, its faults become more obvious. Allowing oneself the leisure to forget how the sentences sound, to let the words slip out of the mental grooves that they have forged in the short-term memory, enables one to read them more critically. There is no better source of critical distance than a desk drawer, where a draft can be put away and returned to after enough time has gone by. But no one has enough time, of course, to make this practical. There is a lesson in this, however, that all writers can apply, even when the time available for composing is short: Don't procrastinate. Students who put off a writing assignment until the last minute have deprived themselves of any time to revise critically. What they hand in will always be a first draft. No matter how much time is available, you should take advantage of all of it, and this means a certain amount of time between drafts to let the distance between you and your words increase. Returning to a draft of an essay after having done something else for a day or two—or a week or two, if possible—can provide just enough critical distance to make revision effective.

Lacking time, you can create other sources of distance. Writers are known to do some wacky things just to alienate themselves from their own prose so that they can revise it from a new point of view. I heard about one writer who tapes his manuscript to a distant wall and revises while reading it through binoculars. A friend of mine revises by turning her manuscript upside-down to read it. Another reads her writing in a mirror. I don't advise any of these tactics; these writers obviously worked them out to suit their own needs. What works for them won't necessarily work for others. But I can suggest two practices that are less "far out" but effective: First, *read your writing to yourself out loud.* Just the sound of the words is often enough to reveal flaws that you might otherwise miss. The rhythm and balance of your sentences can often be improved after you have heard them. Second, *have someone else read your writing out loud while you listen.* This will not only allow you to hear what you have written, but it will reveal trouble spots wherever the reader stumbles or gets the intonation of your meaning wrong.

2. A second obstacle to revision is an unwillingness to allow anyone to see our writing until it is "finished." Perhaps we fear the possibility of negative judgments. Perhaps we only want others to read what we have written so that they will praise us. But such attitudes are not helpful to a writer. It is especially important to develop a positive attitude toward the honest criticism of others. By seeking this criticism, we learn new things about our writing, and thereby learn how to make it better.

Most writers rely on a circle of trusted readers who will comment on their drafts. These "test readers" can often ask questions or make observations that the writer had not thought about. To have the benefit of a critical reader's response is enormously helpful to writers who wish to revise thoughtfully. Choose your readers carefully, therefore. Friends who will only flatter you or readers who do not know how to read critically will be of no help. This raises the issue of a third potential obstacle to effective revision.

3. To revise well you must be able to take criticism without offense and be willing to make critical judgments about your own writing without damage to your ego. Yes, writing does come from the depths of our minds and hearts, but it is also separate from ourselves once it is on the page, and we can attack it *as writing,* without attacking our own souls in the process. Thus, to revise well, you must be able to separate the personality in your writing from your own personality. This is especially important in college, and in a writing class in particular, since teachers and other members of the class must be able to talk about your writing without making judgments about you as a person. Only if you are able to make this adjustment to your own writing—to see it as a thing that you can manipulate without discredit to yourself as a person—will you be learning all that you can about your own writing, so that you can make it better.

In reading others' writing, and in accepting the comments of others about your own, the golden rule should apply: Comment about others' writing as you would have them comment about your own; accept the comments of others as you would have them accept yours. If we could accept all advice about our own writing as if it were given solely for the purpose of helping us to write better, we would be fortunate. But advice, like other aspects of human relations, can come with hidden intentions and can be defended against by rationalization—sometimes beyond our conscious control. It is necessary, therefore, to make a real effort to accept criticism gladly and to respond to it thoughtfully.

4. Student writers also sometimes fail to revise because revision is a part of the writing of others that is invisible. When we read the writing of others, we see only the final product, and the changes and decisions that occurred to the writer are not part of what we normally encounter. It is easy to forget that all writers struggle somewhat, since the final product appears to us as effortlessly composed. When we read printed prose, as on this page, it looks neat, it contains no errors or scribbled changes in the writer's handwriting. Yet some of what we see is not the result of the writer's art at all, but of the typesetter's. What the writer of the essay actually submitted may have been a manuscript with lots of messy changes, or even one with words misspelled or punctuation missing. What we see in the printed version may have been checked by a professional editor. It is easy to become intimidated by the perfect appearance of the writing that we generally encounter as readers and to assume that the way it looks on the page is the way it emerged, full-blown, from the writer's head. Not so. What we do not see is that the writing went through several drafts, often with false starts, massive eliminations or other changes, or holes to be filled in later. What we don't see, in other words, is revision. But that doesn't mean it didn't take place.

Editing as Rethinking

Revision occurs at any point in the writing process, whenever a writer reassesses some choice, on the level of the reasoning, or the structure, or the style. Any question that you can ask yourself about any of these matters you can re-ask, at any time. Let us return, however, to the matter of style and consider some techniques for revising that are suggested by the kinds of questions raised in the previous chapter. For the sake of distinguishing these kinds of questions from revision as a more all-encompassing process, let's call this "editing." Editing is the deliberate revision of the style of a complete rough draft, for the purpose of improving the word choice, sentence structure, and tone of the composition. Editing is a kind of analysis of one's own writing, and as such it provides the writer with a source of critical distance. By deliberately looking for certain qualities in your writing, with the idea of making it better, you can separate yourself somewhat from your own thoughts about the content. In editing, you can focus on one aspect of writing at a time. Since the question of whether any specific editing change actually improves the writing will depend on the purpose of the writing and the context of the whole composition in which change occurs, editing also leads to rethinking the ideas.

We have already encountered an editing procedure suggested by George Orwell's "rules" for a good style. Let's look at those rules more closely and apply them.

Using figurative language

Orwell's first rule refers to the use of figurative language: *"Never use a metaphor, simile, or other figure of speech which you are used to seeing in print."* Notice that Orwell is not telling us to avoid figurative language, but cautioning us against using it thoughtlessly. When certain figures of speech become overused, they lose their power to communicate and become clichés. Perhaps Orwell should have said "used to seeing in print or hearing in conversation." Idiomatic expressions found frequently in the speech or writing of others often come readily to mind when we are composing, but that does not mean that they precisely communicate our intended meaning. Because such phrases are overused, they often cease to convey a precise idea and reflect instead the writer's disregard for precision.

A figure of speech is simply a means by which words are able to say one thing while communicating something else. From this fact comes the power of figurative language—its novelty and ability to suggest unique connections—but this is also the source of its potential imprecision. For example, the philosopher Aristotle took advantage of the suggestive power of language when he wrote, "Poverty is the parent of revolution." He assumed that his readers would know that he did not mean "parent" literally and that they would understand him to mean something by it other than "parent" in the dictionary sense. He assumed that they would associate the relation between poverty and revolution with the relation between parent and child. If he could not assume these things, he would have risked being misunderstood. If I tried to adapt his figure of speech and said something like, "The dean is the parent of the junior faculty," I might achieve a different effect from the one I had intended, since the literal meaning could not be so easily overlooked. Since figurative language works by suggestion, one must be especially careful to control figurative language to get just the right effect from it.

When writers use figures of speech that have become clichés, this control is surrendered. Consider this passage:

> The administration is grasping at straws in its policy toward apartheid in South Africa. We hear harsh words being spoken about racial seg-

regation on the one hand, and on the other we hear glowing praise of
the South African government. Our waffling Congress should get its
act together and tell the White House to get off its horse. The bottom
line is whether we are going to support any government that condones
the moral blood-bath taking place in the name of economic necessity.

The only clear idea being communicated here is that the writer wishes
the Congress to impel the Administration to condemn apartheid un-
equivocally. Apart from this, the writer's words communicate a stri-
dent anger but no additional meaning. In fact, the overuse of figures
of speech makes the meaning harder to find than necessary, since the
reader is distracted by the metaphors that seem to clash with each
other. "Straws" and "waffles" clash in meaning, "house" and "horse"
in sound. Some of the phrases are simply not clear. This writer blurts
out commonplace sentiments without giving them much thought—
an impression that does not depend on whether the reader agrees with
the stance. A few of this writer's phrases might survive careful editing, but most of them should be axed.

Figures of speech and clichés are not always easy to find, since
some "dead" metaphors seem to have become literal. You probably
identified the following as clichés:

> grasping at straws
> waffling Congress
> get its act together
> get off its horse
> moral bloodbath

These are the obvious ones. They stick out (like a sore thumb?) because they seem inept. The writer must have been too lazy to find
substitutes. But other figurative phrases are more subtle, and these
too contribute to the overwhelming impression of this writer as clumsy
in choice of words. Did you also identify these?

> harsh words
> glowing praise
> on the one hand . . . on the other hand
> White House
> bottom line
> in the name of

These metaphors have become so common that we can easily forget
they are metaphors. The writer chose them with the same lack of
consideration as the others. Perhaps they are clear, perhaps not.
Whether a metaphor communicates the writer's meaning precisely is

a question that must be asked of all such phrases, no matter how literal they may sound. This is why a careful assessment of one's own metaphors, such as Orwell prescribed, is important.

Figurative language nearly always works by means of comparison. A simile ("He worked on that project like a fiend") is a direct comparison. A metaphor ("He sweat blood to get it done") is an implied comparison. Figurative language thus gets its power from its ability to relate one realm of experience to another, usually in a way that suggests unstated connections. The reader associates qualities of the metaphoric subject with those of the literal subject, even though those qualities are left unstated. Figurative speech is so common that as readers we perform this act of interpretation without hesitation. In the Declaration of Independence, Thomas Jefferson wrote, "When, in the course of human events, it becomes necessary for one people to dissolve the political bands which have connected them to another . . ." As we read those words, we associate qualities that we understand "dissolve" and "bands" to have in their literal sense with the new context in which Jefferson used them. Bands do not literally connect people, nor was Jefferson calling for bands to be literally dissolved. But because we know that to dissolve something is to dilute its power, and that bands can inhibit freedom, we are not confused by his meaning. We understand it all the more powerfully because it is communicated in well-chosen figures.

Forgetting that figurative language draws on one aspect of experience in order to describe another can lead to losing control of its use. As in the example from Jefferson, there must be an appropriate connection between the kinds of experiences being associated. Examples of experiences inappropriately connected may be found today in the popular application of metaphors deriving from computers. For instance, consider these phrases:

> I will provide my input to our discussion of Plato's concept of beauty.
> Abusive parents have difficulty interfacing with their children.

The metaphors here seem inappropriate to the subject matter because there is no reason to compare the experiences under discussion to associations that we have with computers. "Input" was originally technical jargon for entering data into machines, but it has now become a common metaphor for "thoughts" or "opinions" or "ideas." Similarly, "interface" is jargon for the capacity of computers to combine functions, but it is often used to refer to human relations as well—such as "talking" or "understanding." As these terms lose their metaphoric power through overuse, it becomes easier to apply them to experiences for which they are inappropriate. It is not part of the purpose of these writers to say that Plato's concept of beauty is able to be calculated by machine, according to the manipulation of bits of data, or that the relationship between parents and children ought to be machinelike. Yet, the sentences contain these unintended implications. I often feel insulted when someone asks for my "input," as if my ideas would be counted, like bits of data, rather than considered carefully for their rationality. The popular overuse of this kind of language to refer to human actions or problems (as well as other metaphors taken from business or military or education jargon, such as "bottom line" or "window of opportunity" or "gifted") can change the way we think about people or issues, if we do not remember that they are metaphors. You probably have your own favorite examples of metaphors that affect how people perceive reality when they are taken too literally.

It is not possible, and certainly not necessary, to write without ever using expressions that are commonplace. Avoiding all such phrases could produce a style that is sterile and officious, lacking a human voice. Figurative expressions exist in our language for good reasons, even if they are often abused. They give our speech color and liveliness, they suggest the personality of the writer, and they communicate special meanings. Orwell's rule cautions us against using worn-out and commonplace figures of speech, but it does not prevent us from using occasional figures that contribute to the effectiveness of the writing. Everything I said in Chapter 6 about "risk," however, applies to the use of such phrases, because their effects cannot be predicted. I took such a risk, for instance, when I used *survive* and *axed* metaphorically to end an earlier paragraph. I thought you would notice, and I hoped you would wonder whether I should have used those words in that way. My ear for metaphor often fails me, as does everyone's.

Let's consider another passage in which the use of figurative language is less out of control than in the first obvious example:

> The recent popularity of tanning studios has raised the question of whether artificially induced suntans damage the skin. The community of scientists has not yet rendered its verdict; there is no authoritative evidence on either side to say whether these studios are safe or at what point exposure to their lamps becomes too much exposure. If people continue to seek the body beautiful without caring about side effects, then perhaps these questions are moot. It is another case of "let the buyer beware." But we live in a time when consumers are correctly demanding to know what troubles they are buying along with their services, and there is no reason that the tanning studios should be exempt from the requirement to warn patrons that the potential dam-

age to which they can subject themselves is not yet known. Even in a
tanning studio, you can get burned.

The few figures of speech used by this writer are more consistent and
effective than those in the previous example. But should they remain
in the writing, or should they be cut or changed? A careful writer
would have to consider these alternatives.

If I were editing this passage for effective use of figurative language, I might start by making a list of the figurative expressions:

> community of scientists
> rendered its verdict
> the body beautiful (?)
> questions are moot (?)
> you can get burned

Without deliberately searching for such expressions, I could easily
have overlooked some. I'm not even sure that some of them qualify
as figures of speech, but that doesn't matter, since there's no reason
not to ask whether they belong. The first thing I notice is that two
of these expressions are adapted from the language of the courtroom:
rendering a verdict is what a jury does and moot questions are those
that a court need not decide. The courtroom metaphors seem somewhat too obvious for this discussion of scientific evidence, so I might
decide to eliminate one or both of them. A literal substitute for "these
questions are moot" could be something like "these questions aren't
relevant." Then I notice that the reference to scientists as a "community" isn't consistent with the "verdict" metaphor, since juries
reach verdicts, not communities. No effective use is made of "community" in this context, so that metaphor can be taken out without
harming the passage in any way.

Now I notice that three of these expressions, "the body beautiful," "troubles they are buying," and "you can get burned," suggest
an attitude of scorn for those who patronize the tanning studios. Is
this appropriate? Well, the purpose of the passage is to argue that
these patrons should be warned, and the paragraph doesn't really argue that suntans are dangerous. The scorn that the writer apparently
feels toward the people who use this service is not the main point, so
it should probably not be overdone. At least the first one, which is
the harshest in tone and the least original, might be eliminated. It
shouldn't be hard to find a nonjudgmental alternative to "those who
seek the body beautiful." Looking closely at this expression makes
me realize that the only function of the reference to "let the buyer

beware" is to imply that these people are suckers of some tanning scam. Why make this gratuitous slam? The sentence can go.

So, having scrutinized the figurative expressions, I find some of them to be effective and appropriate and some to be overdone or unnecessary. The result of this editing is a passage that is a bit more graceful and honest:

> The recent popularity of tanning studios has raised the question of whether artificially induced suntans damage the skin. Science has not yet provided authoritative evidence on the questions of whether these studios are safe or at what point exposure to their lamps becomes too much exposure. If people desire to have artificial suntans without caring about side effects, then perhaps these questions do not matter. But we live in a time when consumers are correctly asking to know what risks they take when using professional services, and there is no reason that tanning studios should be exempt from the requirement to warn patrons that the potential damage to which they subject themselves is not yet known. Even in a tanning studio, you can get burned.

Having restricted the figurative expressions to those that serve some purpose helps to make those expressions more effective than they were before. The last sentence is more powerful now that it is not competing with other, weaker figurative phrases. If I don't like the sound of the edited version, once I have tried it out, or if some new expression occurs to me that might add power to the ideas, I can always change it again.

The process I have just illustrated is a simple one, even though it cannot be applied mechanically to get guaranteed results. Identifying and analyzing your figurative language cannot by itself make you a better writer. But it can lead to a greater sensitivity in your use of language. Editing such expressions may result in the discovery of other ways to improve the style of your writing.

Inflated diction

Orwell's second rule, *"Never use a long word when a short one will do,"* returns us to ideas I discussed in the previous chapter, specifically the caution against inflated diction. They are worth going into further as they apply to editing. Don't assume that "long" words will make you sound more intelligent or that "short" ones will make you sound simple-minded. Let the meaning choose the "right" word and length will take care of itself. What Orwell is getting at is the habit common to many writers of automatically substituting polysyllabic monstrosities for the simple, direct terms of everyday English. As an editing technique, Orwell's rule would lead us to examine the long words we use, to see whether we have chosen them because they are right or simply because they are long.

The way some writers try to imitate a "learned" style, editing for precision can seem like translating from one variety of English to another. Here's an extreme case:

> Utilizing civil disobedience methodologies pursuant to the conceptualizations of Thoreau facilitated the efficacious attainment of the primary objective of civil rights activists, namely the modification of statutory prohibitions deleterious toward racial minorities.

Translated into plain English, this means:

> Using civil disobedience methods according to the ideas of Thoreau made it easier for civil rights activists to reach their main goal of changing laws harmful to racial minorities.

Although the meaning is much the same, the effect on the reader is much different.

Notice that the goal of the editor of this sentence was not to get rid of all words over two syllables long. That would be silly. Rather, the goal was to get rid of long words for which perfectly good short ones exist. Thus, the phrase "civil disobedience" remained, because no shorter phrase could be substituted for it without changing the meaning. The same is true for "activists" and "minorities." But because all of the other monstrosities found in the sentence have simple equivalents, they are easily replaced:

utilizing	=	using
methodologies	=	methods
pursuant to	=	according to
conceptualization	=	idea
facilitate	=	make easy
efficacious attainment	=	reaching
primary	=	main
objective	=	goal
modification	=	change
statutory prohibitions	=	laws
deleterious	=	harmful

Some long words are perfectly appropriate in some contexts, but they are misused by writers who habitually prefer the puffed-up to the plain. Orwell blames politicians for overusing such words, which get parroted by others—those who can be fooled into thinking that "selective disinformation" means something other than "lying." Many long words cannot and should not be avoided. But the English vocabulary is so vast that many words have become popular whose only function is to bedevil those who wish to express themselves clearly.

The accompanying list illustrates some more words that you can nearly always replace with shorter ones. You might want to add your own favorite buzz words to this list, ones that you discover in your reading or perhaps find yourself using. Consulting such a list might help you to edit your writing by making you aware of the possibility of looking for shorter words to replace your long ones. You may

commence			considerable	
inaugurate			substantial	
initiate			numerous	
originate	= begin/start		multiplicity of	= many
endeavor			inadvisable	
attempt	= try		adverse	
acquire			counterproductive	
obtain			undesirable	= a bad idea
procure			initial	
secure	= get/buy		primary	
accomplish			principal	= first
execute			contingent on	= depends
effectuate			regarding	
implement	= do		concerning	
discontinue			pertaining to	
terminate			as regards	= about
conclude	= stop		requisite	= needed
advise			cognizant of	= aware of
notify			practicable	
inform			feasible	= possible
disclose			additional	
divulge	= tell		further	= more
demonstrate			subsequent to	= after
exhibit			inception	= beginning
indicate			cessation	= ending
reflect	= show		supersede	= come after
ascertain			enumerate	
determine	= find out		itemize	= list
eventuate				
transpire	= happen			
fabricate				
construct				
formulate				
devise	= make			

sometimes find that some of these words sound all right and mean just what you intend. I've used a few in this book. Remember that you aren't trying to achieve the fewest possible number of syllables. You are trying to avoid the ponderous effect of "wordiness." This brings us to Orwell's next rule.

Cutting

"If it is possible to cut a word out, always cut it out." This editing principle is meant to correct a problem most writers have: using too many words. Clumsy writers not only use longer words than necessary, they also crowd their writing with empty words and roundabout phrases. "Empty words" contribute no meaning to the sentence in which they occur. "Roundabout" phrases are those that substitute several words for one. Think of editing as exercise, aimed at good muscle tone. To do a job, words must be strong. Verbal flab is easily reduced, but it takes self-discipline.

Almost any word can be an empty word if it contributes no additional meaning to a sentence. Here are some examples:

> Her decision was painful in nature.
> I am majoring in the field of accounting.
> Despite various minor flaws, the essay shows a good reasoning process.

Each of these sentences could be made more economical by cutting words that have no function, thus:

> Her decision was painful.
> I am majoring in accounting.
> Despite minor flaws, the essay contains good reasoning.

No reader would respond to these sentences by wondering, "Do you mean painful *in nature?*" or "Do you mean the *field* of accounting?" or "Do you mean a good reasoning *process?*" or "Are the flaws *various?*" These words contribute nothing essential. Yet they are all words that in other contexts might have a specific function:

> By nature, people question authority.
> You have to choose one field for your major.
> Writing is a process, leading to a product.
> The same end can be reached by various means.

The words that were not contributing meaning before are doing so here. So, it isn't the word itself that is empty; it depends on the role it plays. The context of a sentence within the whole composition will determine if any words are superfluous. Editing for economy thus requires a writer to re-examine the meaning carefully and to ask what each word adds and whether that addition is necessary.

Here's a passage in which the writer would face many such considerations as he or she edited for economy. I have exaggerated the wordiness on purpose to illustrate several different ways that language can be inflated.

> The question to pose now is whether or not the acceptance of the basic concept of renewable energy resource production is justified at this time. Each and every kind of nonfossil fuel energy source, such as hydroelectric, nuclear, solar, and wind, etc., has recognized advantages over fossil fuels, but due to the fact that each also has unsolved problems attendant with its use, there is no consensus of opinion up to this point in time that the various benefits tend to outweigh the actual costs. Hydroelectric power resources make use of abundantly available supplies of water, but nevertheless there is opposition against their use from many who view the protection of lakes and streams from negative effects as a higher priority than meeting the energy needs of this nation. The reason why nuclear power is a controversial issue is that the extent to which nuclear waste materials will have lasting effects on the surrounding environment cannot be determined at the present time. Notwithstanding the fact that wind power is a feasible approach technologically, it is not practical from the standpoint of cost-effectiveness. Solar power is dependent on the climate situation to a large degree, and in consequence its maximum possible potential may be viewed as restricted to certain regions of the country. But yet it is the one other alternative that does not have drawbacks sufficient enough to prevent us from directing our efforts toward its further development on a widespread scale.

Get out the blue pencil. Let's start cutting words. (In the following discussion, be prepared to refer to this passage, since I will make lists of words from it, out of context.) This gassy writer has used more than twice the number of words necessary to say what he has to say. Does anybody really write this badly? Maybe not, but many writers slip into one or another kind of wordiness, all of which are illustrated here. Some of the gas results from the kind of empty words we have already discussed. These phrases add no meaning to the passage, in context:

> to pose   (What other kinds of questions are there?)
> basic   (The word is just noise.)
> the concept of   (More noise.)
> attendant   (Can problems ever not be attendant?)

various   (Sheer humbug.)
situation   (More noise.)

Getting rid of these is a start, but the writing would still overflow
with other kinds of waste. It is polluted by many other phrases that
are simply redundant.

>   now . . . at this time
>   whether or not
>   each and every
>   such as . . . etc.
>   unsolved problems
>   consensus of opinion
>   this point in time
>   but nevertheless
>   opposition against
>   reason why
>   controversial issue
>   surrounding environment
>   possible potential
>   but yet
>   other alternative
>   sufficient enough
>   further development

Eliminate half the words and they say the same thing. (You may en-
joy listing samples of such phrases as you encounter them. They are
called "pleonasms," and one could make a hobby of collecting them.)

Another kind of redundancy persists in the passage (not "continues to persist"). It results from including words that refer to concepts
already clear from the context, as in these cases:

>   resource production   ("Production" is understood in context.)
>   energy source   (In context, "source" is redundant.)
>   recognized advantages   (If they were unrecognized, would we be de-
>   scribing them?)
>   problems . . . with its use   (More empty words.)
>   up to this point   (Implied by the use of the present tense.)
>   tend to outweigh   (Either they do or they don't.)
>   available   (How could they be abundant but not available?)
>   protection . . . from negative effects   (Who protects anything from
>   positive effects?)
>   the energy needs of this nation   (We weren't thinking of any other
>   nation.)

nuclear waste materials   (What else could the wastes be if not materials?)

at the present time   (We weren't thinking of any other time.)

feasible . . . approach   (Just wind.)

practical . . . cost effectiveness   (Cost is practical by definition.)

maximum . . . potential   (A useless modifier.)

regions of the country   (Could it be regions of anything else?)

Practice the art of not saying the obvious by eliminating such repetitions. The paragraph is shrinking before our very eyes.

The passage contains yet another kind of wordiness. Many of its phrases consist of strings of words that can be replaced by one word that means the same thing. These stringy "roundabout" expressions should be translated into their economical equivalents:

due to the fact that	= because or since
not withstanding the fact that	= although
from the standpoint of	= in
to a large degree	= largely
in consequence	= so
may be viewed as	= may be (or is)
directing our efforts toward	= trying
on a widespread scale	= widely

With these changes, the passage is really shaping up. It may even be starting to sound human.

But before we finish with it, we still have to attack one last source of wordiness, the extended noun phrases that hide verbs. One way in which writers unknowingly add extra words is to transform verbs into nouns by attaching suffixes and auxiliary words to them, as in these examples from the paragraph:

the acceptance of	= accept
make use of	= use
there is opposition to	= (someone) opposes
the protection of	= protect
is dependent on	= depends on
directing our attention toward its development	= trying to develop

In the last example, we had already made a change, substituting "trying" for its long-winded equivalent, which made it necessary to change the noun *development* into the verb *to develop*. In other cases, we have the option of the long noun form or the short verb form.

When you edit your writing for economy, then, look for verbs hidden inside noun phrases. The offending nouns often contain these suffixes:

-ive   ("is indicative of" instead of "indicates")
-sion   ("made a decision" instead of "decided")
-tion   ("gave consideration to" instead of "considered")
-ment   ("made an improvement" instead of "improved")
-ance   ("has the appearance of" instead of "appears")
-al   ("made an arrival" instead of "arrived")

Sometimes no suffix is needed to turn a verb into a noun, although it does require adding words, as in

"do harm to" instead of "harm"
"is in need of" instead of "needs"
"effect a change in" instead of "change"

You might keep track of other examples of hidden verbs, especially if you find them in your own writing. None of these phrases by itself will make your writing clumsy, and there may be times when any such phrase is more appropriate than its shorter equivalent. But the habit of substituting noun phrases for verbs will result in wordiness if it is not kept under control.

It may seem that editing for economy is fairly mechanical: Remove empty words, cut redundancy, transform hidden verbs. These are good principles, but they do not automatically result in a neat, economically worded product without further editing. Applying the blue pencil to our long passage of overwritten prose might result in some sentences that are still in need of polishing. The result of cutting—or of any revision—can be quite messy, as in the illustration on page 160. Editing like this is not intended for your readers' eyes. A rough draft is like a sketchbook, a record for your thoughts-in-process.*

Having edited the passage for each kind of wordiness, we may still have to touch up the prose. When you cut words from a sentence, you will often have to rephrase some parts of the sentence to make it sound right. But a virtue of brevity is that it enables you to

---

*Of course, if you edit on a word processor, the result won't look like this; it will always look tidy. But don't be fooled by the finished appearance that the word processor seems to give to prose; you will have to reread it to hear how it sounds. (I've been surprised to find that some students who edit on word processors make more mistakes than those who edit by hand on paper, possibly because they do not feel the same necessity to reread their prose as those do who must recopy it.)

The question to pose now is whether or not the (acceptance of
the basic) concept of renewable energy resource production is
justified at this time. Each and every [kind of] nonfossil
fuel energy source, such as hydroelectric, nuclear, solar,
and wind, etc., has recognized advantages over fossil fuels,
but [due to the fact that] each also has unsolved problems
attendant with its use, there is no consensus of opinion up-
to this point in time that the various benefits tend to
outweigh the [actual] costs. Hydroelectric power resources
make use of abadundantly available supplies of water, but

find a better rhythm for a sentence than it had when it was lumbering
along like a hippo. So, now that we have cut out the verbal fat and
put the sentences back together, here is the result:

> The question is whether using renewable energy resources is justified.
> Each alternative to fossil fuels has advantages, but since each also has
> problems there is no consensus that the benefits outweigh the costs.
> Hydroelectric power uses abundant supplies of water, but many op-
> pose it who view protecting lakes and streams as a higher priority
> than more energy. Nuclear power is controversial because the extent
> of lasting effects on the environment from nuclear waste cannot be
> determined. Although wind power is feasible technologically, it is not
> cost-effective. Solar power depends largely on climate, so its potential
> is restricted regionally. Yet it is the one alternative that does not have
> drawbacks sufficient to prevent us from developing it further.

The edited version of the paragraph could probably be reduced still
further, although not much would be accomplished by cutting alone
at this point. It now has 117 words to the 243 of the original version. That's a "flab factor" of 52 per cent. I don't recommend that
you literally count your words, since there is no formula for the right
number of words for any idea. Readers are not ordinarily conscious of

the number of words they read—and they do not know how many words were present before the writer cut out the unnecessary ones— but they are conscious of writing that seems padded, and they judge the writing accordingly. You should edit for economy of expression, not because there is some ideal numerical goal but because you do not want the reader to think you are faking it.

An editor is not a machine for milling words but a writer trying to achieve a purpose effectively. We have certainly improved the tone and readability of this paragraph by the cutting that we did. Its structure is the same; the passage still has seven sentences and each has the same function in developing the writer's argument. Is that structure good? Is the argument working? Are the points sufficient? Are there any ideas that might also be cut? Are there some that might be added? These important considerations require rethinking the intention of the paragraph. This is easier now that the passage is rewritten in its brief form (although we cannot answer those questions now because we do not have the whole essay to use as a basis for judging the function of this paragraph). The service that is performed by cutting and rewriting for economy does not end with the writer's satisfaction at having turned many words into few. The writer also has a better chance of looking squarely at the quality of the ideas. This is why Orwell said "Simplify your English . . . and when you make a stupid remark its stupidity will be obvious, even to yourself."

The passive voice

Orwell's next rule is *"Never use the passive where you can use the active."* Some writers overuse the passive voice, out of habit, and the result is confusion. The passive voice can result in unclear statements or in deceptive ones. A simple example shows how it works. Here's a sentence in the active voice:

The chicken crossed the road.

In this sentence the *agent* of the action is "the chicken"; that's what's doing whatever the verb indicates is happening. The *object* of the action is "the road." In the passive voice, the agent and the object change places, thus:

The road was crossed by the chicken.

These two sentences describe the same action, but the change in syntax changes the emphasis, from the chicken to the road. Both sentences are clear, although the second one is wordier. What makes the passive voice potentially unclear is that it permits a writer to ignore the agent, as in:

The road was crossed.

This is a grammatical sentence, whereas if we tried to get rid of the agent while keeping the verb in the active voice we would not have a complete sentence: ". . . crossed the road." This is what makes the passive risky, or convenient, depending on how you look at it: It permits you to get rid of the chicken! Actions take place in the passive, but nobody *does* them. Thus, in these passive sentences, the agency of the verbs disappears:

The need for higher standards is established.
It is believed that the strike should be cancelled.
The new theory is regarded as practical, but it has not yet been tried.

Because they eliminate the agent, these sentences also hide information. The reader is left to wonder what that information is: "Is established" by who? "Is believed" by who? "Should be cancelled" by who? "Is regarded" by who? "Hasn't been tried" by who? When writers habitually use the passive voice, they seem to be hiding something. In fact, the passive voice has gotten its bad reputation because it is often used when people do have something to hide: "A decision was made to cut your budget," an administrator might say, so that she can avoid having to admit that she decided it. The deliberate use of the passive to deceive is probably rare, but unintended deceptions happen frequently when writers habitually use passive verbs and fail to ask whether the excluded information is relevant. In editing, you should first identify the passive verbs and then ask whether the information they exclude is necessary for honesty, clarity, or completeness.

A short example illustrates how you might go about this:

Once the idea of a lottery has been raised as one way in which the state's economy may be improved, the first question that should be asked is whether gambling ought to be given implicit moral approval. It is also said that under such a revenue plan the poor are taxed more heavily than the rich, since people in families with smaller incomes have been shown to spend more for lottery tickets than where more money is earned.

These two sentences sound cumbersome. When you reread your own writing, you may not hear the awkwardness produced by your passive

verbs, so it is a good idea to search for them deliberately, to see just
how much you may depend on the passive voice without knowing it.
In this case, such a search would yield a relatively long list:

> has been raised
> may be improved
> should be asked
> ought to be given
> is said
> are taxed
> have been shown
> is earned

In each case, a reader might ask "by who?" since the writer has used
the passive without stating who the agent is. Asking whether the
agency of these verbs is relevant to the argument will enable us to
decide whether active verbs would be more appropriate. No writer
can edit in this way without asking "What am I really trying to say?"

If I were editing this passage, I would probably let one of the
passive verbs—"are taxed"—stay, because it does not hide relevant
information or otherwise sound awkward. It is not relevant in this
context exactly who is doing the taxing, whether some specific agency
or just "the state." I would be saying the obvious if I said something
like "The state bureau of taxation taxes . . ." But in the other cases,
I think the agency of the verbs is necessary, to prevent the reader
from being misled or just to make the prose more economical. The
result might be a paragraph such as this:

> Those who support a lottery because it would improve the state's
> economy need to respond to two further objections. A lottery would
> imply that the state government approves of gambling. Also, Senator
> Peterson claims that with a lottery the poor are taxed most heavily.
> Her study shows that families with smaller incomes spend more for
> lottery tickets than those who earn more.

In two cases, the active voice required me to provide specific information not in the original. By not saying at first that the source of
my argument was Senator Peterson and her study, I was trying to
get away with larger claims than I had a right to. The argument is
now more honest because it permits the reader to assess the source of
my information. By not naming that source, I was hedging. Now I
am direct. My argument is helped by this change, even if the reader
might think that Senator Peterson is not a good source, because I
no longer appear to be trying to deceive anyone. When readers encounter phrases like "it has been shown that . . ." or "it is well known

that . . ." they associate the passive voice with equivocation. Identifying the agency of your verbs will help you to reassess the strength of your case.

Passive verbs are not always dishonest and, in fact, are preferable to active verbs in some cases. Here are some sentences from my own discussion of the passive voice above:

> In fact, the passive voice has gotten its bad reputation because it *is often used* when people do have something to hide:
> When you reread your own writing, you may not hear the awkwardness *produced* by your passive verbs. . . .
> But in the other cases, I think the agency of the verb is necessary, to prevent the reader from *being misled*. . . . My argument *is helped* by this change. . . .

As I edited this discussion, I changed other passive verbs to active ones, but I decided that the passive was the best choice in these cases. In the first case, the subject of the sentence is "passive voice" not "people," so I kept the verb in the passive so that the pronoun "it" would not be too remote from that subject. In the second one, I decided that the emphasis of the sentence would change if I used the active: I wanted "awkwardness," the object of the verb "produced," up front for greater impact. In the third one, the agent of "being misled" seemed obvious in context, and any reference to the implied subject would be redundant. In the fourth sentence, I decided that I preferred the passive construction for reasons of emphasis and rhythm. "This change helps my argument . . ." just didn't sound as good to my ear.

The point of editing in this way is not to eliminate all passive verbs, as if they were obvious symptoms of bad writing. The point is to choose them for a reason, rather than to let them choose you because you are inattentive to your own style. This editing principle, like the others, is not absolute. It is subject to your best judgment. That means that as you edit, you have to consider sound, clarity, and honesty, all within the context of what you want your writing to accomplish. Your choices may sometimes be wrong—mine probably are in many cases—but you will at least have made them consciously, and by doing so made it easier to make better choices in the future.

Jargons

A long discussion of Orwell's next rule would repeat too much of what I covered in Chapter 6. It too concerns diction: *"Never use a foreign phrase, a scientific word or a jargon word if you can think of an everyday English equivalent."* This rule hardly needs much explaining. Jargon words and scientific words belong to the specialized vocabulary shared by a specific group. If you are writing for an audience that cannot be expected to share such terms, avoid them. If a jargon term or a scientific term is more convenient because it is precise and eliminates the need to repeat a string of plainer, explanatory words, use it, but not without being sure that your audience will understand it. If your motive for using jargon or scientific language is to impress the reader with your knowledge, or to make your ideas sound more important than they really are, forget it.

The same might be said for foreign expressions, if their meaning would be obscure to the intended audience, unless there is some particular reason for using another language. If you were writing an essay about the way in which American tourists use foreign idioms, for instance, you could hardly do the subject justice without giving examples in the foreign languages. Or, if you were arguing that a translation of a poem sacrificed emotional intensity for literal meaning, you would want to use examples to clarify and support your thesis. In such cases, you would have to depend on your knowledge of the audience to decide what examples to use and whether to provide translations. If you are unreasonable in your expectation that a reader knows the meaning of foreign expressions, then they may be functioning, like some jargon and scientific terminology, to bluff rather than to communicate.

Orwell was not referring to obscure foreign phrases so much as to those that have become clichés in English usage and that we may be tempted to use when we wish to sound cosmopolitan or educated. Here are some examples:

    a priori
    c'est la vie
    coup de grace
    de facto
    ergo
    ex post facto
    non sequitur
    raison d'etre
    sine qua non
    status quo
    vis a vis

The occasional use of such phrases, in just the right context, may not call attention to itself, but their overuse will make you seem self-indulgent. Most of the time there's no reason not to stick to English.

Some abbreviations for Latin phrases do not seem to damage the tone of formal writing, possibly because they carry no connotation of pedantry for most readers. Yet, I still see very little advantage in using them in place of English phrases that bring no risk at all of sounding stuffy:

>   i.e. = in other words
>   e.g. = for instance
>   etc. = and so forth

Some others drag along a heavy risk of pomposity:

>   ibid   = in the same place
>   op. cit. = as before
>   q.e.d.   = therefore
>   supra   = above
>   vide   = see
>   viz.   = that is

If you are tempted to use these, resist. If you haven't developed the habit yet, don't start.

Rules are not laws

Orwell's final rule is the least specific and the most interesting. *"Break any of these rules sooner than say anything outright barbarous."* What Orwell is saying, perhaps, is that rules can only take you so far, and if you rely on them slavishly, they might result in making your writing worse instead of better. Rules are for convenience, but they cannot replace good sense. Applying these editing rules can help you gain control over your writing, and thereby develop a better sense of when to break one of them on purpose. To be in control of your writing means that *you* decide how to phrase what *you* have to say; it is not control to let rules decide for you. But you earn the right to break rules when you know your options and have good reasons for choosing one way instead of another.

What does Orwell mean by "barbarous"? I'm not sure I know. I think he chose the word on purpose to make us think about what it means to be educated and civil, or whatever we think of as the opposite of "barbarous." Although the word is usually applied to behavior in general, it has special connotations when it is applied to language. To write barbarously is to write without care, without respect for the reader or the subject, without intelligence. It is to mimic the prevailing style of others, without thinking. But, ironically, to write in an "educated" way can often mean the same thing, when the writer uses big words or padding or passive verbs to bluff and bluster and impress rather than to speak honestly and clearly. The "educated" writer may be the most barbarous of all, if he or she has learned how to imitate official-sounding prose without at the same time learning how to think more responsibly. Thus, once again, ideas come first. The educated writer should be one for whom reasoning well is the most important goal. Editing well is a responsibility that follows from this goal and that helps the writer achieve it. It can't be faked.

Sentences

Orwell's rules apply to word choice and do not apply to other stylistic considerations, such as variety of sentence length or rhythm. As we have seen in some of the examples, the control of word choice can make sentences sound more natural. Improving the diction of individual sentences can make a whole passage of prose sound more rhythmical. Orwell stressed diction exclusively, perhaps because he believed that attention to word choice will provide the writer with a necessary basis for controlling how sentences work together to form smooth and effective writing. A careful editor can look at the shape of sentences themselves, however, and how they relate to each other, to improve the effectiveness of the composition. I will add two "rules" to Orwell's list that might help you to control some of the subtler effects created by your sentences.

First, *vary the shape and length of your sentences to avoid monotony.* Writing that habitually depends on only a few ways of making sentences or that contains sentences of a uniform length, whether long or short, can produce dullness. Sentences should be constructed to promote the "drama" of ideas, rather than to work against their inherent meaning by being numbingly the same. To discover the best shape or length for a sentence, it helps to look deliberately at the structure of one's sentences and to consider options. Long sentences may be divided. Short ones may be combined. Similar sentences may be reworded. Differently shaped sentences may be made to have similar shapes. The decision is the writer's to make freely, according to the emphasis required by the ideas or the ease with which they may be read.

Here is a short passage in which the sentences are all constructed according to the same grammatical model:

The parents' group attacking "porn-rock" claims that albums should be labeled with ratings, like those found on movies. It says that such a system would not be considered censorship, since it would be voluntary. The defenders of the industry argue that such ratings would not satisfy the critics, who want to intimidate recording artists.

This writer is in a syntactic rut. Each sentence is shaped the same and is roughly the same length. If the writing went on like this for very long, the reader would soon become annoyed by its monotony. Limitless options are available to the writer for revising these sentences so that their rhythm helps the meaning along more effectively: restructuring sentences, combining ideas in different ways, reordering the sequence of thought, using grammatical patterns to create different kinds of emphases. Here are two possibilities:

> The parents' group attacking "porn-rock" claims that albums should be labeled with ratings, like those found on movies. Because such a system would be voluntary, the group denies that it could be considered censorship. But the defenders of the recording industry refute this by saying that the critics would not be satisfied with ratings. What the critics really want is to intimidate recording artists.
>
> Rock albums should be labeled with ratings, like those found on movies. This is the view of a parents' group that is attacking "porn-rock." The group is aware that some might see this as a move toward censorship of the recording industry, but it denies this intention by stressing that such a rating system would be voluntary. Defenders of the industry, claiming that its critics are attempting to intimidate artists, do not believe that such groups would be satisfied with ratings.

A simple chart comparing the lengths of the sentences in these three passages would look like this:

1. ——————————————
——————————————
————————————

2. ——————————————
——————————
————————————————
——————————

3. ——————————
——————————
————————————————————
————————————————

The variety in the length of sentences in the revised versions combines with variety of sentence structure to produce different emphases. The writer's ear must finally tell him or her what particular combination of length and structure will produce the best effect, but revision is the only way to achieve improvement if the sentences are too much the same. So, the best advice is to listen to your own sentences, analyze their length and structure, and devise ways of creating variety.

Transitions

My second supplemental rule is: *Use transitional words and phrases to link ideas, if any shortage of them might cause confusion.* As you can see, this is a rule with a condition. It does no good to add a lot of transitional words and phrases when the relationship between ideas is clear without them, and it may do harm. Here is a passage in which there are no transitional devices:

> Terrorism against U.S. citizens abroad must be stopped. It cannot be retaliated against. The individuals responsible for the terrorism are not affiliated with official governments. Taking foreign hostages in response to the taking of U. S. hostages would punish innocent people for the crimes of others. Taking additional precautions against terrorism is better. It restricts the freedom of Americans abroad.

These separate statements may be connected in the writer's mind, but without transitional phrases to help the reader understand the connections they might be easily misinterpreted. How many transitional words might be added? Here's the passage again, with many transitions added:

> Everyone agrees that terrorism against U. S. citizens must be stopped. But the problem is that it cannot simply be retaliated against, since the individuals responsible for the terrorism are not affiliated with official governments. Therefore, to cite one example, taking foreign hostages in response to the taking of U. S. hostages would punish innocent people for the crimes of others. Rather than to follow a policy of retaliation, then, a better policy would be to take additional precautions against terrorism. There is a problem with this policy too, however, and that is that it would restrict the freedom of Americans abroad.

In this version, the connections that are understood by the writer are made explicit. But do you get the feeling that no reader would need this many clues to the relationships between the ideas? The use of too many transitional phrases leads to clumsiness and to a sense that the writer is faking the connections. It's easy to say *therefore,* but not so easy to earn a logical connection. So, although you want your transitions to be clear, you also want them to be honest. Don't add a transitional word or phrase in order to make a relationship seem to exist that the ideas don't warrant. But do add such words and phrases when a relationship between two ideas is thereby clarified. In the above example, only a few of the relationships need help with transitional words. A no less clear, but more economical, revision might be:

> Terrorism against U. S. citizens abroad must be stopped. However, it cannot be simply retaliated against, since the individuals responsible for the terrorism are not affiliated with official governments. Retaliating against the taking of U. S. hostages by taking foreign hostages would only punish innocent people for the crimes of others. Taking additional precautions against terrorism is a better policy than retaliation, even though it would restrict the freedom of Americans abroad.

Here's another passage without transitional devices, followed by a revision in which the writer has tried to make the connection between the thoughts stronger:

> The president of the college represents the school's image to the larger community. He seeks to explain how the educational policies of the faculty contribute to a healthy local economy. The school cannot function without support and encouragement from the community. This duty to maintain good relations with the public should not go so far that the president puts the interests of the community ahead of the goals of the college. This would be the effect if he were to give in to public pressure to seek defense contracts, when the faculty has voted against classified research on campus. The change in policy might please the public. It would erode the faculty's control of educational policy.
>
> The president of the college, more than any other person on campus, represents the school's image to the larger community. When the president tells the public about the educational policies of the faculty, he therefore seeks to explain how those policies contribute to a healthy local economy. The school cannot function, after all, without support and encouragement from the community. However, this duty to maintain good relations with the public should not go so far that the president puts the interests of the community ahead of the goals of the college. This would be the effect, for instance, if he were to give in to public pressure to seek defense contracts, when the faculty has voted against classified research on campus. The change in policy might please the public, but it would erode the faculty's control of educational policy.

Each of the phrases added in the revised version adds to the coherence of the whole argument by relating thoughts to each other in specific ways. Some of them, like "therefore" and "for instance," indicate logical or subordinate relations between ideas, while others, like "more than any other person on campus," strengthen distinctions essential to the argument. Transitional phrases perform many functions, but they should always be an aid to clarity, where their absence might provoke doubt about the writer's meaning.

These "rules"—Orwell's six and my two—do not exhaust the possibilities of revising for style. They are a good start, however, and by practicing them you will become more conscious of your style. You will also be substituting good habits of composition for careless ones and, in time, you will find that you no longer practice some of the worst writing habits that may once have characterized your writing. No writer ever reaches the point, however, where revision becomes unnecessary, simply because the act of rereading one's own writing critically reveals new possibilities and opportunities for improvement.

Proofreading

Revision generally occurs in rough draft, when a piece of writing is meant to be recopied. The final draft is the actual manuscript that a writer recopies and submits. The reader of this version assumes that the writer intends no further changes. Proofreading refers to the limited kind of revising that a writer does to a final draft, one that will not be recopied. Proofreading appears to the reader as "last minute" changes that the writer has made, usually to correct typographical or spelling or grammatical errors, or to make minor stylistic changes overlooked in earlier drafts.

Proofreading, then, is the writer's final responsibility. Careful proofreading is a sign that the writer has said exactly what he or she intended to say, and the responsibility to make corrections on that final manuscript, therefore, follows from the same commitment that led the writer to want to compose in the first place. If it matters to a writer that his or her ideas are communicated, the burden of making all parts of the writing work—from the reasoning and structure to the style and finally to the correctness of mechanics and grammar—is assumed by the writer. Proofreading is the final check that what the reader actually sees is what the writer intends.

It is during the proofreading stage that writers must think about aspects of grammar that may not have occurred to them earlier. Most of the time, grammatical errors will be caught and corrected during revision, so the following advice applies to revision and to proofreading. If there is any aspect of grammar that you are uncertain about, take the trouble to look it up, or ask someone who knows the answer, like your teacher. You may make some mistakes in English usage that you do not know are mistakes—and you shouldn't be afraid to make them because you should hope to learn from having them pointed out to you. But at this point in your education, you probably know those areas of grammar that give you trouble. When in doubt, find out. Not knowing when to use *who* and *whom,* for instance, is not a sign of stupidity or of moral negligence, but such a mistake may distract your reader from your ideas. You can avoid such errors and learn the grammatical principle involved by consulting a good handbook. The conscientious writer will keep such a reference handy to consult when any question of grammar arises. Many good writers are uncertain about some aspects of grammar. The difference between them and bad writers, however, is that good writers continue to try to find out what they do not know. Grammar becomes less mysterious for those who bother to look up any grammatical question that turns up in their writing. Proofreading is the last opportunity to do this, if you care whether the writing that you submit reflects your best effort.

Proofreading merely consists of neat, legible corrections added to the final draft. The most typical proofreading changes are corrections of spelling or punctuation, additions of words accidentally left out or deletions of words accidentally typed twice, or other mechanical corrections. They should be made in such a way that they produce a neat appearance, but the mere appearance of the page should not be the writer's major worry. The reader should not be distracted by such corrections. Too many of them might mean that you should consider recopying, but it is better to include all necessary corrections than to give the reader the impression that you did not see errors, or did not care whether they existed. The example on page 173 shows part of a manuscript that has been carefully proofread and corrected. Notice that most of the changes are minor. A stylistic change here and there does not detract from the writer's credibility; it suggests that the writer is still thinking.

Be sure that you understand any particular kinds of proofreading marks that your teacher may prefer or require, since there are many ways of indicating such changes. A good handbook will describe specific proofreading conventions. In school, the main objective of careful proofreading is to make sure that the final manuscript says exactly what you want it to say. If you were proofreading your manuscript for publication, a special set of proofreading marks exists to tell the typesetter exactly what to do. These may also be easily found in a

The film attempted to explore the question of what is

"normal" behavior in our society by having the main

characters reverse roles and putting them in situations

where their otherwise "abnormal" attributes make them more

able to cope. Tom, the radical drop out, does not suffer

the anxietes of his fellow workers because he does not take the

business world all that seriously. And Sarah, who is

~~equally~~ her fanatic in desire to be upwardly mobile, is never

persuaded that the revolution is just, but she makes it more

efficient with her businesslike approach to organizing

people. As ~~light~~ farce, the film leaves too many issues

unexplored, however and ~~this reviewer~~ I missed the depth of

questioning found in films like One Flew Over the Cuckoo's

Nest or King of Hearts. Compared to these, this film

suffers from myopia. It cannot see beyond the narrow

reference book, but a student writer ordinarily doesn't have to worry about them.

Teachers appreciate careful proofreading because it tells them exactly what the student understands about his or her own writing. A writing teacher is justified in thinking that any error you leave in your writing is the result of your ignorance of some aspect of English usage, and the teacher will therefore mark your errors for you in order to teach you. Sometimes these uncorrected errors can affect the reader's judgment of your credibility. So, if you allow errors to go uncorrected in your writing when you do understand the correct way, you are not getting credit for what you know, and you may be putting an unnecessary obstacle between your reader and your meaning.

Responding to Criticism

Most teachers have experienced something like this: They have spent a lot of time reading student essays, writing comments intended to show each student where the writing is working and where the student might rethink the ideas or revise the writing, and they have finally determined a final grade to assign to each paper based on all such considerations. Then, they have returned the essays to the students and observed that some of them immediately turn to the grade, react with pleasure or with dismay, and then put the paper aside without reading the comments. Teachers can usually tell when students have not read their comments, when subsequent work shows that no significant changes have resulted from trying to apply them. The thought and effort that the teacher has put into making comments, in other words, has been wasted. Or so it seems.

Students are certainly justified in their concern for the grade that each assignment receives, but if this concern overshadows their assessment and application of the teacher's critical comments, they have not learned all that they can from the teacher. Although a grade determines what kind of credit a student receives for the assignment, it does not communicate what the teacher thinks about the student's work. A grade alone says nothing about how the student has written, or might write again. A grade is a kind of conclusion, and comments are the reasons that support it. Like any conclusion, a grade is only as good as the line of reasoning that justifies it. To understand the grade, the student must understand the basis on which the teacher determined it. For this reason, many teachers, especially writing teachers, choose not to include a final grade on the returned essay itself, but to communicate the grade separately later. This is an attempt to ensure that students will not read the comments in a defensive or perfunctory way, as they sometimes do when their knowledge of the grade may already have prejudiced their reaction to the comments, for better or worse.

Many students do not respond to grades in this way, of course. You will have to examine your own experience to know whether any such "typical" way of responding applies to you. Whether it does or not, some considerations about how to apply critical comments can lead to making the best use of them.

Although it seems obvious, it is helpful to remember that a teacher's comments on an essay may be intended for a variety of responses. The way in which you should respond to comments will differ, for instance, depending on whether the teacher expects the essay to be revised or not. Some teachers like to comment on drafts of a composition and require a revision. Other assignments are, in effect, finished after the teacher has evaluated them. If a teacher expects revision, the student has an opportunity to respond *directly* to the comments, by applying the teacher's specific advice about a particular essay to continued work on that same essay. If no revision is required, however, the teacher's comments can only be applied *indirectly* to future essays. The direct application of comments is perhaps the easiest kind. If the teacher has pointed out stylistic infelicities, the student can follow the teacher's specific advice. If the teacher has commented that a particular passage is unclear or in need of further support, the student can attempt to clarify or explain or add reasons to that portion of the essay. And, if the teacher has made general comments about the logic or the structure of the argument, the student can rethink those aspects of the essay.

Direct responses to comments in revision, because they are guided by the teacher's observations, can also be the most perfunctory kind— for the student who is content to do the minimum that a teacher asks for. It is always tempting to respond to a teacher's specific comments without understanding fully why those comments are there, or what difference the revisions actually make to the quality of the essay. It is too easy, in other words, to make changes just to satisfy the teacher, but not to improve the essay in any way that also satisfies the writer. A teacher's comments are meant to guide students in rethinking what they have done, and if students respond by automatically doing whatever the teacher asks for they have not taken the opportunity to use those comments to their best advantage. A teacher's comment is not a commandment; it is a suggestion. Only the writer can decide whether the comment will lead to a better way of writing, and only the thoughtful application of that suggestion can produce a change that will benefit the student writer in the future.

So, if revision is required based on the teacher's comments on a draft of an essay, the student is not meant to change the essay only in ways that the teacher has suggested and in no other, nor is the student meant to adopt the teacher's suggestions without thinking about their effect on the rest of the essay. Comments are meant to nudge the student into further thought. The outcome of that thought should be a revision that goes beyond the teacher's suggestions. It may even be a revision in which some of those suggestions are not adopted. The important thing is not to make every change the teacher says, but to know why such changes are necessary. At times, they may not be. Teachers are human; as they read your essays, they respond in different ways, just as any member of your audience might. This doesn't mean that teachers are "unfair" if you disagree with them. If you choose not to follow a teacher's specific advice—assuming you have understood both that advice and your own reasons for doing it your way—you might want to explain why to your teacher, who may be more impressed finally by how thoughtfully you approach writing than by how slavishly you follow instructions.

It is important, therefore, that you read the comments carefully and attempt to see what has elicited them. Rereading your essay along with the comments will often make otherwise cryptic comments clear. If a teacher's comments are expressed in ways that you do not understand, it becomes your responsibility to consult with the teacher, to be sure that you and the teacher are reading your essay in the same way. I'm not talking about arguing with the teacher over your grade, but seeking to understand the intention and the source of whatever troublesome comments the teacher may have made. Most teachers respond positively to this kind of inquiry, even if they may not, understandably, respond favorably to complaints about grades. Your teachers may have had some bad experiences with students who habitually whined about their grades; you don't want to seem to be one of those. When discussing your essay with your teacher, then, it is best to leave grades out of it. Make it clear that what you want is a genuine understanding of your own writing. A good deal of the learning that takes place in a writing course can happen in the teacher's office during such conferences.

It helps, further, to remember that comments differ in degree of importance. Typically, a teacher's comments will follow the structure of the essay, usually because it is most convenient to write them in the margins alongside the relevant passage in the essay. (Some teachers have their own methods of making comments, such as putting them all at the end of the composition, or using one form of comment to talk about mechanics and another form to talk about ideas.) Comments that appear side by side are not necessarily equally significant. A teacher may mark a split infinitive in one of your sentences and observe that the logic of the next sentence is not valid. Your response to those comments would necessarily be of a different order. On the one hand you need only make a simple correction. On the other hand you would have to reconsider what you mean and how you might best argue it. The change you are expected to make in the first instance is predictable, but in the second case the teacher has no "right response" in mind other than that you should look critically at your reasoning. The first is a mechanical correction and relatively trivial; the second may be crucial to the success of your argument.

If the teacher's comments do not appear in a hierarchical arrangement of importance, then you need to sort them out yourself, according to the kind of thinking they require. In revising an essay, it would be pointless to make all the minor corrections the teacher has marked at the same time that you attempt to respond to comments about the structure and the argument. As in the case of original composition, your attention should be on the nature of the case you are trying to make and the structure of the argument first, letting matters of lesser significance have your attention only when those are under control. So, you should determine which of the teacher's comments address the most basic aspects of the essay—its reasoning and structure—so that you can respond to those comments first before editing the essay.

It may be that a teacher's comments suggest problems with the thesis itself, or with the general approach you have taken in arguing it. In that case, an appropriate response would lead you to reconsider the thesis and the logic, which might result in a revised essay that has a different argument and structure from the original. If what is most in need of revision is the thesis of your essay, your revision may well turn out to be a wholly new composition based on a revised intention.

Some students assume that writing teachers should only respond to form and have no right to criticize students' ideas. A writing teacher is not simply an editor, whose job is to make sure that all formal aspects of the writing are under control. He or she is also part of the community of critical, inquiring minds to which your essay is addressed. As an expert on matters of usage and structure, a writing teacher may help you to learn about writing from a formal point of view. But as a critical reader, one who responds intelligently to ideas and their support, a teacher also helps you to learn about your thinking. The two are inseparable, and it is unreasonable to expect a writing teacher, as a thinking person, to ignore ideas for the sake of teaching form alone. If a teacher makes a comment about an idea that he or she thinks is not well thought out or adequately argued, it isn't because he or she disagrees with that idea but because it needs further thinking. As a person whose task is to help you toward better writing, your teacher cannot ignore that "good" writing requires well-reasoned ideas as much as it requires effective and correct composition. Your teacher is not determining the success of your argument on the basis of whether he or she agrees with your conclusion, but, as a critical reader, is evaluating the adequacy of the means you have used to reach it.

If a teacher's comments refer to form, consider that your teacher is someone well experienced in English composition who wants to help you understand the intricacies of writing. If the comments refer to your ideas, your teacher's expertise may be limited to that of any other member of your intended audience. You might, in some cases, feel that your idea is better than your teacher thinks it is. But in that case, you have not managed to make your idea understandable or persuasive for a reader whose basic intelligence enables him or her to think about what you have to say. A critical comment from such a reader can only help you in the attempt to further clarify and justify your ideas. You are not being asked to change your mind when a teacher questions what you have to say. You are being asked to think about it, to develop your ideas, and by that means to improve your writing. By challenging you to think harder about the ideas contained in your writing, your teacher is providing you with an essential educational opportunity: to learn for yourself what you think and why you think it.

If you are not required to revise an essay based on the teacher's comments, you will still benefit from analyzing those comments in all the ways I just discussed. It isn't necessary to revise each essay in order to get the benefit of a teacher's evaluation. But a somewhat different strategy for applying comments is necessary, if you aren't going to revise, since you have to apply concepts that you derive from the comments to new writing situations. In other words, although comments that refer to particular aspects of one essay may not apply to another essay, *principles* derived from those comments can still be applied to any new composition. It is necessary for you to derive those principles yourself.

One specific practice may help you to do this most effectively. When you read a teacher's comments, keep notes to yourself of any problems your teacher has found in your writing, so that you can keep track of them apart from the context of any given essay. Say, for instance, that your teacher has marked sentence fragments, or suggested that in several places in your essay you have not supplied a clear transition. On a separate page, in a note intended only for yourself, you might write: "Watch for fragments," or "Concentrate on clear transitions." (It would be best to have separate pages for different kinds of problems—one for words you have misspelled, another for grammar, another for more general concepts—tailored to your own needs.) These notes, no matter what kinds of advice they contain, will be invaluable to you as you revise your next essay by providing a guide for focusing on problems that you especially need to work on. You can add new features to the list as you receive comments on each essay you hand in, and over the course of time you will find yourself gaining more control of most of the writing problems that your teacher has pointed out to you. If you simply read comments once and make no such attempt to remember and apply them, you risk repeating mistakes or getting yourself into the same logical or structural problems.

Speaking of progress, this may be the time to remind you that, as I said in the introduction to this book, writing skills improve slowly and that even as they do, writers continue to feel the frustration of not being able to write easily. Even though principles derived from previous experience can be applied to a new writing situation, each writing task is unique and the degree to which any principle will provide a satisfactory solution to its problems is unpredictable. When it comes to responding to a teacher's criticism, then, it is important to remember that writing is not like mathematics—you cannot rely on a procedure to work in the same way each time to produce an answer that is either right or wrong. A conscientious response to a teacher's comments may still yield writing that is subject to criticism. There is no point at which the process must end.

The difficulties—and the rewards—of writing come from its dependence on the intuitive and intractable dance of the mind at work. Your teacher tries to help, by providing you with comments that derive from outside your particular and individual thought patterns, but these come from inside the thought patterns of the teacher's own mental experience. Those comments represent another point of view, but not the only other one. They will only be as helpful to you as you make them, by being open to discovery while at the same time self-disciplined. The experience of writing is defined by seeming contradictions of this sort—freedom and discipline, individuality and convention—and the challenge of learning to write better is the challenge of feeling at home with such experiences. The frustrations and confusions that come with entering this universe of discourse, in which, for instance, your teacher may at times not understand you and you may not understand your teacher, often seem worthwhile only when you reach the point where you understand that for a thinking person they are inevitable. The worst thing that a person seeking to grow intellectually can do is to give up by trying to avoid the frustration. Embrace the struggle, and you will discover for yourself the value of writing well.

QUESTIONS FOR THOUGHT, DISCUSSION, AND WRITING

1. In your outside reading, locate several examples of figurative language used effectively and ineffectively. What reasons do you have for judging the examples in these ways?
2. Find examples of metaphors common in speech and writing that have the power to affect how people perceive reality. What gives them this power?
3. Find a piece of writing that you completed some time ago for a different class. Then:

    a. Locate and list all the metaphors. Do they work? Would you want to eliminate them? Why?

    b. Edit this writing by looking carefully at the diction, cutting unnecessary words, changing passive verbs to active ones in appropriate cases, changing the length and shape of your sentences, and trying to find effective, honest transitional phrases where they might be needed.

4. Once you have a complete rough draft of an essay done for this class, revise it according to principles discussed in this chapter. Try first to get someone to read it to you out loud. Listen carefully. By hearing it read, what do you learn?

5. After you receive an essay back from your teacher, analyze the comments according to the advice in this chapter. Reread your essay. What do the comments *teach* you as you think about applying them?

CHAPTER 8

ᥥᔰ *Research* ᔰᥥ

Research and Argument

Much of the writing that students do in college requires some kind of research. Because students sometimes produce writing that looks like research, but really isn't, we should consider for a moment what the term means in a college setting. Research is inquiry into the unknown. It is the pursuit of answers to questions that are yet unanswered. Research takes different forms, of course, but all research derives from a basic desire: to find out what is true.

Given these definitions, you can see why I said that the writing of college students sometimes resembles research but is, in fact, something else. The standard "term paper"—sometimes called a "research paper"—might not involve any genuine research at all, if, for instance, the writer only repeats information found in "sources" to confirm a conclusion that was never in doubt. Merely going to the library and compiling information is not research; it is more like reporting on the research of others. Thus, a "research paper" is misnamed if the writer only repeats what others have asserted, without in some way testing that knowledge or using it to solve a problem. Yet, the "term paper" often turns out to be just such an exercise, in which greater importance is placed on the bulk of information gathered and the formalities of footnotes and bibliographies than on the search for answers.

A long essay, with correctly documented footnotes from many bibliographic sources, is only a research paper if it results from the writer's having sought and found an answer to a question that was previously unanswered. (In some situations, this means not previously answered by anyone, and in others it means not previously

answered by the researcher.) Research writing is the process of arguing that answer in such a way that the knowledge the writer has
discovered can be shared with others. Research is like learning: It
proceeds from not knowing to knowing. Research writing is like argumentation: It shows why answers should be accepted.

Research and argumentation thus have much in common. The
writer of a good argument seeks to develop the best case for believing
a conclusion in response to a question at issue. The researcher seeks
to answer a question that is open to inquiry. Argumentative writing
derives from a quest for good reasons, and the responsible conduct of
that quest implies the possibility of the writer changing his or her
own mind in the process of trying to develop the best case. The
search for a satisfactory thesis statement is a kind of research, in the
sense that it involves a search for a genuinely defensible conclusion,
rather than one that seems true but is untested by any rational process. Testing thesis statements against the possible reasons and assumptions that might be used to support them is like what a researcher does when searching for satisfactory explanations and more
or less certain knowledge.

In writing argumentative essays, you base your arguments on
premises that derive from thinking about your ideas and those of your
audience. Your class discussions, therefore, serve some of the functions of research. In your writing you are potentially able to make
use of everything you know about an issue, and when you need to,
you can venture outside your own thoughts to seek to add to what
you already know. In doing research, too, one extends the boundaries
of one's thoughts by seeking knowledge about an issue before committing oneself to a conclusion. Argumentation is open inquiry into
one's reasons. Research is open inquiry into one's questions.

Research is not a process that begins with complete uncertainty
and ends with complete certainty; it is, therefore, not possible to
become "fully" informed first and then to decide what to believe.
There are always gaps in one's knowledge—even if one reaches the
point, after years of research and study, of becoming an expert. One
learns by doing research that there is always something more to know,
before absolute certainty is possible. Thus, the research writer must
always argue for his or her discoveries on the basis of the best information available. The research writer, in other words, must know
how to argue well and responsibly without having "all" the answers.
The researcher, as a writer of argumentation, must seek clarification
and belief within the limits of what it is possible to know. As a
writer of argumentative essays, you should be learning to measure
conclusions against the quality, not the quantity, of the reasons avail-

able. This is exactly what a good researcher also needs to know how to do.

Speculative inquiry is not confined to the library or the laboratory. If research were limited to experiments and to "looking it up" in the library, it would result in the compilation of lots of information, but no real answers. The answers to most research questions involve more than data; they require the creative acts of synthesis, interpretation, and evaluation. A researcher is a creative thinker, not just a compiler of data. Research goes beyond adding to one's store of information. Researchers are also people who *do* something with it, by thinking independently, formulating problems, and applying information or theories to their solutions. Like artists, researchers make something new out of the resources at hand. The resources must be there to work with, but without the spark of imagination, they do not ignite into knowledge. The researcher must not only know how to find something out, but also how to recognize a problem and how to apply knowledge to its solution. Does this sound like writing? Part control and part spontaneity, part deliberation and part intuition—well mixed.

Having acknowledged the intuitive and spontaneous side of research, we can see nevertheless that the process can be guided by some general principles. No matter what kind of research you conduct, you will go through certain steps. These do not necessarily happen in linear order, neatly divided from one another, but the activity of doing and writing research is not complete without some thought to each. As we go through these steps, you will continue to see that they resemble the process of argumentative writing. (You will also notice that I do not include "using library reference guides," "making notecards," "summarizing sources," "listing bibliographical data," and all of the other clerical tasks that sometimes pass for advice about "research." I will mention documentation in the proper context, but these matters should not be confused with what research is all about. You can find descriptions of these activities in any good college writing handbook, if you need them. Suffice it to say that as you go through these stages, you should keep track of your activities by writing them down, including the sources of whatever information you discover along the way.)

Formulating the question

How can you conduct an inquiry until you know what kind of problem you are trying to solve? Even though inquiry may be open-ended, it is not unrestrained by some sense of a destination to be reached. A geologist, for instance, might be interested in volcanoes, but until she has focused on a problem related to this topic, there is no way of knowing what sort of information to seek or experiments to conduct. She already knows some things about volcanoes, but many things about them remain a mystery. How does she know, then, what kind of knowledge to seek? Research questions emerge from the limits of what she already knows, the conflicts produced by that knowledge. Research begins where one's present understanding leads to an intriguing question. It may be the kind of question that seems to jump up and beg to be answered, or it may be one that has to be constructed carefully and deliberately. In any case, the researcher's first obligation is to ask, "What am I trying to find out?" and then "What kind of a question have I got here?"

The nature of the question being pursued will determine how the inquiry will proceed. What do I mean by "the nature of the question"? In Chapter 3 I discuss some different kinds of questions at issue, which I will expand on here to describe some kinds of questions of inquiry that might become questions at issue in arguments. This list of six kinds of questions makes finer distinctions than the earlier list of four kinds:

> questions of fact
> questions of definition
> questions of interpretation
> questions of consequence
> questions of evaluation
> questions of policy

But even this list is not complete; further distinctions are possible. It is enough, however, for you to get a sense of how different kinds of questions may be asked about the same subject matter, and how they might affect the inquiry. I will illustrate the differences using a literary topic mainly, but include brief comparisons with topics from other fields.

Suppose I have been reading Shakespeare's *Othello*. Depending on my previous experience with Shakespeare, or with drama, or with history, certain aspects of the play make sense to me and other aspects do not. I begin with a feeling of curiosity about what I do not understand—or perhaps a feeling of unrest or confusion. Perhaps I begin with an idea about the play that I can't support, and this leads me to ask whether it is true. In any event, I can ask many different questions, based on my experience reading the play. Those questions will be of a certain kind.

Among the *questions of fact* that I might ask are:

When was *Othello* first performed?

How long did it take Shakespeare to write it?

From what sources did Shakespeare derive the story?

Were the characters based on real people?

What verse forms are used for Othello's soliloquies?

Such questions have in common the determinacy of their possible answers. In each case, the answer is a matter of verifiable fact. If the answer could not be verified somehow, then the question must remain unanswered. The answers to questions of fact are either correct or incorrect, true of false, yes or no. Such questions will be more or less interesting—either important or trivial—depending on the subject matter. Research might end with the answer to any of these questions about *Othello,* but these answers might also lead to other, more interesting questions. Inquiries into facts of this sort may open up larger issues, or they may prove satisfying in themselves.

There is no absolute test of whether a question of fact is worth pursuing for its own sake. In matters of literature, say, or political science, such questions may have less inherent interest than they would in matters of, say, chemistry. I might find an answer to any of these questions about *Othello,* and then find myself asking, "so what?" At that point I would have discovered that the question I had been pursuing was only a doorway into a question of larger significance, a question of a different sort. The decision to formulate a question for inquiry need not be final; it may prove to be a way of finding out how to reformulate the question.

Among the *questions of definition* that I might ask about the play could be:

What does Iago's word *tupping* mean?

What are "Anthropophagi"?

What did the word *gross* mean in Shakespeare's day?

What words change meaning for Othello as he becomes jealous?

What different meanings are given to the term *nature* in this play?

Questions of definition concern the meaning or meanings of words. The answers, however, are not always straightforward, as in the case of answers to questions of fact. Perhaps, as in the question about "Anthropophagi," the answer is resolvable by verification, as a matter of "fact." More often, however, the answer depends on the researcher's consideration of more than, say, a dictionary or a glossary. Consider the third question above, for instance. A researcher putting together notes for an edition of the play may wish to find out what *gross* meant to the Elizabethan audience, since the meaning of the word may have changed for the present-day reader of the play. But there is no Elizabethan dictionary in which to look up the word. The researcher would have to examine many uses of the word in the play itself and in contemporary works, and determine, by examining context and apparent intention, what the contemporary audience was most likely to have understood the word to mean. An even more difficult question of definition is contained in the fifth question above, since it assumes that Shakespeare changed and broadened the meaning of the word *nature* in different places in the play for his own reasons. The researcher could only answer the question by combining knowledge about the word with speculation about Othello's character and Shakespeare's intentions. Like questions of fact, questions of definition may be ends in themselves or may lead to the formulation of different kinds of questions.

Questions of interpretation may involve words, or they may involve the "meaning" of larger utterances, events, actions, structures, or concepts. Changing a question of definition only slightly may make it into a question of interpretation, as in:

> Why did Shakespeare use *nature* in these ways?

This question goes one step beyond definition by posing a question of significance as well as meaning. Other questions of interpretation might be of these sorts:

> Is Othello an Aristotelian tragic hero?
> Why did Shakespeare include the clown?
> How does the first scene of the play foreshadow Othello's fate?
> What has Othello learned about himself in the last scene of the play?
> How is Desdemona like Cordelia in *King Lear?*
> What does *Othello* owe to the tradition of the morality play?

Like questions of fact, these may seem to have a right or wrong answer—"Yes, Othello is an Aristotelian tragic hero." But unlike questions of fact, the possible answers are not verifiable as a matter of information alone; they depend on more than data. Hence, they are not true or false in quite the same way as factual answers may seem to be. "It is a matter of interpretation" is a phrase meaning that a given answer is subject to change according to one's point of view, or according to certain conditions. "Insofar as he is blinded by his own pride, Othello exhibits one quality of a tragic hero as defined by Aristotle," one might say, and thereby acknowledge that this interpretation exists within certain limits. Notice how these questions of interpretation involve looking at one thing from the point of view of another. These perspectives, and the limits they impose, are part of what the researcher must establish.

Questions of interpretation arise in most fields, especially when the subject of inquiry is discourse or human action. That Hannah Arendt called evil a "banality" is a fact I can verify by citing her work. What she meant, however, is a question with which historians and social theorists have had to struggle. What is the significance of a phrase or an idea found in the writing or speech of Karl Marx, or Mother Teresa, or John Maynard Keynes, or . . . anyone! Anthropologists may seek to interpret a ritual act or a social relationship. Sociologists may seek to interpret data collected in surveys. Questions of interpretation result whenever the significance of a word, or an idea, or an event, or a fact is not self-evident. No discipline (save, perhaps, mathematics) can escape them.

Does the potential uncertainty of questions of interpretation make them less important than questions of fact? We have seen just the opposite. Questions of interpretation often attempt to answer the "so what?" questions that matters of fact can raise. Yet, they seem equivocal because they cannot be established absolutely. Here we confront something very interesting about knowledge. What we know often has more significance to our understanding as it becomes less certain. As we attempt to go beyond facts and to establish interpretations, we are dealing with our own relation to the subject matter as much as we are with the raw "data" itself. What we are learning about when we interpret is twofold: We learn about the subject and we learn about ourselves. Because we must exercise interpretive judgments, applying our understanding to such questions, the facts do not speak for themselves; we must say what we understand them to signify.

Of course, the degree to which questions of interpretation are more or less significant in this way also depends on the subject matter. In the study of literature, for instance, interpretation is always a central problem, since we are dealing with human creations and our responses to them. But questions of interpretation are no less relevant to research in other areas. There may be no significance to the question of whether "pi" should be carried out to eight decimal points in a certain calculation (a matter of interpretation). Then again, there may be.

By *questions of consequence,* I mean those that seek to establish causes or effects. Among questions of this kind that I might ask about *Othello* are:

How does Othello use logic to convince himself that Desdemona is unfaithful?

In what way do political circumstances affect the main plot?
What motivates Iago to destroy Othello?
To what extent is Iago's hatred the result of Othello's race?
How do Elizabethan attitudes toward marriage influence the characters' actions?

Answering questions about causes and effects also requires interpretation. But what is being interpreted is a special kind of relationship. Causality may be known with varying degrees of certainty. These questions about *Othello* cannot be answered with more certainty than other questions of interpretation. Literary issues do not lend themselves to the kind of experimental analysis that might enable one to be much more certain about the causes of, let's say, a chemical reaction. In the case of some scientific issues, questions of consequence resemble questions of fact more than they resemble questions of interpretation. If I wanted to know what the result would be if the chemical dioxin were added to the growth medium of carrots, I could construct an experiment, with a control group, to derive a fairly certain answer. "Cause" in this case is known as a direct result of being able to control a specific variable. But *whether* dioxin causes changes is still a different kind of question from *how* it does, which may be more difficult to answer with as much certainty. And what if my question is, "What is the effect on the environment of dioxin use?" The whole environment cannot be put in a laboratory; not all the variables can be controlled. Researching this question would involve some speculation. Yet, we would not want to abandon the effort for this reason. Many vital questions of consequence demand our thought, even though understanding "cause" and "effect" in many contexts is subject to interpretive judgments. A pyschologist might wonder "what causes crime," but may come up with a different answer from that of a sociologist asking the same question. As difficult as many questions of consequence are to answer, they are often fundamentally important to our understanding of any subject.

Among the *questions of evaluation* that I might ask about *Othello* are:

Is Iago a coward?
Is *Othello* a "well-made" play?
Is it better theater than *Romeo and Juliet?*
What does *Othello* teach us about the nature of evil?
Does the play encourage racist attitudes in its viewers?

Such questions have in common the application of some standard of "good" to determine value. When we judge anything according to its value, we seek to place it within some kind of ethical context. Such contexts may or may not be absolute ones, or they may or may not be ones to which the researcher subscribes. But some kind of ethical judgment is necessary to say whether, or how, a thing is "good" or "bad." These examples range from evaluative issues that are within the fictional world of *Othello* itself ("Is Iago a coward?") to those that go beyond the values defined by the play ("Does the play encourage racist attitudes?"). Neither can be satisfactorily answered, however, without engaging the researcher in an examination of what standard of value to apply. Whether Iago is a coward may seem like an issue that confines itself to his actions within the ethical standards Shakespeare has created, yet to answer it we must be able to recognize Shakespeare's values, and to do that we must, to some extent, relate them to our own. If our conception of cowardice differs from those that the play presents, our answer to the question will reflect that difference. It may seem that the question of whether the play encourages racism could be asked in a "value free" way—either the play does or it doesn't encourage this attitude. Yet, in the same way, our answer will necessarily depend on how we view racism as an ethical issue. I can hardly reach a conclusion without judging it according to the degree to which I think plays ought not to encourage such attitudes. By asking the question itself, I have revealed an ethical interest, and to answer it I have to apply an ethical standard.

There are those who think that because questions of evaluation are "subjective," they are not appropriate for research. To such an attitude, I would respond like this: Some of the most interesting research questions are subjective to a degree, as we have already seen by noting that they require acts of judgment and interpretation, and thus subjectivity alone is not a reason to rule a question out of bounds for informed inquiry. If we limit inquiry to questions that are "objective," we might find ourselves unable to decide what to do with the information we have gathered, since that decision must result from our own interests, perspectives, and concerns. The decision to pursue one research question rather than another constitutes an evaluative act, which even the most objective researcher must perform. We must be careful not to associate "objectivity" with "good" research in our minds and "subjectivity" with "bad" research. It is possible to have good or bad research of either kind, if that means careful or sloppy, thorough or pefunctory. The idea that objective research is somehow better may be the result of applying the standards of scientific judgment to all realms of knowledge, but this is risky. There are many kinds of knowledge, some wholly objective, some wholly subjective, and some a mixture of the two. No one kind necessarily deserves the title "knowledge" more than another.

It is true that disciplines differ in the degree to which the questions they ask, and the methods of inquiry they employ, are evaluative. Research in the philosophy of ethics obviously concerns value questions primarily. Is it possible, nevertheless, to have an "objective" view of such questions? Yes, depending on the nature of the question. For instance, a philosopher might approach an ethical problem from a historical or cultural point of view: "Are taboos against incest universal?" This is a question of fact posed about an ethical subject. At the other extreme, it seems that a science such as particle physics would concern factual questions primarily and adopt the strictest possible objectivity to ensure valid results. Yet, our society has recently witnessed many such scientists turning their attention to the religious or political questions raised by their discoveries. Thus, a physicist might approach a factual problem from an ethical perspective: "What are the dangers of nuclear waste disposal?" Who can really say that is not a proper subject for research simply because it compromises the scientific ideal of objectivity?

Questions of value—inquiries into quality and ethics—are frequently investigated by researchers in every field. An important reason for this is that answers to such questions are prerequisite to the investigation of the last kind of research question we consider.

Questions of policy direct the researcher's attention to what should be done. They relate to actions. Among the questions of policy that might be asked about *Othello* are:

> What should Othello have done to protect himself against Iago's lies?
> Should Desdemona be portrayed on stage as guiltless?
> How should the murder scene be staged?
> Should we perform *Othello* or choose a comedy instead?
> Should certain lines be cut from the play for high school readers?

Research questions of this kind are intended to conclude with a recommendation, a prescription, or a preference for some action on someone's part. Once again, such questions may refer to actions of the "inner" world of the subject (in this case those of the fictional characters) or to those of the "outer" world, our own or someone else's actions in the real world. Questions of policy arise from situations in which alternative actions are possible, and the problem confronting the researcher is to find out which of them is best. This is why I said that the answers to questions of evaluation are prerequisite to policy questions. "Should certain lines be cut from the play for high school readers?" Whatever answer a researcher might come up with would have to combine some inquiry into cause and effect (what would the effect be of leaving the lines in or cutting them out?) with some inquiry into value (are these effects desirable?). Questions of policy, then, are not the occasion for the mere statement of preferences. If they were, they would not be research questions, since the answers would be predetermined.

All fields of learning are subject to inquiry from the point of view of policy. Once again, it is not the subject that determines what kind of research question to pursue, but the nature of the problem faced by the researcher. Research in political science, where "policy" is the subject matter, may be directed toward answering questions of fact, or interpretation, or consequence, or value, just as research in a scientific field such as biology may move in the direction of answering questions of policy when the issue becomes application, as it does, say, in medicine. Medical research might be said to focus on questions of policy mainly (What should we do to treat x disease?) even though many questions of fact and of consequence will have to be answered in the process.

Becoming informed

Formulating a research question will be an aid to conducting inquiry. It should enable you to define the unknowns, to determine the boundaries of the inquiry, and to keep the inquiry focused as you seek to become better informed. Of course, the question starts out as a tentative formulation, subject to change. The more you discover, and the more thought you give to the possible answers, the clearer you may become about the kind of question that you wish to answer. Research is seldom so straightforward that no side trips, dead ends, detours, or unexpected changes of plan happen along the road to answers. The process of becoming informed seldom follows a predictable route.

Having formulated a research question, you might ask yourself something like, "What do I need to know to answer this question?" At this point you might sketch out a plan, listing some of the specific areas you need to know more about. Any question can be "broken down" into constituent parts, even if the categories are temporary or turn out later to be irrelevant. You may not yet know what all of the categories are—research is, after all, exploring the unknown. Yet, you are never starting out without some knowledge to begin with, since you had to understand something already in order to perceive the significance of the question you have decided to explore. So, trust that knowledge, for now, and sketch out some possibilities, based on the question you have formulated.

For example, suppose I have been reading some accounts in a sociology textbook of studies of "aggression." Based on this reading,

I become especially interested in the idea that human aggression, like that of animals, may be triggered by "territoriality." It makes me wonder whether this could help explain some of the ways I have seen people act in groups, gangs in my old neighborhood, for instance, or even the fraternity guys I've seen at parties. Anyway, I think about the possibilities and finally decide to explore this question:

> Are people who spray-paint graffiti exhibiting an "instinct" to mark off their territory?

Notice that to have asked this question I have already implied a hypothetical answer. But my "theory" may be wrong, so I let it stay a question rather than phrase it as an assertion. This, I realize, is a question of interpretation. I am asking what the significance of this behavior is. This will help me define a few categories of inquiry. What do I need to know to answer this question? I might list a few preliminaries:

> What groups do this?
> What exactly do they do?
> How am I going to define *territory?* Read Konrad Lorenz! (My textbook mentioned him.)
> What is an "instinct?" Do I mean something else?
> What is known about this behavior? Has anybody studied it?

My questions seem to divide themselves into those that concern the behavior of one of the groups and those that concern the meaning of "territorial instinct." This means that I will be finding out about two separate areas (at least) and have to look for potential relationships between them. Anyway, my list of "unknowns" tells me what to do next. After such a list is put together, the next question becomes, "How am I going to find out?" It is at this point that the researcher is confronted by the task of searching out what is already known, and the search will take place primarily, if not exclusively, in the library.

Libraries are so vast in the resources available that it is, of course, necessary to know how your library is organized and what kinds of catalogs and indexes exist to give researchers access to its holdings. If you have not become familiar with the resources of a research library, you can ask the reference staff for their advice. All good libraries have educational material available to students who wish to acquaint themselves with the basic functions of the library. Descriptions of different kinds of reference materials (subject or author/title indexes for books, indexes to periodicals, bibliographies, abstracts of research, and more) can also be found in a good college writing handbook. Rather than discuss these here, I assume you are able to look them up if you need to. Often, the best way to discover what kinds of resources the library has available in your own areas of interest is to get in there with your questions and begin to follow leads wherever they take you. It isn't efficient, of course, just to plunge in without a good idea of where to look for the information you seek. But it is often adventurous and fun to explore somewhat as a means of becoming familiar with the library at the same time that you seek to inform yourself about your subject. Doing research is often compared to the work of a detective. It's a good analogy, as far as it goes. A researcher, like a detective, has to be watchful for unexpected clues. The library is full of these, and you should be prepared to investigate any that might take you into important discoveries.

Remember that although you are inquiring into a question and not into a topic, the library itself organizes information under subject headings, whether these are found in the library's catalogs, in various indexes, or in reference books. Your list of "unknowns" is a list of questions, but to find sources that deal with them you have to reduce them to topics under headings. The kind of strategy that you work out for yourself in finding library materials will depend on the breadth or specificity of these topical categories, but don't lose sight of the questions you are asking as you find specific sources under the topics. Not all sources that might be found by looking up "graffiti," for instance, will have anything to do with the question you need answered. Sometimes you will have to look at the materials in depth to discover how the topic is treated and whether it bears on your question.

To work responsibly in the library, it is at least as important to have an open mind and to be persistent as it is to know all the ins and outs of reference guides. There is no substitute for a genuine spirit of curiosity. A reference guide can help you to locate potentially relevant books, articles, reports, and so on, but it cannot make you want to read them, or to keep looking. Research in the library too often goes no further than the first few sources discovered—it stops short of being thorough—when the student is content to accept any information rather than to seek the best information available. This will become an important issue when I discuss the process of testing the information you collect. It is important here to remember that libraries contain information the researcher can trust as well as what the researcher ought to question. (Remember the bathtub example in Chapter 2?) It is the researcher's job, not the librarian's, to determine what constitutes a reliable source. The researcher makes this judgment, first of all, by being sure that he or she has not stopped inquiring too early. The student who habitually looks everything up in the encyclopedia and goes no further is not going to experience the genuine rewards of informed inquiry.

Research in the library has one crucial limitation. Only by knowing what kind of question you are researching, and what "unknowns" define the inquiry, can you know whether this limitation will apply to the particular research project you undertake. This limitation is probably best described by distinguishing "secondary" research from "primary" research. Secondary research consists of locating and using the research that other people have already conducted and written about. One way of going about answering research questions is to read the writing of other researchers who have investigated the same or related questions. Primary research consists of investigating any phenomenon on one's own, by working directly with the phenomenon rather than reading about other people's work with it. Secondary research is ordinarily conducted in the library, since this is where one usually goes to find out what others have written. Primary research is ordinarily conducted outside the library.

The distinction between primary and secondary research applies to all fields of inquiry. Science provides the most obvious examples. A biologist, for instance, may be interested in discovering how a particular species of plant reacts to changes in light. There are many things about this question that she might learn in the library. To answer it, she would have to know as much about the plant as possible and about how other species of plants react to similar changes, information that can be found in the published research of other biologists. She would also want to know whether anyone has already discovered the answer to her question, or to questions that bear on it. But having informed herself in his way, the researcher would have to move from the library to the laboratory, to complete the study by conducting experiments with plants and light sources. The "secondary" phase of the research exists as preparation for the "primary" phase. Depending on the kind of question under investigation, primary research takes place in the laboratory, or in the "field," or simply in the privacy of one's thoughts. An anthropologist investigating what kinds of traditions accompany marriage in urban subcultures may learn a lot by reading, but at some point he would want to go out and collect some primary information, by talking to people and observing the phenomena firsthand. A sociologist studying the attitudes of teenagers toward alcohol abuse can learn much by reading in the library, but she would also have to question teenagers to find her answers. A scholar studying the possible influence of impressionist painting on the literary style of Gertrude Stein would learn a lot by finding sources in the library, but her research would enter its primary phase when she made careful observations about the paintings and the writing and compared them. The way in which primary research is conducted varies from discipline to discipline, depending on the kinds of questions being asked, but all research moves from the secondary collecting and assessment of others' ideas to the primary study of the phenomenon under study. Primary research *extends* secondary research. Without both, no research would be complete.

Isolating the "unknowns" for a given research question enables a researcher to make the best use of library sources, which differ in their function and level of complexity. You would not want to spend all of your time in the library looking up information that you already understand, nor would you want to waste time by reading information that you cannot understand because it is written for an audience that knows more than you do at this point. Thus, you want to try to make your research as informative as possible by moving from the general to the particular, if possible, so that you have sufficient background to understand what you are reading. It is helpful to remember that the library contains sources that differ in levels of particularity. For instance:

> Sources of general information, overviews of a subject:
> > General headings in encyclopedias. Introductory textbooks. Popular journals. Abstracts or summaries of research. Book reviews. Books that survey a field or introduce a subject to a wide audience.
> Sources of more specific or technical information:
> > Specific entries in encyclopedias. Advanced textbooks. Atlases and other reference works. General studies in professional or academic journals. Books that discuss specific topics for a general audience.
> Sources of highly specific or technical information:
> > Detailed studies in professional or academic journals. Government or industry reports. Books that discuss specific topics in depth for an audience of specialists.

Thus, keep in mind that you may have to do some reading that functions to prepare you to read more relevant sources competently. Common sense—and what you already know about your subject—should guide you as you try to sort out where to find information at the appropriate level. If you find yourself reading material that is too complicated, note the source and return to it, if you need to, after preparing yourself with background information. If you find yourself reading material that is too simple for your purposes, see if it contains references to sources or more detailed studies that you might pursue.

Finally, remember that the researcher enters the process of becoming informed without knowing where that process may lead. The research question, like the thesis of an argumentative essay, may change as the researcher discovers more information or complexities and continues to think about them. Further questions may arise. Answers may have to remain tentative. But just as the writer of an argumentative essay has to decide when a line of reasoning is adequate, a researcher must decide when a question can be answered reasonably. In either case, there is nothing wrong with admitting that the answer is only as good as the quality of the evidence that supports it, so that the possibility of further inquiry remains open.

Evaluating and testing

Once you have discovered any source of information in the library, or conducted primary research of some kind, you must be able to evaluate whether it is useful or trustworthy. Obviously, not everything that one reads in the library is true. In some fields, knowledge may become outdated; published information in science, for example, may be superceded by more recent research, which shows it to be false. "What is known" may contradict or qualify "what has been known." Why, then, does the library not discard obsolete studies? One simple answer is that these studies may themselves be relevant to a researcher, if, for example, the question under investigation involves the history of ideas in this field. For a historian of science, past mistakes constitute essential knowledge. Once again, the library does not discriminate between right and wrong information; that is the researcher's task. In other fields, knowledge may not evolve as it does in science. Although philosophers at different times may have given different answers to questions of ethics, for instance, those given by the ancients may be just as relevant to our present understanding of an issue as those given by the latest thinkers. The fact that they give different answers does not mean that the most recent ones necessarily improve on the ones that came before.

Another way in which library sources may be untrustworthy is this: Not all research has been "honest," and some may reflect the ideological desires of the writer more than the quest for truth. A researcher with an "axe to grind" in any field, might leave out or distort information that would result in "undesirable" answers. Thus, a particular study of history, or of politics, or even of science may be intended to promote an ideological preference rather than to arrive at honest answers. Once again, the library has a duty to include a study of this sort. Who's to say that the question of how ideology has affected the study of a subject may not itself become a subject of someone's inquiry? The researcher ought to be aware of the possibility of finding studies that are not honest in this way, and yet consider that all studies have a "point of view" of one kind or another. The

limitations of any study may not be the result of the writer's desire
to deceive, although the conclusions may still be affected by the writer's perspective. Some research may be wholly ideological. If I had
set myself the task of designing a "perfect" government, I would
want to read the works of others who have tried to do the same, as
well as those who have studied the successes and failures of real governments. My subject would be ideological, by definition, and the
ideologies of my sources would be central to my study.

There is no foolproof way to know whether one's sources can be
trusted. An open mind is necessary to ensure that you discover adequate information. A critical mind is necessary to ensure that you
assess that information well. Rather than try to offer a dependable
procedure for knowing when a source is right or wrong, let me describe the worst kind of uncritical research and see what it tells us
about our responsibilities as critical readers. I have seen student "term
papers" in which many sources were cited to support the writer's
idea, but in each case those sources consisted exclusively of the conclusions of studies that agree with the writer. In other words, the
writer's thesis is argued by constructing a list of authorities all saying
the same thing, as if such a list alone "proved" the point. This cat-
alog of authorities does not constitute an argument, however, because
the *reasons* that these sources give for their conclusions are not explored. Such a writer has located many sources and found their conclusions, but he or she has not tried to assess those conclusions according to the process by which they were derived. The resulting
"research paper" does not discriminate between conclusions derived
by adequate means and conclusions derived by inadequate ones. As
an argument, it is weak. As research, it is useless.

Clearly, then, anyone conducting serious research has the responsibility of doing more than skimming through sources to find
conclusions. Once you have found a source that seems relevant, you
must not only know what its conclusions are but also how those
conclusions have been derived. In other words, you must consider the
arguments that have been presented in support of those conclusions
and assess the conclusions accordingly. Whatever the sources, you
must satisfy yourself that you have asked

What does it say?

By what process have the conclusions been derived? What evidence is
presented? What reasons are given?

What assumptions do the reasons depend on?

These questions should remind you of the longer discussion in Chapter 2 (see pages 34–43). Your answers to these questions are just as

important to your research as the conclusions themselves. Research, in this sense, *is* critical reading. Your own presentation of the results of your research must demonstrate that your inquiry has included such questions. Your reader, after all, can be assumed to be capable of asking them about your own conclusions.

It is also the researcher's responsibility to have located and considered studies that do not support whatever potential conclusion he or she may intend to reach. Research questions are open-ended, but researchers often work from a "hypothesis," whether it is defined early in the study or late. Whenever answers begin to emerge, it is essential to know what reasons may contradict those answers as well as what reasons support them. When looking for information, when assessing sources, and when determining your own conclusions, you should consider possible reasons or evidence that would support different conclusions. This way of looking at arguments, whether others' or one's own, is called "falsification."

As a way of testing ideas, critical thinkers try to falsify them. This means simply trying to come up with a serious line of reasoning that would show them to be false. For the researcher, this process has two dimensions: falsifying the ideas contained in sources and falsifying the conclusions that one derives from them. Falsifying the studies that one reads is a good way to determine for yourself how you might use them, whether with confidence or with some qualification, whether to support your conclusion or to illustrate the potential range of its relevance. The process of falsifying ideas is an important mental exercise, involving seriously trying to answer questions like these:

> What if this idea is wrong?
> What kinds of reasons could be used to argue the opposite?
> What would have to be true for those reasons to be valid?
> What assumptions are available to support those reasons?

To be able to consider such questions seriously, a researcher must have the mental agility to shift points of view. (We all probably increase our mental agility simply by trying to answer such questions.) It helps to see the weakness in a given line of reasoning to know how the opposite conclusion might be argued. To learn this requires that we be able to imagine how someone who believes the opposite might defend it. It is one way to learn. No harm is done if by this means we come to question our ideas, or even to change our minds.

The ideas that one discovers during secondary research are also tested in the court of experience. As the researcher makes use of secondary sources to conduct a direct inquiry, moving from secondary to primary research, the usefulness, relevance, accuracy, and correctness of others' observations continue to be subject to scrutiny. Primary research is itself a means of judging the validity of secondary sources, as well as a means of discovering answers. Primary research complements secondary research and fulfills the possibilities that secondary research uncovers.

Evaluating and testing has a somewhat different emphasis in primary research than it does when the published research of others is the source of one's information. Primary research may involve designing and conducting experiments of some kind or it may involve direct observations and interpretations. The methods of primary research differ depending on the kind of question being pursued, and they range from empirical to statistical to theoretical depending on the phenomena being investigated. It might help to discuss these methods briefly in relation to very general fields of inquiry. The broad divisions between the natural and physical sciences, the social sciences, and the humanities and fine arts distinguish areas of inquiry, each with special research techniques. The areas overlap considerably, of course, and the techniques of research that apply to one may be used in another. An art historian may use a strictly scientific means of dating a statue, for instance, or a psychologist may conduct an experiment to verify a theory of behavior. But with this reservation in mind, three general areas of inquiry—empirical studies, social studies, and humanities—may be used to illustrate the kinds of considerations that govern primary research.

Empirical studies. In the natural and physical sciences, empirical studies predominate. This means that the method of discovery is based on observation of quantitatively measurable phenomena, in such a way that the phenomena can be accurately described. Consider, for instance, the technique that a zoologist must use to investigate the structure of an animal's muscular system; he would dissect the animal and make detailed observations of the physical properties of each muscle and where it is located, distinguishing types of muscle according to these observed characteristics. In an empirical study of this sort, where the subject is available for observation, the validity of the result depends on the accuracy and precision of the observations, and these depend, in turn, on the instruments of measurement the investigator uses. For some inquiries of this sort, it may be sufficient simply to observe what is there, but most empirical studies involve the use of measuring devices of some sort that extend or quantify the investigator's power of observation, such as scales or rulers to measure weight or size, meters, or microscopes to increase powers of vision. In empirical observation, precision of observation and measurement is a central concern.

Phenomena that cannot be simply observed are studied empirically through experimentation. If, for instance, the question confronting the zoologist is not the structure of the muscular system but its functions, such as its power relative to the animal's age or how various muscles react to different stimuli, these cannot be observed without the control of an experimental setting. In such cases, the researcher manipulates the circumstances in which the phenomena take place, so that a particular unknown can be observed. The results of such a study continue to depend on the accuracy of the observations, but they depend also on the conditions imposed by the experimenter. For instance, if I wanted to study how an animal's muscles react to diet, I would have to impose special conditions on the study. First, I would have to establish a "control," so that I knew what a "normal" response was like, and then I would have to change the single condition that I was investigating. If, in addition to diet, I changed other conditions, I would not be able to know precisely what I was observing.

The "scientific method" of inquiry in primary research generally follows a well-established path: It begins with a problem and a hypothetical answer that the researcher attempts to verify by designing an experiment in which the hypothetical result is predicted. The predicted result is discovered to be true by controlling "variables" and accurately observing the result. An important feature of this method of inquiry is that the result of a particular study must then be generalized. I might infer, for instance, that what I observe about the controlled reaction of a particular muscle will also apply in other identical cases that I have not controlled experimentally. On the basis of limited observation, I make a larger prediction. Experiments in science, for this reason, must be repeated enough times to make such inferences reasonable. Through the control of variables, precise observation and measurement, repetition and inference, science develops theories that predict the results of experiments that have never been conducted. Scientific reasoning can lead to the prediction, for instance, that a sphere will roll down an inclined plane, not because every single instance has been tested experimentally, but because sufficient observation has led to the formation of theoretical "laws." The law of gravity, the behavior of spheres, the effects of friction have all been investigated experimentally and have led to generalizations that can become the basis of prediction.

We all know from experience, of course, that balls will roll down inclines, so such proofs seem unnecessary. But uncontrolled observation can often mislead us in our search for answers to how the physical universe works, and so scientific investigators attempt to make no assumptions that have not been verified by empirical means.

This is, of course, an impossible ideal, since no scientist can conduct all of the experiments necessary to verify every principle on which a particular investigation is based. Consequently, science itself is a collective body of observations and generalizations that scientists accept and apply. It is for this reason that science sometimes reviews past knowledge and corrects it; old assumptions may prove inadequate to explain newly observed phenomena. Science expands and alters our understanding because of the infinitely flexible nature of its method of discovery—and because of the curiosity and patience of scientists who observe and explain the new unknowns that past observations and explanations have revealed.

Social studies.   The empirical method is not only used to study physical phenomena in the natural and physical sciences. It is also used in the social sciences to study human behavior. The social sciences differ from natural and physical science, however, in the degree to which strictly empirical methods of investigation suffice. Behavior, whether that of individuals or groups, can be observed, measured, described, and made the subject of experimentation, but these methods can be used to account only for the quantifiable aspects of behavior. They cannot be used to give a complete account of aspects of behavior that are not subject to direct observation, such as intention and motivation, emotion, commitment, attitude, dignity, self-consciousness, or thought. Thus, the social sciences seek to combine empirical observation and the formation of predictable "laws," as in physical science, with explanations based on consistent, probable principles.

A simple illustration might clarify this difference: A social scientist might be interested in a question such as, "How does a childhood of poverty affect adults' attitudes toward work?" Is this question subject to empirical study? Yes and no. It is not the kind of question that can be answered by direct observation, since attitudes cannot be seen, except as they influence overt behavior, which can be seen. But the connection between the attitude and the behavior that it creates cannot itself be isolated for observation and measurement. The social scientist interested in such a question understands that the range of potential behaviors is very large, and attitudes are fashioned by a complex of forces that include poverty but cannot be restricted to that variable alone. "Poverty" itself will have different meanings in different social contexts. It isn't possible to construct an experiment by raising children in controlled situations in which only this one variable is manipulated so that the result can be tested by scientific means. It would take a "mad scientist," indeed, to attempt such an experiment, since the effect would be to enslave the subjects. Such considerations limit the ability of an investigator to apply scientific

methods to the question. Nevertheless, the social scientist must conduct an inquiry that is as objective and precise as possible, to avoid
answering the question by guessing or by stating preferences based
on prejudgments. Consequently, the social scientist applies the ideal
methods of science only where observation and inference are
appropriate.

Certain procedures can govern the inquiry that do not plunge
the investigator wholly into speculation. It is a matter of deciding
what aspects of the phenomenon might be observable and testable.
In relation to the question about childhood poverty and attitudes
toward work, a study could be made of people who grew up in conditions of poverty—as defined by the researcher—and these people
could be asked specific questions designed to discover what their attitudes are and how these might have been affected by their upbring-
ing. The researcher would then compare the answers of these respondents with those of people who did not grow up in poverty but who
otherwise resemble the first group. By this means, the social scientist
can produce a statistical comparison and make inferences about the
probable effects of a childhood of poverty. The validity of these conclusions will depend on whether the sample of respondents is representative of the larger population in question, whether it is large and
diverse enough to be statistically relevant, and whether the questions
are designed to elicit answers that can be accurately compared to one
another. Other considerations might also affect the validity of the
conclusion: Are there cultural values, or superstitions, or other influ-
ences that would distort the respondents' answers? It is possible that
some respondents might not want or are unable to answer truthfully?
Has the researcher asked questions in such a way that the answers are
predetermined? Do the researcher's own attitudes affect the way the
respondents' answers are compared? Questions of this sort require
interpretation on the part of the researcher.

Social scientists, then, use scientific methods to create data, but
the validity and meaning of that data are generally subject to interpretation. The definitions of the terms that social scientists use may
not be as universally accepted or understood as those used in scientific
measurement. Social science, because it deals with human behavior,
must go beyond observation, description, and experimentation. The
social scientist must analyze and interpret information based on general premises about behavior. These take the form of "theories" or
"models," which are meant to account for observable phenomena but
which are not themselves subject to experimental validation. Sig-
mund Freud's theory of human motivation, for instance, may explain
the same phenomena as B. F. Skinner's different and incompatible
behaviorist theory. Each of these theories might be appealed to by a

social scientist as a way of interpreting observed behaviors, but the interpretation does not in itself validate the theory. Theories in social science are like the "laws" of science, but they are not subject to scientific "proof" in the sense of demonstration. They explain specific events to the extent that they are consistent and well reasoned, but they provide a framework for interpretation rather than an absolute law for prediction. This makes the conclusions of social science subject to controversy depending on the perspective of the researcher. A Freudian and a Skinnerian can come to different conclusions about the same phenomena because their points of view determine different interpretations. This does not make them "unscientific." The controversies of social science result from the nature of its subject—human action—as much as from its methods, so they are inevitable. This is what makes social science fascinating for those who study it. We cannot ignore the importance of understanding human behavior, but we must qualify our conclusions based on the limits of what can be known about it.

The social sciences are also characterized by controversy over whether the conclusions they reach are "value-free." Some would argue that the proper goal of sociology or psychology must be the objective discovery of "what is true"; others think that the proper function of these inquiries is to improve human life. Researchers may, of course, deal with both, and some theories of behavior may attempt to bridge the gap between "what is" and "what ought to be." Thus, some social scientists strive for neutrality and others advocate change based on qualitative assumptions. When dealing with human action, it is hard to ignore questions of harmful or helpful actions, and social scientists do not ignore them. But insofar as they become researchers into the significance and value of the phenomena they study, they resemble researchers in the humanities more than they resemble scientists. This means that in addition to observing and describing according to a theoretical framework, they must also apply value judgments in a reasonable way.

Humanities. The humanities overlap with the social sciences (these labels have evolved over time to distinguish academic specialties, but for reasons other than any "natural" division of knowledge into neat compartments). The difference is not always clear. In some colleges, for instance, history is considered a "social science" and in others it is considered a "humanity." This may or may not indicate that what the historians in these departments do in their research is different. Social scientists may view history as subject to scientific study—within the limits of the social sciences—and humanists may think of the study of history as resembling the study of literature. At any rate, "the humanities" is a broad category used to describe the study of human creation and thought: the fine arts, music, literature, language, history, philosophy, religion, and other related areas of human thought. The humanities in general is the study of the human condition through the creations of humankind. Thus, the subject matter of the humanities is vast and extremely diverse. Each of the separate fields of the humanities may be approached from within a very specific framework or a very broad one. Researchers in the fine arts may investigate subjects as particular as "Northern Scottish watercolor landscapes of the 1890s" or as broad as "the creative impulse." In the study of literature, the range is equally broad. One researcher may ask "How does Thomas Mann use water as a symbol in *Death in Venice?*" while another may try to answer the question "What is a literary symbol?" or even "What is literature?" One philosopher may seek to discover "Hegel's use of Platonic dialogues in constructing his theory of dialectic"; another may speculate about the concept of "theory" itself. The vastness of "human creation and thought" makes it impossible to think of any subject that cannot come within the humanities—mathematics, for instance, may provide a useful basis for describing abstract impressionist painting, or the human realm of science itself may be studied as a problem of creativity or knowledge from a philosophical point of view. Humanistic subjects, such as "medicine as an art," or "optics in Renaissance painting," or "depictions of social classes in American novels," transcend the distinctions that separate the humanities from the social and natural sciences.

The breadth of the humanities is such that the way research is conducted cannot be prescribed as a systematic process. Research in the humanities is just as dependent on precise observation and accurate description as the sciences, even though its subject matter rarely invites experimentation. The logic of conclusions in the humanities also depends on the consistency of its theories—as in, let's say, the validity of a literary interpretation based on a psychoanalytic or a rhetorical theory of literary meaning. In these senses, humanistic inquiry shares with the social and natural sciences the desire to discover knowledge by valid means and to communicate it clearly. Humanistic inquiry deals with subject matter that is experiential, however, and this affects how such inquiry is conducted. Humanists *test* their hypotheses by applying logic and theory to them, but they often claim that they *discover* their conclusions by means of appreciation and insight. There are no procedures to follow to "appreciate" or to "see" what an artist has done. For this reason humanists must combine knowledge about their subjects with sensitivity and experience. For instance, a drama critic might analyze a play's structure or the way in which its themes are communicated, but that critic, while watching a performance of the play or reading it, wants also to be moved by the sheer experience. A scholar of music will seek to know and understand as much about a symphony as possible, but that scholar will probably admit that the pleasure of hearing it performed goes beyond such knowledge. The scholar's enjoyment is based, in part, on the depth of his or her knowledge and understanding, but without enjoyment the experience would not be complete. Thus, the subject matter of the humanities is often the experience of seeing or hearing or reading the creations of others, and this experience is often not able to be studied as such or wholly contained by description. The way in which humanists "know" is often intuitive, even though they can make use of more direct kinds of inquiry to add to this kind of knowledge. As the examples about Shakespeare's *Othello* show, a humanistic inquiry can be conducted systematically and its conclusions must be subject to logical analysis. But a literary critic attempting to argue that *"Othello*'s greatness comes from its ability to touch depths of passion in the human spirit" would have to make the reader of his or her own criticism feel that passion in addition to attempting to analyze its sources. Thus, criticism in the fine arts, if it is to bring out certain experiential qualities, must be a creative "performance" in its own way.

Conclusions about the same subject in the humanities may be different and yet equally correct, because what the critic deals with is the combination of the subject and the experience. This does not mean that any conclusion is correct. It must be possible to be wrong. But the kinds of questions that humanists pursue are often unanswerable in the scientist's sense of a single, unambiguous explanation. If two scientists conduct the same experiment but achieve different results, the assumption is that one or both of them made an error. But if two violinists give performances of a Mozart concerto that have different tonal qualities and create different feelings, it is possible for both of them to be correct. Two interpretations of a poem may be equally correct—because the language of poetry has many dimensions—while a third reading of the same poem may be demonstrably wrong. The humanities combine knowledge, logic, and precise description with sensitivity and experience to produce an endlessly rich array of results.

Defining the humanities as the study of "the human condition" implies that no matter how limited the scope of inquiry may be, humanists seek to understand and affirm human values. What human creations teach, and what research about them teaches, is the potential range of human responses to life. Humanists do not ignore questions of value, therefore, but consider them central to their inquiries. Thus, issues having to do with quality are frequently argued by humanists in their research. The validity of their procedures is tested, finally, by the shared values and experiences of the community to which the humanist researcher communicates his or her findings. Whether the conclusions confirm values or correct them, the success of a humanist's arguments depends on whether the audience—in a limited or in a broad sense—finds them worthwhile. Researchers in the humanities might be said to do on another level what the artists that they study also do: express the potentials of human achievement for others to use for their understanding and inspiration.

Writing the research paper

Every researcher is also a communicator. Since the progress of research goes from formulating a question and becoming informed to drawing and testing conclusions, these same elements constitute the essence of what the researcher must communicate. These, of course, are the elements of an argumentative essay. The writer of an essay using research faces all of the responsibilities we have encountered in this book. Formulating a thesis, developing a principle line of reasoning, structuring the reasoning into major parts of the composition, revising the argument, structure, and style—these do not change for the researcher. The research paper adds to these responsibilities certain others that follow from having used secondary sources and conducted primary research of some kind. These additional considerations are the only ones that we need consider at this point.

The researcher, in the process of gathering information and discovering reasons to support a hypothesis, has amassed a lot of information and tested its relevance and validity. The research writer must sort this information and these assessments into an order that follows a line of reasoning. Not everything that the inquiry has turned up will necessarily be relevant, and the writer may eventually use only a portion of the actual information he or she has discovered. The writer should include whatever is necessary and sufficient to lead to a conclusion, as well as whatever may need to be said to refute the arguments of others or suggest limitations on one's own. The writer must also consider where in the developing logic of the argument these matters need to be said. The object is to produce a sequence of reasoned steps that permits the reader to follow the researcher from problem to solution, including in its place each premise, example, description, supporting detail, and counterargument that will carry the reader along without confusion or digression. To do this requires planning, along the lines discussed in Chapter 5: The writer can perceive the necessary structure of the essay by analyzing the parts of the whole argument, which can be summarized in an enthymeme. It is important to remember here that *the order in which the research findings will appear in the essay will not necessarily be the same as the order in which the researcher discovered them.* The structure of the final essay should not be based on the *experience* of discovering information in whatever way that occurred; it is not a narrative of what happened to the researcher during the inquiry. The structure of the final argument is a *construct, made up of ideas discovered during research,* in whatever logical order binds those ideas into a whole, developing argument.

The structure of research writing in some disciplines is determined in part by conventional formats. It may or may not be necessary for you to follow them in writing for college courses, since the formats generally derive from the conventions of publication in different fields. Thus, an academic journal of research in psychology may specify that papers submitted for publication have a certain form. Articles in the social sciences often follow the conventional divisions of scientific reports, with all the material organized under headings, such as:

Problem and hypothesis
Review of relevant literature
Experiment design
Results
Analysis
Conclusion and discussion

The specific headings differ from discipline to discipline, and even from publication to publication, so you should not try to reproduce a "standard" format of this kind unless you are fulfilling an assignment that specifically calls for one, or writing for publication in a journal that does. The prescription of headings such as these is intended to provide readers with a set of expectations of where certain kinds of information may be found, so that if they need to consult an argument more than once they can find what they are looking for easily. (One unfortunate result of the use of such conventions, as I suggested in discussing critical reading, is that they may encourage readers to leap to the "conclusion" without having made an adequate assessment of the means by which it is argued.) If your audience expects to find your research organized in such a way, then your use of a conventional format will make their reading easier. If not, you should be guided only by the logical structure of the ideas you present. Do not confuse "structure" with "format." You are no less responsible for structuring your ideas *within* each of these conventional sections, if you use them.

As a research writer you have a special obligation to provide whatever the reader needs to know to assess the validity of your findings. Remember that you are interested in finding the best reasons possible for drawing a conclusion, not in bullying the reader into believing some idea that you haven't adequately supported. This means that you should consider including a description of the methods that you have used in your study and any limitations imposed by those methods. In some cases, this may mean a description of an experiment, or a survey, or some other form of primary research, together with a description of the sorts of conclusions that such methods are not able to support. Or, it may mean that you should inform the reader about any prior assumptions or perspectives that have guided your inquiry. In other cases, this might simply mean acknowledging that your pursuit hasn't gone far enough in some ways, or that you encountered difficulties, or that your terms are less precise than they need to be. If you have doubts about any of your sources, you can say so. If you think there are weaknesses in your conclusions, qualify them accordingly. If you have discovered reasons against your case (by reading sources that disagree or by "falsifying" your conclusions), present them fairly and let the reader assess them as you have done. As a researcher, you will have discovered more information than you will finally use in your essay, but be sure that your reason for leaving anything out is because it isn't relevant or necessary, not because you wish to hide anything. Honest research, like honest argumentative writing, is intended to put the whole case forward, as you see it, so that the reader's agreement is *earned*.

Documentation.   If your readers are to make independent assessments of your research findings, or if they are to pursue your ideas as part of their own inquiry, they must know where you discovered your information or what other sources you used in formulating your argument. Thus, research writing includes complete documentation. Each idea, fact, or theoretical model that you derived from a source other than your own experience or speculation should be documented by giving the reader complete bibliographic information about that source. This is ordinarily done in footnotes or references in your paper and works in a bibliography, which you attach to the essay. Obviously, you should have collected this bibliographic information while doing the research, so that you can use it in this way. I will not discuss *how* to document here, since formats vary in different disciplines and you can easily look such formats up in a handbook. It is enough to say that the important thing about the form of your documentation is that it should be consistent and provide the reader with all the information necessary to find the source. But let's briefly look at *what* to document, and *why*.

In addition to allowing the reader to assess your sources independently and to pursue the issue further, documentation functions to give credit to others for their research or their ideas. Knowledge is a collective activity, and everyone owes most of what he or she knows to others. It isn't necessary to document everything you know, giving the names of all your teachers back to the first grade or every book you ever read, since it is commonly understood that we all have learned what we know somehow. So, what debts should be acknowledged by a researcher and what need not be? Certain kinds of information do not require documentation, since they obviously fall within the common stock of knowledge that you and your readers share, or that anyone could find out by checking a readily available source. Thus, if you were writing about the economy of the United States, you would be wasting time, and testing your reader's patience, if you included a footnote to document the facts that the United States has fifty states and that its economy is based on the dollar. If you were comparing the value of the dollar to a foreign currency, however, or citing the laws that govern imports, you would want to cite your sources, since you had to uncover these details, and your credibility is only as good as the credibility of your sources. It isn't always easy to tell the difference between common information that does not need documentating and special information that does; it is a judgment that you must make. In general, if you have to look it up, or if you can expect your reader to ask "how do you know that?" you ought to document. This means that each time you use information that you have learned specifically from your inquiry into the subject at hand, you should cite the source. There are times when you may not have had to look something up because you already know it, but you should document your information anyway if your reader cannot be expected to share or to trust your expertise.

The responsibility to credit sources does not stop with factual information, but includes the ideas of others that you have used in your study. Thus, for instance, if you are reporting the results of a survey you conducted to see how people reacted to losing their jobs, but designed your questionnaire after one used in a study to see how people reacted to the death of loved ones, you have borrowed a concept from another researcher even if you have not used any of that researcher's data. Since the concept is not original with you, you need to document where you got it. Similarly, if you read a piece of literary criticism claiming that Walt Whitman's poetry revealed his pantheism, and if you then used this idea in your own criticism, you should acknowledge its source, even if your support comes exclusively from your own independent analysis of the poems. The reader deserves to know what ideas are your own and what ideas aren't.

Another kind of documentation functions to refer the reader to sources of further study. In your research you will encounter citations of this kind, and you will be grateful for them, since they will point you in new directions and expand the territory of your inquiry. As you write your research essay, you will brush up against potential lines of inquiry that you cannot go into, but a reader interested in your ideas may well wish to take these paths. Hence, if your study suggests such sources, provide them. For instance, if you are presenting your research on the myths surrounding the Bermuda Triangle, you could include a note citing similar studies of myths about other places of this kind. By doing this you are acknowledging that your own research fits into a context of broader issues about which further inquiry is possible.

The kinds of documentation discussed so far all refer to sources you encounter in your secondary research. There is, finally, the responsibility of documenting your primary sources. For instance, if you are analyzing a poem, you should cite the particular source for the version of the poem you are using. Or, if you are describing a painting, your source might be a reproduction in a particular volume, or it may be the original painting seen in a museum or gallery. In such cases, your specific source is important to the reader, who may not be able to follow your analysis otherwise or who may need to check your observations against the source you used. Not all printed versions of a poem are the same—its first appearance in print may be different from the author's handwritten text or from later revised editions. Many works of literature or scholarship differ from edition to edition or from translation to translation, and accuracy demands that your reader know what version you are using. Not all reproductions of a painting are equally detailed or faithful to the original. Similarly, the information you cite in a study of history might come from the work of other researchers, or it may have been a primary source, such as old newspapers or ledger books, or interviews with people who know the events firsthand. These kinds of primary sources need documenting. In the case of empirical or experimental studies, researchers document the kinds of apparatus they use or the source of their specimens, and so on, as essential information for other researchers who may wish to reproduce or use their results.

Besides the issue of documentation, as a research writer you also face the problem of how to incorporate the research of others into your essay. Do you, for instance, quote your sources directly, and if so do you use long or short quotations, do you paraphrase them, do you merely refer to them in passing, or do you confine any reference to them entirely to notes? The answers are not easy, and you should decide based on the specific function of the source material in your own argument, rather than try to follow a general rule. Direct quotation is often unnecessary and in many cases may distract your reader by interrupting the progress of your argument through its logic. There are times, however, when the words of others actually constitute your evidence, in which case you should include them. If, for example, you are analyzing the Great Depression and find it necessary to argue that the most popular explanation is wrong, you would want to quote a passage representing that explanation so that you could isolate its error as you see it. If you were examining the syntax of Herman Melville's prose, you would want to quote your representative passages, since the reader would need to see them exactly as Melville wrote them in order to follow your reasoning. If, however, you were studying the plot structure of *Moby Dick* as a whole, your paraphrase of the story would, in most cases, be sufficient to provide the reader with the necessary context. Another occasion for quoting secondary sources comes when the words of another researcher are particularly striking or meaningful—when, in other words, you can make your point better by letting your sources speak for themselves. These occasions are rare. Researchers who include numerous or lengthy passages that are not especially interesting in themselves risk losing credibility in the reader's eyes. It is usually sufficient to paraphrase and to provide the reader with the source of the ideas or information in a note.

Of course, you should always make it clear to the reader when you are paraphrasing and when you are quoting. Read the following two passages, for instance:

> Richard Rodriguez has written that bilingual education is "foolish and certainly doomed." He says, "Middle-class supporters of public bilingualism toy with the confusion of those Americans who cannot speak standard English as well as they can. Bilingual enthusiasts, moreover, sin against intimacy."
>
> Richard Rodriguez argues in his autobiography that supporters of bilingual education are not sensitive to the need for intimacy on the part of students who do not speak English, and for this reason he does not think it is a good approach.

You can tell by the conventions of punctuation whether Rodriguez's words are being directly quoted or paraphrased. If you use the exact phrasing of your source, you should use quotation marks or set entire passages off by themselves by indenting them. In either case, your responsibility to cite the source is the same; both these passages would need to be documented by whatever means you are using.* If you quote directly, you must be absolutely certain that you have been accurate: Quotation marks around a passage mean to the reader that

*Richard Rodriguez, *Hunger of Memory: The Education of Richard Rodriguez* (Boston: David R. Godine, 1981), p. 35.

the words are exactly as they appear in the source. If you fail to indicate by quotation marks or indentation that the words are directly quoted, you will have inadvertently committed plagiarism.

Having raised the specter of plagiarism, I'll discuss it briefly. Textbooks about writing always discuss it; it is one of the customary topics of anyone speaking to students about research writing. Although I would not want to ignore an issue so many think is essential, I would like to believe that if you are using this book, and have gotten this far, you are not the kind of student who would be tempted to plagiarize. To have read this far in a book that stresses the responsibilities of a writer and in a chapter that treats research as honest inquiry, you have already demonstrated your interest in using your writing to improve and express your thinking, for the sake of your education. You know that the definition of plagiarism is the fraudulent use of the words and ideas of others as if they were one's own. You know that plagiarism is academic dishonesty and punishable as such. You don't need to be told not to do it. It is enough to say that plagiarism is self-imposed bondage of the intellect—an avoidable first step toward slavery of the mind.

A Final Note

This chapter has only scratched the surface of the subject of research. Each of the methods of inquiry that characterize the disciplines of knowledge might be discussed at length, and whole books have been devoted to teaching "the scientific method" or "the conduct of social science" or "how humanists know." As a student writer, you are practicing these methods as your write research papers, and the exercise might not take you as far into the issues as this chapter suggests you go. But all researchers approach their subjects at whatever level of experience they have been prepared for, and one benefit of doing research is, therefore, that it prepares you to do more research. In college, your research assignments are not ends in themselves. They are intended, at least in part, to provide you with the basis for continuing to find ideas challenging and to approach them with curiosity. This is not a "skill" that confines itself to school. It is what thinking people do as part of the pleasure of being alive.

I could say the same about this whole book. Writing argumentative essays is not an end in itself. It is a great pleasure to have solved a problem by means of reason and to have presented that solution persuasively for others to share and evaluate. But it is a greater pleasure to have learned by this means to face knowledge itself as an endless adventure. The argumentative writer faces in each new essay what the thinking person faces throughout his or her life: the challenge of discovering one's own meaning in the conflict of ideas. I wouldn't have bothered to write this book if I didn't believe this lesson to be the most important one that all students have to learn, and to learn again. I feel toward this book and your education about how Robert Frost felt when he wrote a poem called "A Considerable Speck," in which he tells of encountering an almost microscopic bug on his writing paper. Instead of squashing that bug so that he could get on with his writing, he watched it and let it go. The poem ends like this:

> I have a mind myself and recognize
> Mind when I meet with it in any guise.
> No one can know how glad I am to find
> On any sheet the least display of mind.*

You, too, are "considerable" to me—as writers of real ideas. No teacher wants to "squash" the mental life of students, and I hope this book has helped you to display your mind better in your writing, for your own sake and the future's.

Glossary

This Glossary contains terms that are central to the content of this textbook, defined according to the way in which I have used them. Please refer to the Index for further terms and to locate extended discussions of these concepts. Italicized terms in the definitions are defined elsewhere in this glossary.

Argument The process of finding and presenting *reasons* to an *audience* that shares one's sense of a *question at issue* but not necessarily one's answer to that question. Argumentative writing is writing in which a writer defends a *stance* with reasons. Argument need not end in persuading one's audience; it is an attempt to find the best available grounds for accepting a *conclusion.* Hence, argument resembles, and requires, *inquiry.*

Assent Agreement that results from a process of thoughtful *inquiry.* Agreement, or belief, in an *idea* may be groundless, but assent implies a decision to agree based on the quality of *reasons* offered.

Assertion Any idea that is proposed by the writer as one that the reader should *assent* to. To assert an idea is to imply that one believes it and can offer *reasons* to support it. See *Thesis.*

Assumption Any idea that the writer expects to be accepted by the reader without *argument* and that the writer has therefore used as the basis for developing a *reason.* See *Enthymeme.*

Attitude Those feelings of a writer toward his or her subject, *audience,* and self that are communicated by means of the *style* of the writing. See *Diction, Stance, Tone.*

Audience Those readers to whom a composition is addressed and for whom it is written. One's audience may be well-known, or it may be

214

generally defined as any reader who shares with the writer an interest in an *issue* and a willingness to engage in *argumentation* about it.

Authority (appeal to)   Any *reason* that offers support for a conclusion by referring to a credible source, one that is expected to be believed by the *audience.*

Conclusion   The end and result of a *line of reasoning.* Hence, the answer to a *question at issue.* Whether a given *assertion* is a conclusion depends on whether *reasons* are offered for it. Any conclusion may also function as a reason and lead to another conclusion. See also *Syllogism.*

Consequence (question of)   The kind of *question at issue* that asks how one thing causes another. Questions of consequence are argued when the writer addresses an *audience* that needs *reasons* to believe that one thing is the result of something else.

Critical reading   Reading in which one attempts to adjust the degree of one's *assent* to a writer's *ideas* according to the quality of the *reasons* given to support those ideas. Critical reading requires a willingness to understand at the same time that it requires an unwillingness to agree or to disagree without sufficient cause.

Definition (question of)   The kind of *question at issue* that asks what a word or concept means or signifies. Questions of definition are argued when the writer addresses an *audience* that needs *reasons* to establish how a word or concept should be understood.

Diction   The kinds of words chosen by the writer to communicate an *idea.* Diction reveals a writer's *attitude* toward his or her subject, *audience,* and self. Diction helps establish a writer's *tone* and contributes to the clarity of the writing.

Documentation   The full citation of a writer's sources, giving proper credit to the ideas of others, so that the reader may verify and evaluate the writer's use of these sources and pursue an independent *inquiry* into the writer's subject.

Draft   A version of an essay. A "rough" draft is its first state; later drafts result from *revision.* The "final" draft is the finished version, after *editing* and *proofreading,* as intended to be read by the *audience.*

Editing   The kind of *revision* that focuses mainly on *style.* Editing generally aims toward greater clarity and economy of expression. See *Revision.*

Empirical research   The kind of *inquiry* based on observation of quantifiably measurable phenomena, in such a way that the phenonomena can be accurately described. This is the predominant method of the sciences.

Enthymeme   Two *assertions* related to each other in such a way that one is a *conclusion* and the other is a *reason*. In *argumentative* writing an enthymeme implies a connection between conclusion and reason based on an *assumption*, in order to establish a *line of reasoning* that will appear probable and by that means achieve agreement with a conclusion otherwise in doubt. Thus, an enthymeme implies an underlying *syllogism*. See *Logical thesis statement*.

Essay   A prose composition, generally said to be unified by fulfilling a single purpose, that of earning the *assent* of the *audience* to the writer's *thesis*.

Evaluation (question of)   The kind of *question at issue* that asks whether a thing is good or bad. Questions of evaluation are argued when the writer addresses an *audience* that needs *reasons* to establish the value of something.

Fact (question of)   The kind of *question at issue* that asks whether a thing is or is not *empirically* the case. Questions of fact are argued when the writer addresses an *audience* that needs *reasons* to verify or demonstrate that a phenomenon exists.

Falsification   The process of developing a plausible *line of reasoning* that would refute one's own *thesis*. This process, as a part of *research*, enables one to test hypothetical answers and thereby alter or qualify one's thinking about any *issue*.

Humanities   The kind of *inquiry* that focuses its attention on human creation and thought, in such a way that human nature can be illuminated, understood, and valued. *Research* in the humanities is not confined to any single method but combines the methods of *empirical studies* and the *social sciences*.

Idea   A statement about some subject. An idea is not complete unless it can be stated as a sentence with predication—the use of a verb to relate one concept to another in some way. See *Assertion*.

Inquiry   The process of reasoning about an *issue* for the purpose of discovering what to believe about it. Inquiry is an attempt to find good *reasons*, whether one already knows one's *stance* or not.

Intention   The sense of purpose, to say some particular thing to an *audience* or to accomplish some end by writing, that enables the writer to choose the means of accomplishing that purpose. See also *Stance, Thesis*.

Interpretation (question of)   The kind of *question at issue* that asks what a word or concept signifies. Questions of interpretation are argued when the writer addresses an *audience* that needs *reasons* to establish how a word or concept should be construed, that is, how it relates to some other word or concept in a significant way.

Issue   A question. The *assertion* of any *idea* implies that there is an issue to which it is a response. See *Question at issue*.

Jargon   The specialized vocabulary of any field of endeavor, appropriate only if the intended *audience* shares the writer's special knowledge of this field. See *Diction*.

Line of reasoning   The process by which a writer connects *reasons* to lead a reader to accept a *conclusion*. The *structure* of argumentative writing follows the progress of a line of reasoning as it develops toward a *conclusion*.

Logical thesis statement   A *thesis* with a "because clause," or main *reason*, added to it. Such a thesis statement, in the form of an *enthymeme*, provides the writer with a *line of reasoning* on which to base the *structure* of an argumentative *essay*. If this enthymeme results from considering the possible *assumptions* shared by the writer and the *audience,* it provides a means of basing the reasoning in the *essay* on the beliefs of the intended reader.

Nature of the case (appeal to)   Any *reason* that offers support for a *conclusion* by deriving that conclusion as a logical consequence of the truth of the reason, independent of whether the *audience* desires it to be true or whether the source of the conclusion is credible. See also *Syllogism*.

Plagiarism   Using the writing or ideas of another writer as if they were one's own. Deliberate plagiarism is intellectual dishonesty, taking credit for someone else's work. Unintended plagiarism may be avoided by giving proper credit to one's sources. See *Documentation*.

Policy (question of)   The kind of *question at issue* that asks what should be done in a given situation. Questions of policy are argued when the writer addresses an *audience* that needs *reasons* to establish whether a certain course of action is desirable or necessary. Hence, questions of policy often require that questions of *evaluation* and *consequence* be argued first.

Preference (appeal to)   Any *reason* that offers support for a *conclusion* by referring to the *audience's* desire that it be the case.

Proofreading   The kind of *revision* that one does to the final *draft* of an *essay,* intended to correct mistakes and make other minor changes. See *Editing*.

Question at issue   Any question that a writer and his or her *audience* does not already answer in the same way. Hence, it is the existence of questions at issue that motivates *argumentation*. See also *Consequence, Definition, Evaluation, Fact, Interpretation, Policy.*

Reason   An *idea* offered in support of another idea, which derives or "follows" from it. A reason is asserted by a writer whenever the reader is assumed to need an answer to the question "why?" See also *Authority, Enthymeme, Nature of the case, Preference, Syllogism.*

Research   The deliberate investigation of the unknown, informing oneself about matters that are as yet unsubstantiated. Research may be informal, as in asking questions or looking up information, or it may be formal, as in an extended *inquiry* into a hypothesis that is in doubt. Primary research is a direct inquiry about any phenomenon. Secondary research is an inquiry into what other researchers have discovered. See *Documentation, Empirical research, Humanities, Social studies.*

Revision   The process of reconsidering one's choices, to make sure that they are consistent with one's *intention*. Revision may include rethinking and changing any aspect of an *essay* as it develops in successive *drafts*. See *Editing, Proofreading.*

Social studies   The kind of *inquiry* based on observation of and speculation about human behavior, in such a way that the behavior can be accounted for and understood. This is the predominant *research* method of such disciplines as psychology, sociology, and, to some extent, history.

Stance   The "position" of the writer in respect to any *question at issue*. One's stance determines what one chooses for a *thesis;* it also derives from one's *attitude* toward the subject.

Structure   The relations among the *ideas* in a piece of writing. Structural relations are what enable a reader to understand the connections that make the *line of reasoning* seem to progress from a beginning, through a developed middle, to an earned *conclusion*. See *Transitions.*

Style   The surface features of a writer's prose that are controlled for the purpose of making the sentences readable, the ideas clear, and the voice, or *tone,* of the writer appropriately reasonable.

Syllogism   In logic, the combination of two *reasons* (generally called a "major premise" and a "minor premise") and a *conclusion* in such a way that belief in the conclusion "follows"' from acceptance of the reasons. Informally, a syllogism is implied whenever a stated reason and an assumed reason combine to generate a conclusion. Syllogisms are said to be "valid," if the premises assert categorical conditions that entail a necessary conclusion. (This book does not offer the student the "rules" that must be adhered to in "valid" syllogisms according to formal logic, because informal reasoning does not generally adhere to such rules when ordinary language is used to argue persuasively.) See *Enthymeme*.

Syntax   A technical term for the order of the words, and hence their functional relationships, within a sentence.

Thesis   An *idea*, stated as an *assertion*, that represents a writer's reasoned response to a *question at issue* and that will serve the writer as the central idea of a unified *essay*. See *Intention*, *Logical thesis statement*.

Tone   The qualities of voice that a reader hears in the writer's words. These qualities suggest the writer's *attitudes*. See *Diction*.

Transitions   The structural relationships that function to enable a reader to understand how one idea connects to another as the writing progresses. Transitional phrases may be included in the writing, or they may be implied without being stated. See *Structure*.

❧ *Index* ❧